Megalithic Traditions of North East India

About the Editor

Queenbala Marak is Associate Professor, Department of Anthropology, North Eastern Hill University, Shillong, Meghalaya. She has authored several papers in International and National journals, and contributed chapters in edited volumes. She recently edited *Doing Autoethnography* (2016, Serials), and authored *Food Politics: Studying Food, Identity and Difference among Garos* (2014, CSP) and co-authored *Misimagre: A Prehistoric Factory Site from Garo Hills, Meghalaya* (2017, RIP).

MEGALITHIC TRADITIONS OF NORTH EAST INDIA

Edited by
Queenbala Marak

CONCEPT PUBLISHING COMPANY PVT. LTD.
NEW DELHI-110059

ISBN-13: 978-93-86682-70-3

First Published 2019

Published and Printed by

Concept Since 1974

Concept Publishing Company Pvt. Ltd.
A/15-16, Commercial Block, Mohan Garden,
New Delhi-110059 (INDIA)
T : 91 11 25351460, 91 11 25351794
E : publishing@conceptpub.com *W* : www.conceptpub.com

Cataloging in Publication Data--Courtesy: D.K. Agencies (P) Ltd. <docinfo@dkagencies.com>

Megalithic traditions of North East India / edited by Queenbala Marak.
pages cm
Contributed articles.
Includes bibliographical references and index.
ISBN 9789386682703

1. Megalithic monuments--India, Northeastern. 2. Tribes--India, Northeastern--Social life and customs. 3. Tribes--Monuments--India, Northeastern. 4. India, Northeastern--Antiquities. I. Marak, Queenbala, editor.

LCC GN790.M44 2018 DDC 954.1 23

Foreword

Megalithic erections, such as menhirs and chamber tombs, are usually connected with different functions, such as commemorative, religious as well as cremation ceremony. What is interesting in the present space is that the indigenous tribal people of North East India erected and continue to erect megaliths/monoliths as memoirs, pictogram, passage etc. for the dead, and the living.

Studies on indigenous people of North East India have always been an attraction for academicians and laymen. The unique feature of looking at stones (that speak for the dead and the living) is rarely seen across the world (except in a few pockets) — and thus become a fascinating microcosm to study in the broader spectrum of culture, habits, and customs of indigenous people of the region. In this connection, I am positive that this will be a valuable contribution to the field of Heritage studies, Cultural studies, and more specifically to Cultural Anthropology.

To deliver a delightful reading experience, requires a lot of hard work, commitment and dedication on the subject matter. The intention behind this book by Queenbala Marak will enable students to come to grips with the main principles and potential applications of this tradition of indigenous people at different levels. This book is an attempt to connect us with traditions which may enable to win over the rational. A perusal of this book will certainly help to get an insightful view on customs and reverence of megaliths by the people of the region.

I hope that the insights presented in this book will not only give ideas on Cognitive Anthropology, but will also inspire readers and help them proceed smoothly with their ken on the dimensions of Anthropological perspectives.

18.2.2018

Abdullah Ali Ashraf
Professor and Head,
Department of Anthropology
Gauhati University, Guwahati, Assam

Preface & Acknowledgements

In 1933, James Phillip Mills, the then Deputy Commissioner of Naga Hills, stated that an archaeological characteristic of Assam (in which he included the whole of the North East region) is its wealth of megaliths. Indeed, megaliths of various shapes and sizes dot the whole region — many of them living as myths in the social memory of the people, and a few entering the ethnographic present. These structures have been reported from almost all over the region.

The megaliths of the region are in a class of its own — differing from the ones found in other parts of the country and world. However, it is the functional aspect of these stones that are of extreme value. Diverse functional interpretations are possible since a living tradition is seen in many communities and areas where the structures are found. Therefore, more than a mere archaeological specimen, these are of ethno-historical and anthropological significance.

However, a comprehensive look at megaliths of the region by bringing together the assorted megalithic traditions of North East India within one common platform was long felt in academic circles. This book is an outcome of that long-felt need to fill the gap in academia.

When I approached scholars, irrespective of their academic inclinations, working in the area, I wanted to cover the whole region. Despite my best efforts, the states of Tripura and Arunachal Pradesh remain academically unknown, though a representation from Sikkim was most encouraging. Of course, it goes without saying that the study of pre-historic cultures cannot be straitjacketed or compartmentalised into specific geo-political zones of our own making at the present.

This book is multi-disciplinary in nature with specialists from anthropology, history, archaeology, sociology and folklore looking at the constructs of megaliths and megalithism. I thank all the contributors who sincerely and unfailingly sent me their several drafts in a timely fashion. Most of them were prompt in responding with regard to queries, and additions and deletions that I suggested.

I am grateful to Professor Abdullah Ali Ashraf who agreed to go through the draft and pen a foreword to this book. An eminent anthropologist of the region, Ashraf, was one of my teachers who imbibed the love for all things material from the past—lithics, big and small.

18.2.2018 **Queenbala Marak**

Contents

SECTION-II
SYMBOLIC NATURE OF MEGALITHS

SECTION-III
LAND, CHANGE AND CONTINUITY

List of Contributors

Akoijam Milan Meitei is a Research Scholar in the Department of Anthropology, North Eastern Hill University, Shillong, Meghalaya. His research interest lies in megalithic studies of the Khasi and Jaintia. He can be reached at *milanakoijam93@gmail.com*

Dr. Charisma K. Lepcha is Assistant Professor in the Department of Anthropology, Sikkim University. She works mostly in the eastern Himalayan borderlands but has also spent time in the field in Meghalaya and Manipur. Her research interests include myths, religion, indigeneity, visual anthropology and material culture. She can be reached at *lepchack@gmail.com*

Dr. Ditamulu Vasa is Assistant Professor in the Department of History and Archaeology, Nagaland University, Nagaland. Her research interests lie in the field of ceramic archaeology. She can be reached at *damvasa@gmail.com*

Gangotri Bhuyan is a Research Scholar in the Department of Anthropology, North Eastern Hill University, Shillong, Meghalaya. Her research interest includes ethno-archaeology, ecological anthropology, material culture, museum studies, and field methods in Anthropology.
She can be reached at *gangotribhuyan1@gmail.com*

Dr. Jelle J.P. Wouters is Senior Lecturer at Royal Thimphu College. His research revolves around political lifeworlds, social history, and the state in Nagaland, and North East India more widely. He recently edited (with Michael Heneise) the book *Nagas in the 21st Century* (2017, Highlander Books) and authored the book *In the*

Shadows of Naga Insurgency: Tribes, State and Violence in North East India (2018, Oxford, India).
He can be reached at *jjp.wouters@gmail.com*

Dr. Kalpana Choudhury is Associate Professor and Head, Department of Anthropology, Demoria College. She works on megaliths of the Karbis of the plain areas.
She can be reached at *kalpananjp@rediffmail.com*

Dr. Malsawmliana is Associate Professor in the Department of History, Government T. Romana College, Aizawl, Mizoram. His main interest is the study of megalithic traditions in Mizoram. He recently published the book *Megalithic Culture of Mizoram* (2017). He is the President of Mizo Archaeological Society, Mizoram. He can be reached at *sawmavvk@gmail.com*

Dr. Marco Mitri is Associate Professor in the Department of History, Union Christian College, Barapani, Meghalaya. He works in the field of archaeology in Khasi Hills, and recently discovered the lithic sites of Sohpetbneng and Myrkhan.
He can be reached at *marcommus@yahoo.com*

Prof. Mayanglambam ManiBabu is Professor in the Department of Anthropology, Manipur University, Imphal. He has edited the book *Anthropology of Manipur: Archaeological, Biological and Cultural Dimensions* (in two editions: 2006, 2012, Educare: Imphal) and authored *Ceramic Ethnoarchaeology of the Andros of Manipur India* (British Archaeological Report International Series, Oxford). His areas of interest include ethnoarchaeology, lithic typo-technology, lithic prehistory of South-East Asia, post-processual archaeological paradigms.
He can be reached at *mmanibabu@yahoo.co.in*

Dr. Potshangbam Binodini Devi is Associate Professor, Department of Anthropology, D.M. College of Science, Imphal. She has authored the book *Megalithic Culture of Manipur* (2011). Her research interests include the Prehistoric archaeology of Manipur.
She can be reached at *binodini96@gmail.com*

Prof. Raphaël Rousseleau is Professor of Anthropology at the Department of Religious Studies (IHAR, FTSR), University of Lausanne, Switzerland. His main research interests are the Scheduled Tribes of India (particularly in Odisha) from an anthropological and historical perspective (in particular in relations with the former local kingdoms), as well as the relations of such groups with their environment. Some years ago, he also studied archaeology and particularly Neolithic megaliths in Western France.

He can be reached at *Raphael.Rousseleau@unil.ch*

Dr. Sukanya Sharma teaches Archaeology in the Department of Humanities and Social Sciences, Indian Institute of Archaeology Guwahati, Assam. Her main research interests are prehistoric and historical archaeology and heritage studies of North East India particularly.

Tengnang D. Sangma is an independent researcher from Garo Hills. His research interests include ethnomusicology, traditional craftsmanship with special reference to architecture, and traditional governance. He can be reached at *tengnangdsangma@gmail.com*

Dr. Tiatoshi Jamir is Associate Professor in the Department of History and Archaeology, Nagaland University, Kohima campus, Meriema, Kohima, Nagaland. His main research interests are prehistory, ethnoarchaeology, community archaeology and ethnomusicology. He currently directs a research programme on cave archaeology in the Mimi Formation and the Naga Hills Ophiolite belt adjoining Myanmar in collaboration with the Department of Art & Culture, Government of Nagaland.

Dr. Watijungshi Jamir is Principal, Kohima College, Kohima. Formerly he was Head, Department of Anthropology, Kohima Science College, Jotsoma, Nagaland.

He can be reached at *watijungshijamir@gmail.com*

Introduction

Queenbala Marak

High mountain, wide mountain,
This stone is neither yours nor ours,
From today the stone is no more your child,
And now onwards it becomes a man's soul.[1]

The above Karbi prayer to a megalith succinctly sums up the ethos behind megaliths in North East India. In this region, stones not only have stories connected to them — but they live, breathe, have gendered lives, and even procreate!

In the year 2012, when I wrote a brief chapter on "Megaliths in North East India"[2], I received an overwhelming feedback from the student community. There is still no work consolidating the megaliths of North East India in academia, even though it is clear to scholars and laymen that the stones of the region are a class apart. This is the idea which lays the foundation of this book — in order to fill the gap in the studies of megalithic cultures. However, in opposition to the term 'culture', I have intentionally used the term 'tradition'. This is to state the obvious that in the region under discussion, megalithism[3] is still playing itself out. In archaeology, the term 'tradition' might refer to a set of cultures or industries which develop successively. However, in the context of the region, such a cultural gradation is too early to envisage. A tradition, after anthropologist Shils (1981), refers to a belief or behaviour passed down within a group or society with symbolic meaning or special significance with origins in the past. This term, therefore, aptly suits the present context of North East Indian megalithic tradition.

Despite its occurrence and relevance in the present day, megaliths are known to be of prehistoric or archaic origin — that is, belonging to a time before written records, and possibly much before civilisation appeared. They are said to have first appeared/built in the Neolithic times as the 'stone henges' of later Neolithic Britain and continued through Bronze Age till Iron Age. The origin and chronology of megaliths, however, is still unsettled. These structures largely relate to Iron Age times and are often described as burial complexes. Rather than the archaic nature, it is the present day relevance which makes the study of megaliths in North East India unique and enriching. Except the states of Arunachal Pradesh and Tripura, all the states of the region have been covered in this Book.

Meanings and Definitions

The term 'megalith' refers to a large stone or monument either alone or in association with other stones. The word *megalith* comes from the Ancient Greek *megas* meaning 'great' and *lithos* meaning 'stone'. Megalithic culture, by definition, therefore, refers to a culture distinguished by the presence of monuments of large stone structures used for funeral or other purposes — which can include a variety of functions and uses. Childe (1946) states that the term was introduced by antiquarians to describe a class of monuments in western and northern Europe, consisting of huge undressed stones and termed in Celtic as *dolmen*, *cromlech* and menhir.[4] However, these are not the only type of stones that are classified as megaliths. Daniel (1962) adds that the term can be applied to all constructions using very large roughly dressed slabs of stone.

In reality, however, the meaning of 'megalith' is not always connected with large stones (Marak, 2012a). In 1938, van der Hoop suggested a deeper meaning that megalithic objects are not always made of huge stones, but sometimes smaller stones as well (Yondri, 2006). If the people or community in a certain area could not find suitable stones to make a structure then they used wood as a substitute. Therefore, while megaliths are understood to be huge stones, in some places objects of smaller stones or other materials such as wood should also be classified as 'megalithic' if those structures were used for a certain objective, such as worship of an ancestral spirit (Marak, 2012a). This situation is aptly suited for the region under study due to the use of non-lithic materials as monuments for both funerary and non-funerary purposes.

In the North East Indian context these large (or small) stone structures are known by different names. For example, Lepchas of Sikkim call them *longtsaok* (meaning 'hard stone') — and they are said to be a representation of Mt. Kanchenjunga. Though *longtsaok* stands for a menhir, it also refers to the other kinds of megaliths. Contrastingly, similar looking menhirs are named either as *mawbynna* (memory stone) or *mawshyrang* (male stone) among Khasis; and *kosi* (village foundation stones) and *a'mal* (boundary markers) among Garos of Meghalaya. Within the space of megalithic culture, we can also see a variety of non-lithic structures. In the early 1920s, Hutton (1922a) mentioned that among the Lothas of Nagaland, stones were normally set up as monuments, but Y-shaped posts were sometimes substituted if no suitable stone was available. He further mentions that in the village of Yekhum there existed a clan who was not allowed to set up stones at all, but instead use Y-shaped wooden posts. Such wooden posts, whether substitutes or not, can be seen among the Mizos, Garos and others as well.

North East India — An Overview

North East India comprises of eight states — referred to as the seven sister states of Assam, Arunachal Pradesh, Manipur, Meghalaya, Mizoram, Nagaland and Tripura; and one brother state Sikkim. The former states are connected and contiguous to each other, while the latter is connected through the Siliguri Corridor of West Bengal. This corridor, also known as Chicken Neck, with a width of 21-40 kilometres connects the North Eastern region with the rest of the country. The region shares more than 4,500 kilometres of international border with China (Tibet region) in the north, Myanmar in the east, Bangladesh in the south-west, and Bhutan to the north-west. The region comprises an area of 2,62,230 square kilometres which is 8.0 per cent of India's area.

Possibly, though not proved conclusively, the earliest settlers into the region were the Austro-Asiatic speakers, followed by Tibeto-Burman speakers, and lastly by the Indo-Aryans. The strikingly demographic feature of North East India is that the hills are predominantly inhabited by tribal communities while in the plains non-tribal communities live. It is not easy to determine the ethnic affinities of the population of the region, but broadly speaking the tribal population in the hills and plains have Mongoloid features. The Aryan speaking people in the plains have mainly Caucasoid features. However, in the western side of the plains a blend of Caucasoid with Dravidian and Pre-Dravidian elements are seen, while in the east a blend of Caucasoid and Mongoloid features (Majumdar, 1980).

This region occupies a prominent place in the archaeological map of the world because of its rich megalithic remains. It is one of the few places in the world where monuments of this type are still erected. Megaliths are found distributed over a large area — the greatest concentration being in the Khasi-Jaintia Hills of Meghalaya, where large fields occur at Cherrapunjee, Mawphlang, Laitlyngkot, Laitkor, Jowai and Nartiang. In Manipur, megaliths are found spread over the Naga dominated areas of the districts of Chandel, Ukhrul, Tamenglong, Senapati and Churachandpur. A large number of megaliths are also seen in Vangchhia in Mizoram. In Dima Hasao of Assam, megaliths are found at Nenglo, Bolosam, Kobak, Derebora and Kartong. They are also found widely in the Hamren sub-division of Karbi-Anglong in Assam. In Nagaland megaliths are found extensively in the Kohima and Phek districts populated by Angami and others.

The first report of megalithic remains of this region was published by H.H. Godwin-Austen (1872), followed by G.B. Clarke (1874), T.C. Hodson (1911), P.R.T. Gurdon (1914), J.H. Hutton (1921, 1922a, 1922b,1923) and others. Much needed regional studies were undertaken by D. Roy (1963), A. Bareh (1981), N.C. Shadap Sen (1981), O.K. Singh (1985), P.B. Devi (1993, 2011), C. Mawlong (1996), W. Jamir (1997), D. Bezbaruah (2003), K. Choudhury (2004), T. Jamir (2005), Z. Venuh (2005), Malsawmliana (2011, 2016), D. Sarma (2011), R. Khongreiwo (2015), and M. Mitri (2016) among others. In recent years some of the analytic works in the area of megaliths include those of Mawlong (2004, 2009), Marak (2012c, 2015), Rousseleau (2012), Burke (2014), Khongreiwo (2014), Wangjin (2014), Wouters (2015), and Meitei and Marak (2015, 2016).

Types of Megaliths

Megaliths in the region are of a wide variety both in terms of structure and function. Due to the wide-ranging differences, classification of these stones is rather difficult. However, most of the authors while making a regional study have tended to group them into either funerary or commemorative types. In the following some of the basic types found in the region are discussed.

1. *Menhir*: These are the most common types found all over the region. There is a wide variation in terms of size – from the largest menhir seen in Nartiang in Jaintia Hills standing at 823 cm × 227 cm × 76 cm (height × breadth × thickness) to a menhir of 10 cms in the form of *a'song kosi* in Garo Hills. They are seen at different places in the village, near village paths leading to habitation areas, *jhum* fields, and near burial spots. They are raised during the lifetime of a person to attain the highest position in the social ladder, or after death. They also act as memorials and commemorations for various events. Alignments, consisting of carefully oriented row or series of menhirs in a plan; and avenues, consisting of two or more parallel rows of megaliths, are abundant in Churachandpur District (Manipur) and Vangchhia area (Mizoram). Sometimes menhirs form a constituent part of a complex — such as a stone circle, or in association with a number of dolmens. At Willong Khullen in Maram area (Manipur) one stone circle is constituted by fourteen menhirs out of thirty two stones in the circle (Devi, 1993). In Iawmusiang of Nangbah village (Jaintia Hills) the stone circle comprises a circular arrangement of nine menhirs with eleven dolmens and two stone slabs (Marak, 2012b).
2. *Dolmen*: These 'table stones' are found either singly or in cluster. Clustered dolmens are a common occurrence in areas occupied by the Karbis, Maos, Poumais, and Khasi-Jaintias. Among the latter, these structures are erected in front of a row of menhirs and usually in front of the tallest menhir (termed as 'maternal uncle stone'). One of the largest dolmens is seen in Laitlynkot in Khasi Hills. The horizontal slab measures 914.4 cm × 411 cm with an average thickness of 46 cm. It rests on ten upright pillars standing at 168 cms.

Among them, dolmens make up various complexes and the local terms (for the similar looking structure) enumerate their usages. For example, dolmens are known as *mawkynthei* (female stone) as well as *mawshongthait* (resting stones). In the context of North East India, a dolmen might appear like a cist[5] — but the difference being that the former is merely a table stone, while the latter is a box-like structure. It is also understood that the cist would possibly hold bones or ashes of the dead along with other offerings. Thus, in differentiating the two, I propose the former as a non-funerary structure, and the latter as a funerary structure.

3. *Cist*: A cist refers to a small stone-built coffin-like box or ossuary to hold the bodies of the dead, and these are usually underground or half underground (by definition, a dolmenoid cist). Therefore, in terms of defining them, these are box-like stone chambers buried underneath the ground. They vary in size from a few centimetnes in diameter to large ones. Many times these chambers are opened periodically by removing one of the vertical stones for depositing ashes or bones. Cists are rare in distribution in North East India, and is found abundantly only in Khasi—Jaintia Hills of Meghalaya. Stone cists of different shapes and sizes are seen among Khasis — of the individual, family and clan. From an archaeological context, Mushrif-Tripathy *et al.* (2009) reported different cists — oblong cist with primary/secondary inhumation, oblong cist (with transept wall) with primary/secondary inhumation, and jar-burial with secondary inhumation from Jotsoma near Kohima. A passage chamber leading to a cist, an exceptional feature in the region, was also reported from Nartiang in Jaintia Hills (Meitei & Marak, 2015).
4. *Capstone*: These are stone slabs, either circular or rectangular and of varying sizes. They are placed directly on a pit for primary/secondary inhumation along with grave offerings. At times, it covers the pit where skulls of human beings and bones of hunted animals are buried. They are generally found inside or outside the village settlement areas in Manipur. Some authors prefer to differentiate between capstones and stone slabs — the former are stones with funerary functions and are used as a cover for a pit, while the latter are stones

placed directly on the ground and are usually without any funerary functions. These stone slabs are also referred to as stone seats or seats for resting. These kind of stone slabs/ seats are seen in almost all the megalithic sites.

5. *Cairns*: Cairns consists of a heap of stones or rubbles of smaller but somewhat regular slabs either enclosed within a circle of small or considerable sized boulders or freely raised on the ground by piling up the stones one above the other without any enclosure. Cairns are abundant in Mao-Maram-Poumai areas of Senapati district in Manipur. Devi (1993) states that every Maram village has at least three cairns in every clan habitation area which also function as watch tower. One of the finest structures is seen at Willong Khullen, a Maram village, in Senapati district. This structure has a flat top surrounded by dressed slabs at regular intervals to serve as seats. This is at a height of over 355 cms. This cairn possesses two staircases on each side to reach the top of the platform. On the other hand, cairns as burial stones are seen in Shangpung in Jaintia Hills (Meitei & Marak, 2015).
6. *Trilithons*: Trilithons or 'three stones' (from Greek, *tri* meaning 'three' and *lithos* meaning 'stone') refers to a structure consisting of two large vertical stones (posts) supporting a third stone set horizontally across the top. These types of stones are usually seen to act as a gateway, i.e. entry or exit gates to the villages. In the village of Nongbareh in War Jaintia area, the structure *dwarkor* is morphologically a trilithon. This stone acted as the entry and exit into the village. The pillars stand at 102 × 52 × 2, while the slab at the top is 82 × 22 × 2 in breadth (Meitei, 2017). Many of the traditional village gates in Mao Maram areas also appear to be a trilithon.
7. *Stone Jars*: Within the type of megaliths, stone jars are a class apart — not only due to its morphology but also due to its archaic nature. This is the only class of stones which do not have a living tradition attached to it. In 2015 Thakuria and Jamir (Thakuria *et al.*, 2016) undertook an exploration of sites in Dima Hasao mentioned by Mills and Hutton (1932). Similar types are also seen in Saipung reserve forest, Jaintia Hills. In a preliminary exploration[6] in October 2016, we located two sites in Thlangmoi Biate village. These sites

were referred to as *Lungzubel* by the local Biate population ('rice brewing pots' in Biate language). In *Lungzubel* I, eleven intact jars were seen; while in all 30-40 (in various conditions of disarray) stone jars were identified. In *Lungzubel* II, 40-50 numbers of jars were present. We classified these as — *Type 1*: Round jar with flattened top and small central mouth, *Type 2*: Round jar with flattened top with large central mouth, and *Type 3*: Elongated dome-shaped jars. From an uprooted jar we surmised that only one-fifth of *Type 3* protrude above the surface. One interesting structure found were large stone slabs in both the locations. In *Lungzubel* I, three large circular slabs were found, the largest showed dimensions of 17 feet in circumference and 10 inch in thickness.

8. *Wooden Structures*: In some of the tribes of the region, instead of stone, wooden structures are raised. *Maran-tarungs* are forked wooden posts or Y-posts found inside habitation areas in front of the merit seeker's house among the Tangkhul Nagas. These are found in a cluster constituted by five or ten such posts and always in association with one or two menhirs. *Lamal-bam*, a small collection of stones with a stout wooden

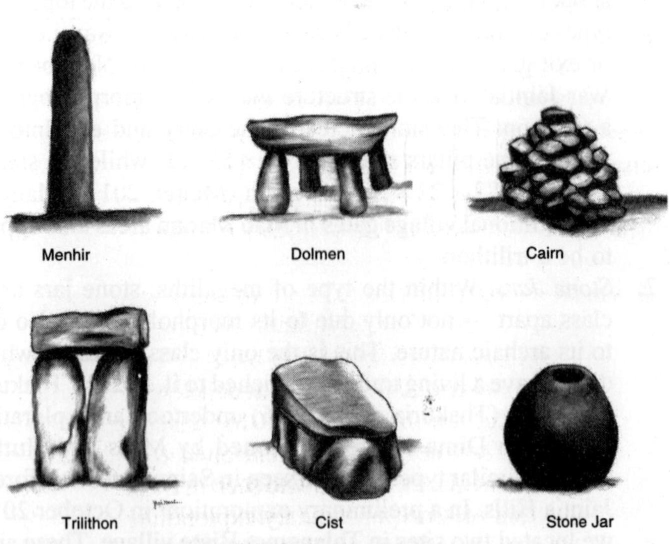

Fig. 1. Types of megaliths found in North East India

post and branches of a special kind of tree along with Y-post, is commonly found in Maring villages of Chandel District, Manipur. Garos use a Y-shaped post, to which they tether bulls before sacrifice in their death ceremonies and more or less round ones called *kima* as memorials to their dead (Playfair, 1909). These *kimas* are at times shaped like a human figure and clothes and ornaments attached to it.

Functional Attributes

Based on use and function, the megaliths of North East India can be grouped into two main types, however, it is clear that there is a wide variation amongst them.

A. Funerary Stones

These are related to funerary functions, and may or may not contain the bones of the deceased. It may either consist of an underground chamber (like a cist) among Khasis, or an upright stone or raised platform with or without a horizontal flat stone directly covering the pit burial or horizontal flat stone resting on three or smaller stones like a dolmen. In both cases, these stones — its erection and usage —will be accompanied with a number of rituals and ceremonies. As mentioned earlier the custom of cist-burial among Khasis takes the form of *mawphew* (individual grave), *mawkynroh* (family grave) and *mawniam* (clan grave). Therefore, for an individual, the bones will move twice, if not thrice, to the final resting place which is the clan cist. *Taideli-atu* among Liangmeis is a burial stone serving as sitting stone. This is also a memorial stone as it is raised in memory of a dead person within three to five years of death.

B. Non-Funerary Stones

1. *Memorial Stone*: Memorial stones or commemorative stones are of two kinds. First, are those in memory of the dead, and second, are those that are raised during the lifetime of a merit seeker. Structurally, they may be either menhirs or alignments but functionally they are memorials. Among Anals of Manipur, *tutangkam* is erected in the memory of an outstanding person who could perform the *Akam*

sacrifices (a series of feasts of merit). On the other hand, *lungpatha* is raised as memorial stone when the performer is still alive. *Anhu* is raised by a Chakesang performer of *Anhu* feast. Today, such structures are also built to commemorative significant events such as the setting up of a church or school.

2. *Resting Stone*: These are stone seats used for taking rest and refreshment. *Maning-toba-tusom* are stone seats with menhir among Liangmeis. *Ranii-atu* is a cairn with resting or seating seats and *arou-atu* are stone seats with or without an upright stone among Marams. *Yosotokho* are cairns or raised platforms or enclosures with stones and *kathi-tokho* are raised platforms of stone seats and miniature upright stones among Poumais. *Bamdon* is raised by wealthy Kabuis as resting places on the way leading to jungles, *jhum* fields or by the side of inter-village path leading to the plains by giving feasts to the village. *Maw-shongthait* or resting stones are also found commonly in different places in Khasi and Jaintia Hills, Meghalaya.
3. *Watch Tower*: Among Angami Nagas, *dahu* is a rectangular pyramidal platform, structurally a cairn that is used as a watch tower in wars with neighbouring clans (Hutton, 1926:74). Devi (1993) mentions that every Maram village in Manipur has at least three cairns that act as a watch tower.
4. *Religious Stone*: These stones comprise different structural types. *Kapet-bam* is a stone circle among Liangmeis connected with a number of religious ceremonies. Marams have a cairn (called *atuchagakamatei*) which is considered sacred and no one is allowed to touch it. *Bhamdon* among Kabuis are menhirs where the village deity resides. These are small menhirs erected in pairs and located outside the main habitation area but within the village gate. Among Khasi-Jaintias, every sacred grove has a deity who resides in a dolmen. On this sacred stone, the priest performs a series of annual rituals.
5. *Witness or Judiciary Stone*: Among the Laingmeis, Marams and Tangkhuls, an oath stone is present — where it is believed that if anyone bears false witness, they will be punished by the spirit of the stone. It is called *atukra* among Liangmeis, *beitung* among Marams and *rihai-lung* among

Tangkhuls. *Mawsmai* in Khasi Hills is also a witness or oath stone, after which the village of Mawsmai was named. It is said that when the feuds between Cherra and Mawsmai villages were settled, the people made peace and swore by the stone which they set up.

6. *Path-stone*: Among Khasis some megaliths are seen showing the way or acting as guiding stones. *Mawlynti* is a group of three menhirs and one dolmen. This group of stones is planted on the way to the cists (burial stones). The slab of the dolmen is referred to as *mawkynthai* and dedicated to the ancestress of the clan. The middle menhir which is the tallest is called *mawkni* and dedicated to the maternal uncle. *Mawaibam* is similar to the *mawlynti* with three menhirs and a slab in front set up after the ceremonial deposition of bones in the clan tomb. They are also planted along the path leading to the clan tomb.
7. *Village Foundation Stone*: Among Liangmeis such stones are raised by anyone who wishes to be the chief of a new village. If there is more than one aspirant, then go to the place where they intend to set up a new village with a rooster each. They spend the night in the new location and wait for dawn. The aspirant whose rooster crows first is believed to be ordained by god and hence accepted as the new chief. Immediately the new chief raises a village foundation stone called *petbam*. The person who raises the *petbam* also constructs *kapet-bam* for keeping hunted heads of wild animals and enemies. Thereafter, the clan members of the new chief under his supervision build a cairn called *tabaolong* on the highest ridge of the village to act as a watch tower. Among Garos whenever a new village is set up the clan members of the founding mother erect a set of menhirs known as *a'song kosi*.
8. *Market Stone*: In Khasi-Jaintia Hills, a series of menhirs and dolmens are seen to mark a market area in the past. These clusters are impressive and dominate the geo-space of the village. Such impressive market stones (a series of menhirs and dolmens) are seen in many places — such as Nartiang in Jaintia Hills and lewdoh in Shillong.

A Living Tradition

Generally megaliths are ancient tombs, but as mentioned in the preceding pages in North East India, there exist a living tradition of erecting megaliths and of adherence to socio-cultural functions. This cultural practice associated with megaliths by living people is referred to as *living megalithism*.

Putting up Megaliths

Megaliths continue to be erected here. Among Mao Nagas, Singh (1985) narrates that the erection of megaliths takes place after a series of feasts given by the merit seeker — each succeeding one more grand and opulent in nature. Among Karbis (both from the hills and plains), erection of menhirs continue to take place regularly as a part of funerary traditions — in the former it is collectively done after a few years, while in the latter it is done on a regular basis for one individual. Among Khasi-Jaintias, the 'maintenance' of clan and burial stones is paramount. I stress on maintenance, since majority of the megaliths are merely maintained — through periodical cleaning by clan members. Interestingly, some broken cists are also spruced up by using modern materials such as cement and mortar. In April 2016, the festival of *Lympung Sengkhilang* was held in village Narwan, Jaintia Hills. This festival commemorates the abiding connection between the Jaintias and Khasis, and leads to the exchange of megaliths (three menhirs and one capstone) between Jaintia Hills and Khasi Hills every alternate year. In 2016, the megaliths were gifted by Mawngap village (Khasi Hills) to Narwan (Jaintia Hills) at a distance of over 130 kilometres — and carried with the help of cranes and two trucks with accompanying rituals.

Feasting for Merit

Feasts of merit given by the merit-seeker are a common occurrence in the erection of megaliths. In the early 1920s, Dewar (1966) witnessed the erection of a megalith among the Angami Nagas after a series of feasts. However, even today such feasts leading to the setting up of a megalith is still witnessed. These feasts are given by anyone for the whole village/villages and meant for the fertility of the people and crops, and thereby achieve the honour of setting up a menhir. Among Mizos, the successful completion of a series of feasts gives the merit-seeker the honoured title of *Thangchhuah*, which allows him certain privileges including the right to set up a menhir. These feasts and ceremonies include the following — *Sakung, Chawng, Sedawi Chhun, Sekhuan* and *Mitthirawplam*, and the final feast *Khuangchawi* which lasts for three days. These feasts successively become more opulent starting with the slaughter of only one pig to many pigs and mithun along with a large quantity of rice beer. One who performs the feasts of merit is also entitled to other privileges — such as the right to use certain decorations on the house — *ceka* and carvings and display of heads on the wall — among the Chakesang Nagas.

Male or Female?

Among Garos, *jikma* is a set of female stones and *jikse* a set of male stones (both alignments), and these together form the village foundation stones (*a'song kosi*) representing the two clans who set up a village. The former symbolizes the matrilineal kin of the founding mother, and the latter the matrilineal kin of the founding father. Among Khasi-Jaintia, an interesting morpho-cultural phenomenon is witnessed — menhirs are referred as male stones (*mawshynrang*), and dolmens as female stones (*mawkynthei*). The 'clan stones' comprise of 3/5 menhirs and a dolmen, sometimes the number of menhirs and dolmens going up to 15 and 10 respectively. Therefore, each cluster of clan stones comprise both male and female stones. Since they represent the matrilineal kin, the male stones represent the maternal uncles and dolmens the ancestresses. In all cases, the central menhir is always taller than those flanking it on both sides, and represents the 'maternal uncle'. The menhirs encompass strength due to its size and shape; guidance since majority of the menhirs also acts as path-stones and boundary-stones; and dominance since it is the tallest structure. On the other hand, femininity entails motherhood: this is exemplified by the flat stones which structurally being opposite to the upright stones, indicate a nurturer-ancestress. This is also supported by the fact that the flat-stones are also used as resting-stones. Furthermore, the goddesses (deities) of the sacred groves reside, not in an upright standing menhir, but in a flat-shaped dolmen (Marak, 2015).

Society and Politics

It is understood that the underlying social structure can also be observed in the way that the stones are put up symbolically. One of the most interesting features that are witnessed in this connection is the relation of matriliny with stones in the Khasi-Jaintia region. Among the Jaintias, after cremation, the bones are carefully kept in the individual family cist, until they are handed over to the deceased's maternal relatives after the performance of certain rites. When a woman dies, her husband does not conduct the cremation, which is done by her children and clansmen. A woman who dies without any children may be cremated by the husband but he cannot collect nor receive the bones which will be done by the deceased's clansmen and women. From these individual cists, the bones are collected in a year or even later and placed in a larger cist of the sub-clan/lineage. Thereafter, after some years when the clan members are able to gather sufficient money for the ceremony, these bones from family and sub-clan cists are gathered and laid to rest in the clan cist. Thus, an individual born into a clan will likely travel thrice if not at least twice to reach its final resting place at the clan cist, even if it takes years to do so. The above ceremonies reiterate the importance of the clan system among the matrilineal Khasi-Jaintia people, and, therefore, a person born into a clan will likely remain in it even after death (Marak, 2012b, 2012c).

Space and Territoriality

Following Renfrew (1976) and Chapman (1981), we can state that the megaliths in North East India are symbols of territoriality. In Khasi Hills, lands and territories are 'marked' by the presence of clan tombs (cists) and clan stones — giving a stamp of identity and ownership over an area. From the study of ancestral clan tombs, it is easy to locate the origin of clans. Selection of the spots where megaliths are located also appear to be planned — since majority of them are found either at the highest point of the area or are visible in the landscape from afar. The concept of territoriality — marking the landscape with 'social memories' — are witnessed extensively in other areas too, including the sites occupied by Nagas, Karbis, Mizos and Garos.

Change and Continuity

Changes have taken place in the cultural milieu due to forces such as modern education, proselytization, industrialization, urbanization etc. which have negatively impacted megalithic tradition in the region, which has been touched upon by most of the authors in this book. It is only among traditional believers like the *Seng Khasi*, *Niamtre* and *Songsarek* in Meghalaya that this culture seems to flourish though with much limitations and modifications among the latter. Unlike the Khasi-Jaintia Hills and the Naga occupied areas, megalithic structures in Sikkim and Garo Hills appear to be in the process of becoming archaic. However, it is the stone jars of Dima Hasao and Saipung reserve forests that have been completely erased from memory — there exists no living tradition connected to them.

The spread of Christianity, along with modernization and development, has impacted on this tradition. Mawlong (2009) states, that as a result of the missionary zeal to dispel ignorance, superstition and the worship of evil spirits, the megalithic tradition was seriously eroded and gradually disappeared. However, in recent times, revivalism in past cultural practices within the fold of Christianity, which earlier was the strongest opponent, is witnessed. The Catholic Church in recent times made efforts to preserve and conserve some of the surviving megalithic monuments which stand within the church premises like the one at Laitlyngkot church compound in Jaintia Hills. Similarly, the Catholic church at Laitumkhrah in the city of Shillong erected a set of menhirs and a dolmen within its premises to mark the centenary celebrations of the Catholic Church in the Khasi-Jaintia Hills in 1990.

A similar feature taking place in Jaintia Hills indicates the secularization of megaliths which were once solely connected to socio-religious life of the *Niamtre* Jaintias (Marak, 2012b). Thus, the stones which traditionally had religious connotations were made 'secular' by taking away its sacred meaning and putting it up within church premises as mere tokens. In this continuance of past tradition the 'politics of culture' is inherent. This revivalism, however, does not in any way reflect a re-sacralization of traditional symbols — but rather a token to counter the challenges of the traditionalists, especially, the Seng Khasi proponents[7] in the context of Khasi-Jaintia Hills (Marak, 2015). This was a counteractive step so that the church could be viewed as pro-tradition. This social reality is supported by the fact that except the structure (megalith), no other socio-religious activity of the past survives within the Christian complex. This reality finds parallel in the revivalism of 'folk culture' traditions in North East India, such as songs and dances, dress and ornaments, celebrations and rituals, leading to a quasi-sacralization of the past.

Dating Megaliths

Archaeological evidences have proved beyond doubt that North East India was occupied in the Stone Age, but a temporal framework is missing. Prehistoric sites, i.e. sites with evidence of early man such as stone tools and prehistoric pottery, have been reported from all the eight states. The Neolithic stage exemplified by ground and polished axes and adzes have been reported from all the states — some in the Colonial period, and many more with reference to sites in recent time. Debate, however, surrounds the pre-Neolithic phase. Though the Palaeolithic stage is still questioned by many, it is beyond doubt that there are indeed 'Palaeolithic-like' tools found in the region. The intervening phase, represented by the Hoabinhian, has been reported from almost all the states in recent years (Sharma, 1988; Ramesh, 1989; Ashraf, 1990, 2006, 2010; Singh, 1997; Sharma, 2003; Sharma, 2007), and it is now quite possible that the 'Palaeolithic-like' tools that were once clubbed under 'Palaeolithic' could likely be Hoabinhian in nature.

In 1981, H.D. Sankalia, the doyen of Indian archaeology, proposed a framework for prehistoric North East India on the basis of typo-technology and stratigraphical evidences provided by S.N. Rajguru. This puts the Neolithic phase to *c.* 5000–2000 BC, the Mesolithic to *c.* 10,000–5,000 BC, and the Palaeolithic to 2,00,000–10,000 BC. Whether this classification is correct, and if so, to what extent, still remains to be seen.

One of the oldest chronometric dates come from Tripura, where N.R. Ramesh dated 'preneoliths' to 34,680±2960 BP by radiocarbon dating certain "peaty material found in the upper part of the formation" indicating an Upper Pleistocene age for the site (Ramesh, 1986:293). The Neolithic, on the other hand, has been dated from 1190±90 to 3450±110 BP (*ibid.*). From Manipur, O.K. Singh procured two dates. A charcoal sample from the corded ware stratum at Nongpok Keithelmanbi was dated to 4460±120 BP, and a TL sample from Napachik to 1450 BC (Singh, 1997). In recent times, M. Mitri and others procured C^{14} dates from four samples of charcoal from Lawnongthroh ranging from 2960±30 BP to 1640±30 BP, and one charcoal sample from Myrkhan to 3500±30 BP (Mitri *et al.*, 2015). However, older by a couple of hundred years is the AMS date procured from an ash deposit of the basal level at Ranyak khen by T. Jamir and his team. This pushes the prehistoric occupation by humans in the region to 5560±40 BP (Jamir *et al.*, 2017).

Going by typo-technology, cord impressed pottery reported from various locations (Sharma, 1967; Roy, 1977, 2004; Rao, 1977; Singh, 2008) is taken as a marker of Neolithic culture in the region. However, in a recent study in Bambooti an interesting fact emerged. That around the same time, indigenous handmade pottery was also in use in Bambooti at the foothills of Garo Hills. From OSL dates procured from three sites, an average date of 3226±0.6 years can be taken (Ashraf & Duarah, 2013-14).

When it comes to megalithic cultures (possibly post-Neolithic), which are chronologically seen to appear in the intervening phase of historicity – one can argue that perhaps metallurgy or the simplistic use of metal is required to construct them. In this connection, the mining of iron ore become important. Two Polish scientists working on geo-environment recently dated charcoal and residual iron slag from several sites in Khasi Hills. The site of Nongkrem gave a date of 2140±80 BP, and the site of Raitkteng to 1110±30 BP (Prokop & Suliga, 2013) – thus identifying the earliest iron smelting centre in North East India. It is pertinent to note that almost 25 years ago, Ashraf, while undertaking a study in Parsiparlo, mentions the stage of 'ferrolithic' in the context of the frontier state. By this he meant a stage where the Neolithic intrudes into iron using stage (Ashraf, 1990) — and this could be true to many sites in the region.

From the megalithic zones, a few dates have been procured — which give some clue to the temporality of these stones. The C^{14} date procured from Jotsoma gives a *very* recent date of 200±30 BP (Mushrif-Tripathy *et al.* 2009). This pushes the Jotsoma cist burials to 17th century AD. However, the megalithic site at Marakdola in Khasi Hills gave a comparatively older date. Here, from a single cultural horizon cord-grooved kaolin pottery found in association with menhirs and dolmens were carbon dated to 1296±100 BP (Rao, 1991). From the same area (which Ashraf and his team refers to as Maragdola), a recent excavation revealed a large number of potsherds of kaolin ware from the foundation trench of a menhir which were

OSL dated to 15th century AD. These dates prove beyond doubt that megalithic culture of the region is rather of recent origin, and it flourished approximately 1000 years ago. This supposition is supported by oral traditions especially connected to the Jaintia and Kachari kingdoms.

Organisation of the Book

This book is thematically organised in three sections. Section I is titled "Regional Specifics" and gives a regional overview of megalithic traditions existent in North East India today. Six chapters encompassing six states are discussed herein. The first chapter by **Marco Mitri** gives an overall discussion of the megaliths of Khasi-Jaintia Hills of Meghalaya. Being a Khasi himself, he puts forward an insider's classification of the megaliths which is unique — for instance, he distinguishes between different types of dolmens, on the basis of nomenclature which plays itself out in structure and function. He also brings in a socio-cultural and political analysis of these stones found in the region. Chapter 2 is by **Potshangbam Binodini Devi** who gives a comprehensive morphological and functional discussion on Poumai Naga megaliths in Manipur. Of interest are stones which are very unique in terms of nomenclature as well as usage — for example, there is a stone referred as "cat killing stone", where a cat is actually killed. The next chapter discussing the megaliths of Nagaland is **Watijungshi Jamir**'s chapter on chronology and affinities of Naga megaliths. He looks at the different hypotheses and theories existent in megalithic cultures of the world, and tries to place the Naga megaliths within its fold. Chapter 4 is by **Kalpana Choudhury** who brings in the process of megalithic erection among the Plains Karbis of Demoria in Assam. It becomes clear in her chapter that the process of selection, transportation, erection, and post-erection stages are connected to a number of rituals. In chapter 5, **Mawlsamliana** presents the megalithic perspective from the Mizo worldview. The Mizos are found to raise megaliths to commemorate important events such as the achievements of the chief and the *thangchhuahpa*, and their structures may be of both wood and stone, on which the figures of humans and animals were carved. These carvings provide valuable insights into several aspects of early Mizo society. In the last chapter in this section, a first of its kind, **Charisma Lepcha** discusses the megaliths from Sikkim. She states that the cultures of these stones are in essence a celebration of Mt. Kanchenjunga which is of great symbolic and social value among the Lepchas.

Section II is titled "Symbolic Nature of Megaliths" and presents very interesting perspectives and analyses of the stones of the region in many and varied ways. **Mayanglambam ManiBabu**, in the first chapter in this section, discusses how ideas are stored and exposed through megaliths and is a unique manifestation of human cognition. He argues that large stones are exploited, materialised and used as 'external symbolic storage' by the indigenous Naga people (Mao, Maram and Poumai) of Manipur. In chapter 8, **Tiatoshi Jamir** discusses the conception of monumentality and landscape among the Nagas and how it is connected to social memories. He states that memorials carry not only personal memories of one's attainment of status in the Naga milieu, but also are manifestations of a collective past. In chapter 9, **Akoijam Milan Meitei** discusses how the religious practices of the Jaintias of Meghalaya is intrinsically connected with their mortuary rites which find manifestation in a variety of megaliths — ranging from cairns to cists to dolmens. Of interest are also the passage chamber tombs that he touches upon, which are rather unique in the North East Indian megalithic map. **Jelle J.P. Wouters**, in the next chapter, states that megaliths both produce and communicate the form and substance of social life. Keeping a Chakhesang village at the core, he narrates how stones are transformed from a 'natural entity' into a 'social repertoire' of feelings, emotions, and beliefs, finally positing that stones can speak. In the last chapter in this section, **Raphael Rousseleau** brings in interesting narrations of the Nartiang site – of colonial accounts, Khasi/Jaintia scholars, and complementary ethnographic enquiries. This encompasses the socio-economic and political contexts of the impressive megalithic market complex.

The only constant in culture studies is change itself, and this is exemplified when we look at the changes that take place which leads to complete annihilation or modification. The final Section "Land, Change and Continuity" of this book deals with this important aspect. Chapter 12 is by two young authors who are currently undertaking a study on megalithic cultures in Garo Hills. Here, **Gangotri Bhuyan** and **Tengnang D. Sangma** gives an overview of the type of megaliths that are found in the region — specifying the changes that have taken place and the 'modified' structures — of wood and bamboo — that have now appeared. In chapter 13, Ditamulu Vasa discusses the non-lithic privileges that a feast-giver achieves after giving a series of feasts – the *ceka*, for instance, a projection that only a 'rich man' can put up on his house. These non-lithic structures appear to be an extension and a modification to the lithic structures that a feast-giver has the right to put up. Chapter 14 by **Sukanya Sharma** succinctly sums up the changes that have taken place in the town of Cherrapunjee (in the context of megaliths) and the reasons thereof. In lines of cultural resource management, she presents a list of 'how to' conserve the megaliths. Perhaps, Sharma's 'how to' could be applied in other regions as well. This chapter, in essence, concludes this book most meaningfully.

NOTES

1. This Karbi prayer is a part of the ritual which precedes the transport of a stone from its natural context to the social context. For more details, see Choudhury — this book.
2. This chapter appeared as "Megaliths of North East India" in T.B. Subba (ed.), *North East India: A Handbook of Anthropology* (2012), and published by Orient Blackswan, New Delhi.
3. Even though the term 'megalithism' is mostly used in relation to funerary, I prefer to use it to refer to various cultural practices (both past and present) — both funerary and non-funerary — that is connected to the erection of *usually* large stone structures. However, in North East India, we see the erection of smaller stones as well as non-lithic structures such as bamboo and wood which also can be clubbed under 'megaliths'.
4. Dolmen, cromlech and menhir are the basic classification of megaliths used in the context of European archaeology. A dolmen [from Brittonic language; possibly Irish *dolmain* meaning table stone], also referred to as a table stone, is a single-chamber megalithic tomb consisting of two or more vertical stones supporting a flat stone. The term cromlech is no longer used in academia [from Welsh *crom* meaning bowed/arched, and *llech* meaning flat stone], but if used it is taken to be synonymous for a dolmen and other stones like menhirs — but, if differentiated, then a cromlech usually stood for a number of stones arranged in some manner. Menhir [from Brittonic languages, *men* for stone and *hir* for long], refers to long and large upright standing stones. These appear to be the most common type of stones erected anywhere across the world.
5. A basic distinction between the terms dolmen, cist, and dolmenoid cist lay in the manner of laying these structures, even though not everyone

agrees to this distinction. A dolmen is a structure which lies above the ground; while in opposition to it, a cist is a structure that lies completely underground. Therefore, a dolmenoid cist is a structure that is half above the ground and half underground.

6. This exploration was undertaken by the Department of Anthropology, North Eastern Hill University, Shillong in the month of October 2016.
7. Established in Shillong in 1899, the founders of the Seng Khasi were men who had a liberal education, business opportunities and had found government employment. The Seng Khasis were witness to the zealous efforts of missionaries propagating the faith and were concerned that large numbers of Khasis were being converted to Christianity. The Seng Khasi initiated the process of revivalism and reformation of the Khasi religion and remains an active religious group even today.

REFERENCES

Ashraf, A.A., 1990. *Prehistoric Arunachal: A Study on Prehistory and Ethnoarchaeology of Kamala Valley*. Itanagar: Directorate of Research.

_____. 2006. "Autochthons of Meghalaya in Anthropo-Archaeological Perspectives". *Humankind*, 2: 31-36.

_____. 2010. *Stone Age Traditions of Meghalaya: A Study of Variation and Continuity*. Oxford: Archaeopress.

Ashraf, A.A. and A.G., Duarah. 2013-14. "Bambooti: A Late Neolithic site in the foothills of south-western Assam". *Bulletin of the Department of Anthropology*, XV: 23-32.

Bareh, A., 1981. *Megalithic Culture among the Khasis with Reference to Mawiong Village*. Ph.D. Thesis, North Eastern Hill University.

Bezbaruah, D. 2003. *Megalithic remains in Karbi Anglong District: A study in the Context of Karbi Culture*. Ph.D. Thesis, Gauhati University, Guwahati, Assam.

Burke, D.. 2014. "*Jingkynmaw*: Memories written in stone". In T. Jamir & M. Hazarika (eds.), *50 Years After Daojali-Hading: Emerging Perspectives in the Archaeology of North East India* (Essays in Honour of T.C. Sharma). New Delhi: Research India Press, pp. 360-75.

Chapman, R., 1981. "The emergence of formal disposal areas and the "problems" of Megalithic Tombs in Prehistoric Europe". In R. Chapman, I. Kinnes & K. Randsborg (eds.), *The Archaeology of Death*. Cambridge: Cambridge University Press, pp. 71-81.

Childe, V.G., 1946. "The distribution of Megalithic Cultures and Their Influence on Ancient and Modern Civilizations". *Man*, 46:97.

Choudhury, K., 2004. *The Megaliths and their Associated Remains in*

Dimoria Area of Kamrup District, Assam. Ph.D. Thesis, Gauhati University, Guwahati, Assam.

Clarke, G.B., 1874. "The stone monuments of Khasi Hills". *Journal of Royal Anthropological Institute*, 3: 481-93.

Daniel, G., 1962. *The Megalithic Builders of Western Europe*. Harmondsworth: Penguin Books.

Devi, P.B., 1993. *Studies on the Megalithic Remains of Manipur*. Ph.D. Thesis, Gauhati University, Guwahati, Assam.

_____. 2011. *The Megalithic Cultures of Manipur*. Delhi: Agam Kala Prakashan.

Dewar, S., 1966. "The Ceremony of Erecting a Megalith among the Angami Nagas". *Folklore*, 77(4): 264-69.

Godwin-Austen, H.H., 1872. "On the Stone Monuments of Khasi Hills tribes". *Journal of the Royal Anthropological Institute*, 1: 122-36.

Gurdon, P.R.T. [1909]1914. *The Khasis*. London: MacMillan & Co.

Hodson, T.C., 1911. *The Naga Tribes of Manipur*. London: MacMillan & Co.

Hutton, J.H., 1921. *The Angami Nagas: With Notes on Neighbouring Tribes*. London: MacMillan & Co.

_____. 1922a. "Carved Monoliths at Dimapur and an Angami Naga ceremony". *The Journal of the Royal Anthropological Institute of Great Britain and Ireland*, 52: 55-70.

_____. 1922b. "The Meaning and Method of the Erection of Monoliths by the Naga Tribes". *The Journal of the Royal Anthropological Institute of Great Britain and Ireland*, 52:242-49.

_____.1923. "Carved Monoliths at Jamuguri in Assam". *The Journal of the Royal Anthropological Institute of Great Britain and Ireland*, 53:150-59.

_____. 1926. "The Use of Stone in the Naga Hills". *The Journal of the Royal Anthropological Institute of Great Britain and Ireland*, 56: 71-82.

_____. 1929. "Assam Megaliths". *Antiquity*, 3: 324-38.

Jamir, T., 2005. *Megalithic Burial Tradition of the Nagas (with special reference to the Angami and Chakhesang Nagas): An Ethno-archaeological Perspective*. Ph.D. Thesis, Deccan College P.G. and Research Institute.

Jamir, T., D. Tetso and Z. Venuh. 2017. "Recent Archaeological Investigation around the Naga Metamorphics and Ophiolite belt of the Indo-Myanmar Border". In K. Paddayya & B. Basak (eds.), *Prehistoric Research in the Sub-continent: A Reappraisal and New Directions*. New Delhi: Primus Books.

Jamir, W., 1997. *Megalithic Traditions in Nagaland: An Ethno-archaeological Study*. Ph.D. Thesis, Gauhati University, Guwahati, Assam.

Khongreiwo, R. (2014). Landscapes, Monuments, Collective Memories: Understanding pre-Christian belief systems and Socio-religious Practices of the Nagas. In T. Jamir & M. Hazarika (eds.), *50 Years After Daojali-Hading: Emerging Perspectives in the Archaeology of North East India.* New Delhi: Research India Press, pp. 292-317.

_____. (2015). *Archaeologies of Landscapes: A Social and Religious History of the Nagas of Nagaland and Manipur.* Ph.D. Dissertation, University of Delhi, Delhi.

Majumdar, D.N., 1980. "North East India: A Profile". In T.C. Sharma & D.N. Majumdar (eds.), *Eastern Himalayas: A Study on Anthropology and Tribalism.* New Delhi: Cosmo Publications, pp. 23-62.

Malsawmliana. 2011. *Megalithic Monuments of Mizoram: A Descriptive Study.* Ph.D. Thesis, North Eastern Hill University, Shillong.

_____. 2016. *Megalithic Culture of Mizoram.* New Delhi: Research India Press.

Marak, Q., 2012a. "Megaliths of North East India". In T.B. Subba (ed.), *North East India: A Handbook of Anthropology.* New Delhi: Orient Blackswan, pp. 34-53.

_____. 2012b. "Megaliths, Types, and Its Living Traditions among the Jaintias of North Eastern India". *Journal of Indo-Pacific Archaeology,* 32: 45-53.

_____. 2012c. "Matriliny and Megalithic Practices of the Jaintias of Meghalaya". *Indian Anthropologist,* 42(2):67-82.

_____. 2015. "Megaliths and Living Cultural Traditions". In S. Sengupta (ed.), *Explorations in Anthropology of North East India,* New Delhi: Gyan Books, 31-51.

Mawlong, C., 1996. *Megalithic Monuments of Khasi-Jaintia Hills: An Ethnoarchaeology Study.* Ph.D. Thesis, North Eastern Hill University, Shillong.

_____. 2004. "Megaliths and social formation in Khasi Jaintia Hills" Playfair, A. [(1909)]1998]. *The Garos.* Delhi: Spectrum Publications.. In M. Momin & C.A. Mawlong (eds.), *Society and Economy in North East India,* Vol.1. New Delhi: Regency, pp. 35-56.

_____. 2009. "Christianity and the Megalithic Tradition in the Khasi-Jaintia Hills: A Preliminary Study of the Processes of Deculturation and Enculturation". In T.B. Subba, J. Puthenpurakal & S.J. Puykunnel (eds.), *Christianity and Change in North East India.* New Delhi: Concept, Publishing Company, pp.194-202.

Meitei, A.M., 2017. *Megaliths and Jaintia Culture: A Study in Archaeological Anthropology.* Ph.D. Thesis, North Eastern Hill University, Shillong.

Meitei, A.M. and Q. Marak. 2015. "A Study of Traditional Mortuary Practices of the Jaintias of Meghalaya, India". *Journal of Indo-Pacific Archaeology,* 39: 74-80.

_____. 2016. "Giant Stones: A Study on the Significance of Menhir(s) in Jaintia Hills, Meghalaya, India". *Nritattva: The Anthropology*, 8(10)/ 9(11): 33-48.

Mitri, M., 2016. *The Living Megalithic Culture of Khasi-Jaintia Hills, Meghalaya*. Shillong: Don Bosco Centre for Indigenous Cultures.

Mitri, M.B., D. Kharmawphlang and H. Syiemlieh. 2015. "A Preliminary Report on the Excavation at the Neolithic Site of Lawnongthroh (Sohpetbneng Hill), Khasi Hills Meghalaya". *Man and Environment*, XL (1): 33-42.

Mushrif, V., T. Jamir, D. Vasa and S.R. Walimbe. 2009. *Human Skeletal Remains from Jotsoma, Nagaland: Osteobiographic Studies*. Kolkata: Centre for Archaeological Studies and Training.

Playfair, A. [1909]1975. *The Garos*. Guwahati: United Publishers.

Prokop, P. and I. Suliga. 2013. "Two thousand years of iron smelting in the Khasi Hills, Meghalaya, North East India". *Current Science*, 104(6): 761-68.

Ramesh, N.R., 1986. "Discovery of Stone Age Tools from Tripura and its Relevance to the Prehistory of South-east Asia". *GEOSEA V Proceedings* Vol. II, *Geol. Soc. Malaysia, Bulletin,* 20: 289-310.

_____. 1989. *A Study on Geomorphology, Quaternary Geology and Associated Cultural remains of West Tripura District*. Ph.D. Thesis, Gauhati University, Guwahati, Assam.

Rao, S.N., 1977. "Continuity and Survival of Neolithic Traditions in North Eastern India". *Asian Perspectives*, XX (2): 191-205.

_____. 1991. "Megalithic Practices among Khasis and Nagas of North Eastern India". In J.P. Singh & G. Sengupta (eds.), *Archaeology of North Eastern India*. New Delhi: Vikas Publishing House, pp. 106-25.

Renfrew, C., 1976. "Megaliths, Territories and Populations". In S.J. De Laet (ed.), *Acculturation and Continuity in Atlantic Europe*. Brugge: De Tempel, pp. 198-220.

Roy, D., 1963. "The Megalithic Culture of Khasi Hills". *Anthropos*, 58 (3 & 4): 520-86.

Rousseleau, R., 2012. Megalithic landscapes: Cultures and Identity in North East India. In Nicolas Laîné & Tanka B. Subba (eds.), *Nature, Environment and Society: Conservation, Governance and Transformation in India*. New Delhi: Orient Blackswan, pp. 17-35.

Roy, S.K., 1977. *A Study of the Ceramics from the Neolithic to Medieval Period of Assam: An Ethno-archaeological Approach*. Ph.D. Thesis, Gauhati University, Guwahati, Assam.

_____. 2004. *Ceramics of North East India: Ethno-archaeological Perspective*. Delhi/Itanagar: Himalayan Publication.

Shadap Sen, N.C., 1981. *The Origin and Early History of the Khasi-Synteng People*. Calcutta: Firma KLM. Private Limited.

Sarma, D., 2011. *Megalithic Traditions of the Karbis in the Hills and the Plains of Assam*. Ph.D. Thesis, Gauhati University, Guwahati, Assam.

Sharma, H.C., 2003. "Prehistoric Archaeology of North East India". In T.B. Subba & G.C. Ghosh (eds.), *The Anthropology of North East India*. New Delhi: Orient Longman, pp. 11-29.

Sharma, S., 2007. *Celts, Flakes and Bifaces: The Garo Hills Story*. Oxford: Archaeopress.

Sharma, T.C., 1967. "A Note on the Neolithic Pottery of Assam". *Man* (NS), 2(1): 126-28.

_____. 1988. "Discovery of Hoabinhian Cultural Relics in North East India". In N.C. Ghosh & S. Chakrabarty (eds.), *Adaptation and other Essays: Proceedings of the Archaeological Conference*. Viswa Bharati, Shantiniketan: Research Publications.

Shils, E., 1981. *Tradition*. Chicago: University of Chicago Press.

Singh, O.K., 1985. "A Live Megalithic Culture in Manipur". In V.N. Misra & P. Bellwood (eds.), *Recent Advances in Indo-Pacific Prehistory*. Proceedings of the International Symposium held at Poona, 19-20 December, 1978. New Delhi: Oxford & IBH, pp. 491-96.

_____. 1997. *Stone Age Archaeology of Manipur*. Imphal: Amusana Ins. of Antiquarian Studies.

_____. 2008. *Pottery Through the Ages in Manipur*. Imphal: Amusana Ins. of Antiquarian Studies.

Thakuria, T., T. Jamir and M.K. Chauley. 2016. "Stone jar burials in North Cachar District, Assam". *Man and Environment*, XLI (1): 44-51.

Venuh, Z. (2005). *Megaliths and Megalithic Traditions of the Chakhesang Nagas: Myths, Facts and Interpretations*. Ph.D. Thesis, Dibrugarh University, Assam.

Wangjin, W. (2014). "Ideologies, Identities and Memories: Interpreting Stone Structures of the Konyak and Angami Nagas". In T. Jamir and M. Hazarika (eds.), *50 Years After Daojali-Hading: Emerging Perspectives in the Archaeology of North East India* (Essays in Honour of T.C. Sharma). New Delhi: Research India Press, pp. 318-32.

Wouters, J.J.P., 2015. "The Social Lives of Stones: Studying the Past in the Chakhesang Naga Village of Phugwumi". *Anthropology Today: North East Institute for Research in Anthropology*, 1(1): 21-41.

Yondri, L., 2006. "A Short Review of the Megalithic Functions in Indonesia". In T. Simanjuntak, M. Hisyam, B. Prasetyo & T.S. Nastiti (eds.), *Archaeology: Indonesian Perspective: R.P. Soejono's Festschrift*. Jakarta: LIPI Press, pp. 295-302.

Section-I

Regional Specifics

1
The Enchanting Monuments of Khasi-Jaintia Hills

Marco Mitri

Introduction

The Khasi root word *kynmaw* or memory, which literally combines the words 'mark' (*kyn*) and 'stone' (*maw*), shows how stone monuments have become so important in the life of the people who have no art of writing (Burke, 2014). The Khasis are among the several groups of people in the Indian subcontinent where Megalithic tradition still survives as a 'living practice'. This has created attraction for many colonial writers who curiously wrote about the preliterate Khasi society and their prehistoric practice. Their reports have become an important source of information on the subject as they recorded the practice at the time when the native people were yet to be influenced by foreign culture.

The earliest detailed Report on Khasi megaliths was provided by H. Walters (1832), followed by the work of H. Yule (1842). The megalithic monuments have also attracted the attention of various workers starting with J.D. Hooker (1854), H.H. Godwin-Austen (1872), C.B. Clarke (1874), P.R.T. Gurdon (1914), J.P. Mills (1929), J.H. Hutton (1928), C. von Fürer-Haimendorf (1943), and others. From the academic circle the unpublished dissertation of Angeline Bareh (1981) although concentrated on a single megalithic site in Khasi Hills is one step which has taken the subject of Khasi megalithism to the academic level. Then followed by Cecile Mawlong's unpublished Ph.D. dissertation in 1996 touched a far larger area of study, and expanded the subject matter of Khasi megalithism towards the socio-political realm.

In this chapter, author has given an overview of megaliths of the Khasi-Jaintia region.

Types of Megaliths in Khasi-Jaintia Hills

Since megalithic practice is a 'living' tradition in Khasi-Jaintia Hills of Meghalaya, detail information regarding the significance of the monuments according to their types has been recorded by the colonial workers and also by local writers (Lyngdoh, 1962; Kharakor, 1988). However, a known typological classification will be helpful in understanding the pattern for monuments in the archaeological context as well.

In order to understand the variations of the megalithic monuments distributed along the Khasi-Jaintia Hills of Meghalaya, the following class are typical to the monuments as far as their shapes, functions and meanings are concerned.

Fig. 1.1: Megalithic cluster at Nangbah village, Jaintia Hills

Menhirs

Here, menhir refers to an undressed upright monolith. These stones occur sometimes alone or in alignments comprising 3, 5, 7, 9, and occasionally, 11 to 30. Their height varies from 1 m to 4 m. These stones are hewn from materials like sandstone, gneiss, and granite

Fig. 1.2: Fallen monuments at Laitlyngkot, Khasi Hills

depending on the availability of the raw materials. Most of the menhirs found in the Khasi-Jaintia Hills, are in an alignment of 3 or more and they always occur in association with one type of table stone. These standing stones are locally called the *maw shynrang* or the male stone. The tallest recorded monument measures 8 m in height from the ground, with a maximum breadth of 0.78 m, and it is found at the village of Nartiang in Jaintia Hills. The largest cluster of monuments consisting of 11 upright stones and table stones is found in a place called Laitlyngkot in the Khasi Hills.[1] The tallest stone measures 5.72 m from the ground, and the largest table stone weighs about 21.2 metric tons (Godwin-Austin, 1872:141).

Within this category of megalithic monuments is also another class of monuments called trilithons where two upright stones support the horizontal stone slab on top. This form of monuments is rare and only stray evidence claimed that they are found in the Khasi Hills (Chowdhury, 1996). Clarke (1874) provided a sketch on the sort of monuments that resembles a trilithon although he never mentioned its location. However, there is absolutely no information from any sources about their antiquity or functional purpose.

Dolmens

Dolmens refer to all stones having a horizontal slab supported by two or more vertical slabs, forming a table like structure. On the basis of their structural and functional variations, the Khasi dolmens can be grouped under the following groups:

(1) *Dolmen Type 1*

These refer to table stones found in association with standing stones. They are rough and simple with sometimes oval or irregular shapes. Technically, they are always known as the *maw kynthei* or the "female stones".

(2) *Dolmen Type 2*

These are known in local dialect as *maw shongthait* literally translated as "resting stones". Although, these monuments have altogether no relation with the dead, it is important to note that since their manner of occurrence and their identical forms, might lead to confusion with other similar structural monuments having altogether different implication. They are usually square, oval and even circular in section. Most of them are made from the rough and undressed stone slabs, and there are four supporting vertical slabs. They generally serve as a resting place for travellers as in many cases they are found on the side of footpaths leading to farms or market places.

(3) *Dolmen Type 3*

They are known in local dialect as *maw shyieng* literally translated as "bone stone" and are associated with placements of the bones. Those, which are also referred to as the cists, are categorized under this class of dolmens. They vary in shape and form, and are rectangular to circular. Most of them are found to be very well dressed to form a fine circular section. The overlying top-slab is supported by four or more vertical stone slabs equally dressed into fine pillars.

Menhirs with Dolmen Type 1

Mawbynna Niam

These are memorial stones of proclamation erected to proclaim the completion of the funeral rites and rituals pertaining to the bone-placement ceremony. They are primarily erected in memory of the deceased ancestors from the maternal side of the clan or the great maternal uncle. They are basically stones of purificatory rites. They are generally formed by 3 upright stones and 1 table stone. The middle upright stone is always ascribed to the *kni rangbah* or the "eldest maternal uncle of the clan". The other upright stones on the sides are called *maw pyrsa* or "stone of the nephew", who will eventually take up the role of maternal uncles in the future. The table stone is always placed in front of the middle upright stone, and this stone is ascribed to the *iawbei tymmen* or the "great ancestress of the clan" or to the *iawbei kpoh* or the "great grandmother of the family", or to the *iawbei khynraw* or the "grandmother of the family". They are called purificatory stones because they are associated with the performance of religious rites and sacrifice particularly those related with funeral practice.

Functionally, these classes of monuments in terms of its meaning based on their local nomenclature are classed under the following types:

(1) *Maw Lynti or Maw Kjat*

Literally translated as 'foot stones' or 'path stone', these stones are erected at the time when the family of the deceased is on the way to deposit the cremated bones or ashes into the dolmenoid cist. They are always erected halfway on the side of the road leading to the destination. If the number of upright stones is more than 3 having more than 1 table stone, then it is associated with the second bone placement ceremony, since 3 upright stones represents a single family, and every additional three upright stones with additional table stone is associated with an additional number of family which participates in the bone placement ceremony of the clan (Lyngdoh, 1962).

(2) *Maw Umkoi*

Maw umkoi literally refers to the "purificatory stone". They are erected at the time when the bones of the deceased person dying of unnatural death are washed in a small artificial tank before placing them on the stone cist. This tank represents the last ritual bathing of the deceased to cleanse the impurities attending the unnatural death and also to remove the curse of such death to the clan in the future.

(3) *Maw Klim*

Maw klim can be literally translated as "stone of adultery". These stones are erected only at the time when the family of the deceased performs a rite and a sacrifice to remove the bond of marriage between the deceased and his wife in the case of the deceased being a male, or her husband if the deceased is a female. After such a stone is erected a person is allowed to remarry. The stones here act as a witness to this declaration (Lyngdoh, 1962).

(4) *Mawbynna Nam*

Mawbynna nam literally refers to "memorial stone", a general name for all types of memorial stones, which may or may not be associated with the performance of rite and ritual. They are erected on certain occasions or at any given time, as one would feel like. The number of upright stones also varies like 1, 2, 5, 7, 9,11, and even up to 30, sometimes with 1 or 2 table stones or without any. The erection of these types of stones are also ascribed both to the maternal and the paternal sides of the family or clan. The tallest stone in the alignment is always ascribed to *u thawlang* or the father of the clan, and the table stone in front is always ascribed to the *kiawkha* or the paternal grandmother.

(5) *Maw Ksing*

Literally referring to "drum stone(s)", these are erected during the performance of *Ka Phur Ka Siang* or the ceremonial dance. These stones are always erected alongside the *maw thawlang* or the "father stone" and the *maw kiawkha* or the "paternal grandmother" stone. The number of these stones depends upon the number of families from the paternal side who participate in the dance ceremony.

(6) *Maw Kait*

"Stone of banana offering" are stones of offerings, erected at the time when the relatives of the paternal family visit the house of their in-laws and offer banana to a newly born child.

Within the class of monuments mentioned above are arrays of other memorial stones that are erected on other occasions besides those that are mentioned above. In this category would also be included stones erected to commemorate a newly founded village. Then there are also types of monuments which are erected in places where regular religious activities are conducted. An important example of such places where these stone monuments are found lies at the old market place of Shillong known as *Iewduh* and at Nartiang in Jaintia Hills. Another spectacular stone alignment formed by 30 upright stones without any table stone is also found at Sutnga village in Jaintia Hills. Legend has it that these stones were erected in the memory of a woman who had 30 husbands. Although the story has no reliable source, yet it provided important information which thereby suggests that certain peculiar achievements in the society are also commemorated in stones (Shadap-Sen, 1981). The death of a chief is also marked by erecting a megalith. As in the case of the megalithic monuments at Cherrapunjee, which are also one of the most exquisite of all monuments in design and ornamentation, they are said to have been raised in honour of the ancestress when the clan began to prosper after her death (Godwin-Austin, 1872). Besides many of the place names in the Khasi Hills originated with some form of megalithic practice. As mentioned above, Yule (1844) brought out the names of the villages which were derived from stone monuments. Thus, he explains that out of the lapping of salt from the sword (being a Khasi form of taking oath), the name Mawmluh village was derived, and out of an oath between two parties the name Mawsmai village appeared. There are many other examples where villages derived their name from the megalithic practice. Godwin-Austen (1872) therefore described through his first-hand account that these monuments are also erected for such a reason as the following — During the illness of a person, every kind of propitiation and exorcism either by the breaking of eggs, sacrifice of fowls, pigs etc., and by the examination of the liver and viscera, having been made, and then failing to restore him. The sick man may vow that should he recover, he will erect a set of stones to one of his ancestors, who, it is presumed, on knowing of the intention, will do his best to save him.

Stone Enclosure

Besides, the commonly occurring megalithic monuments mentioned above, there are the cenotaphs or the resting place which are locally known as the *kors*. They are dry masonry structures built with well-dressed squarish stone blocks to provide (seating) resting facility. In many cases there are two such walls and are separated by 1-2 m gap, thus forming a kind of enclosure. The normal height from the ground is 1-1.5 m, and the seating facility is raised to about 0.5 m high without any superstructure. These can be considered as megalithic monuments because apart from their primary function as resting place, they are also forms of memorial monuments for the dead, and are, therefore, erected by the family or relatives or even the village, in memory of some dead person.

Cairns

Cairn is another form of megalithic monument that appears in published literature. They are covered by a heap of stones after a primary burial was completed. These forms are mostly confined to the northern side of the Khasi Hills plateau and in some areas in the Jaintia Hills. Godwin-Austen (1872) claimed he saw this type of structure south of Jowai in Jaintia Hills district. He even recorded artifacts of bangles and wristlets of brass along with calcite bone pieces from the spot. He speculated that it was very old pointing from the fact that no information was derived regarding their antiquity, from the local inhabitants.

Stone Jars

Found widely scattered in Laos, these are another class of megalithic monuments which calls for serious investigation and there is no ethnographic information available for this class of megaliths. These types of monuments are also found scattered at different areas of North Cachar Hills of Assam and along the Saipung Reserve of Jaintia Hills of Meghalaya. They are built in the shape of hollow jars hewn from locally available rocks and are sometimes pear-shaped or taper towards the tip. They are buried below the ground and only the flaring mouth is left exposed to the surface. These monuments are considered megalithic because earlier scholars who studied them in North Cachar Hills claimed to have found remains of human bones inside this hollow monolith and hence they can be classed as mortuary monuments.

An Overview

The first information that any observer would like to understand about the Khasi megaliths are their location pattern. A general survey showed that the monuments are always placed at the highest point of the landscape and can be seen from a great distance when the area is devoid of vegetation cover. Such points are mostly the ridge-top of a hill overlooking either two sides or one side of a valley(s). This location pattern is clearly discernable in many of the cluster sites especially in Khasi Hills. No straightforward answer can be forwarded regarding the choice made in these particular spots of the landscape for erecting the monuments. The selection of the ridge-tops for erecting megalithic and other funerary monuments indicated that the area are marked as territorial boundary of a village or a settlement. In line of this argument, it may, therefore, be stated that the Khasi megaliths are primarily territorial markers of the physical landscape which in a way exhibited clan solidarity and clan-based settlement.

But as has been observed from the ethnographic study of Umniuh-Tmar village in the southern part of Khasi Hills, where the tradition is a living practice, the megalithic cists cluster are built on a raised platform and keenly visible from the village at that time. Correlating this information, the Khasi people in traditional practice avoid building their houses or their settlement at the ridge-top. Houses were usually built in areas below the ridge-top on a slope of a hill or some natural terrace on a hill slope. The selection of the ridge-tops for erecting megalithic and other funerary monuments indicated that the area was marked as territorial boundary of a village or a settlement. In line of this argument, it may, therefore, be stated that the Khasi megaliths are primarily territorial markers of the physical landscape which in a way exhibited clan solidarity and clan-based settlement. A more symbolic explanation to the location pattern of these monuments on the ridge-tops could be linked to the belief system of the people and their construction of the after-life, whereby the highest point in the landscape becomes a vantage point of interaction between the living and their ancestors and this could only be understood through the funeral rites of passage.

Fig. 1.3: Clan Cist at Nongkseh Rim, Khasi Hills

Distribution of Megalithic Sites

A systematic mapping on the distribution of the Megalithic monuments in the Khasi-Jaintia Hills is imperative to provide the necessary information of these monuments in their respective landscape. A total of 19 clusters of megalithic monuments of different types have been mapped to generate a pattern on the distribution of the monuments in the landscape (Mitri, 2016). The primary objective of mapping these monuments is basically to provide information into the settlement pattern of their authors. In an effort to bring to light the distribution patterns of the monuments in Khasi-Jaintia Hills, an attempt is, therefore, made to map some of the major clusters which are assumed to represent a concentration of habitations. As already noted, since all aspects of life are written in stones, it is only probable that sites with concentrated megalithic monuments or clusters have direct relationship with concentrated habitation.

The preliminary mapping of the hills reveals the following figures:

(a) 8 major clusters in East Khasi Hills District.

(b) 7 major clusters in Jaintia Hills District.
(c) 2 major clusters in West Khasi Hills District.
(d) 2 major clusters in Ri-Bhoi District.

It has been observed that the larger clusters are always found in settlements which were known to be centres of socio-economic and political importance. The megalithic clusters found in present day villages such as Nangbah, Raliang, Shangpung in Jaintia Hills; Mawpat, Mawpdang, Marngar, Lawnongthroh and Diengiei villages in Khasi Hills and Ri-Bhoi, are located close to areas of large agricultural and fertile valleys with large tract of paddy fields.

There are also megalithic clusters in the villages of Nongtalang, Lamin of southern Jaintia Hills, Umniuh-Tmar/Nongjri, and Sohra of southern Khasi Hills located close to the plains, the Surma Valley, that were once important trade routes, and traces of such commercial importance still survive till recent past.

Clusters of megalithic sites are also found in the villages of Nongspung, Nongkrem, Laitlyngkot, and Mylliem-Mawiong of Khasi Hills, which were known to be centres of iron smelting and manufacturing, the traditional iron industry that continue to thrive well till the last century.

Finally, the megalithic clusters in the villages of Nartiang, Moopat (Moakinpat) of Jaintia Hills, Nongkseh Rim and Nongkhlaw of Khasi Hills represents areas where early tribal state formation in both the Khasi-Jaintia Hills are said to have made their first appearance. These areas also represent centres of nascent political activities where the ruling elites made their first appearance in the area.[2]

At the first glimpse the general picture that appears regarding the location of these megalithic clusters in Khasi-Jaintia Hills clearly reflects the stable socio-economic positions of the community. The presence of these monuments in a certain selected landscape of the hills indicates the significance of these areas and the activities that were thriving at the time. The monuments and their clusters also strongly affirms the presence of a regulatory mechanism which was operating within the socio-political system, indicating a dynamic cultural process taking place in the formation of tribal identity.

Socio-Economic and Political Implication

Looking at the monuments from an ethno-archaeological perspective, they represent a wide range of meaning allowing us to infer clearly on their role as symbols of power and control in the socio-economic and political system of early Khasi society. Some of the megalithic clusters like those at Nangbah and Nartiang in Jaintia Hills and Iewduh in Shillong on the basis of oral history are directly linked with market places. The importance of markets or more appropriately areas of exchange, calls for a different interpretation of these monuments. Exchange centres came to acquire a new meaning with these monuments in context. The importance of exchange, which could invariably be in the form of barter centres, is also seats of organised religion which culminate into centres of power. The uniformity of exchange in a barter economy or may be a very rudimentary monetary economy, demands stringent moral conduct among the participants, which thereby allow social mechanism to appear. Thus, religion and political system operate symbiotically for the smooth functioning of these exchange centres. The market monuments in Khasi-Jaintia Hills are good indicators of that transitory phase of early Khasi society. The clusters where such monuments are recorded in the study region are all linked to the erstwhile headquarters of a commune or chiefdom. Thus, oral history recorded that the monuments at Nartiang are directly linked to the relocation of an exchange centre, which used to be at the neighbouring village of Raliang. The monuments at Nangbah village on the other hand are remnants of an exchange centre before it got shifted to modern Jowai town. Again, the monuments at Iewduh in Shillong represent the shift of exchange centre from the erstwhile capital of the Shillong chiefdom at Nongkseh rim.

Megaliths in Khasi-Jaintia Hills representing the above mentioned centres of exchange are clear indicators of the socio-economic and political transition of early societies of these hills. Today these clusters assumed a sanctified position where in some case only certain clans and while in others only the chiefs can perform religious rites and ceremonies on these sites annually. Although sacred as they are seen today, these sites are different from those which are directly linked to the mortuary practice of the people. Archaeologically, these market monuments can help to understand the concentration and logistics of settlements.

Other clusters which are also linked to the socio-economic and political system are those found at Nongtalang in Jaintia Hills and Laitlyngkot of East Khasi Hills. These are ascribed to be seats of village assemblies. The presence of these monuments that are generally constructed from big size stones are good indicators of the nascent political structure of early Khasi societies composed of villages and communes. The time and labour involved in their construction reflected the emergence of socio-political order and its necessity. These groups of monuments are similar to market monuments as both types belonged to a class of memorial stones, which are not specific to family or clan concerned but of broader socio-economic bonding, antecedents to political structure.

Chronology

It is not an easy task to date the Megalithic culture in the Khasi-Jaintia Hills as there has not been any effort to excavate any of the megalithic graves. Based on the recent excavations from two Neolithic sites[3] of Khasi Hills, which produced earliest dates of 1900-1200 BC respectively, the cist burial monuments are recorded at the upper most layer of both the sites which, therefore, suggest a general continuity from the Neolithic to the Megalithic phase. The upper most layer of the site of Lawnongthroh has been dated to 5th century AD. From the site of Myrkhan, a stone enclosure which resembles those associated with clan cist has been found at the upper most layer of the Neolithic site. Although the upper most corresponding layer from the site has not been dated, dates between 1st century BC to 1st century AD could be assigned for beginning of megalithic culture in these hills.

Fig. 1.4: Excavated stone enclosure at Myrkhan Neolithic site, Khasi Hills

Conclusion

While studying the megalithic culture of the Khasis, there would be a space for certain speculations regarding the origin of this cultural practice which dominates the worldview of the community. There are no dates as of now which could be placed as a time period that can be associated with the monuments of these hills. However, there is a clear pointer that the megalithic practice had struck deep roots in the culture of Khasi-Pnar community of Meghalaya. If this community had migrated into the present habitat, they should have left trace of such monuments on their route. A detail study of the stone jars found in Jaintia Hills and North Cachar Hills in Assam which are generally found very close to megalithic monuments that are widely seen in Khasi-Jaintia Hills could be a clue which may lead to some kind of understanding on the antiquity of this practice and the people responsible for it.

There are numerous questions that will emerge out of the relationship between the monuments and ethnic group responsible for their erection. The stone jars have been postulated by some scholars to be the product of the Mon-Khmer language speakers (Colani, 1935). Thus, the Khasi-Pnar community being the only ones speaking this language in North East India could certainly be the authors of these stone jars. But interestingly, these stone jars are not found anywhere west of the Saipung Reserve Forest in Jaintia Hills. Instead, the megalithic monuments in the hills are quite inferior in terms of workmanship and labour investment compared to the stone jars. If the arguments being that the authors of the stone jars are the Khasi-Pnar community, then the degeneration could have been caused by depletion of resources. Thus, when the Khasis moved further west in search of resources[4], their symbolic cist burial could be a reminiscence of the stone jars. This would invariably show that the people could no longer afford to create the elaborate stone jars and thus, the cist burial was the symbolic reminder of the megalithic culture of the Mon-Khmer speaking groups.

NOTES

1. According to Godwin-Austen (1872), the megaliths at Laitlyngkot in Khasi Hills were the largest collection of huge stone slabs recorded

from the hills and on the unique form of arrangement, he speculated that they were erected for a different purpose and was probably a place of meeting of the chiefs or elders of the clan. He estimated that the weight of largest stone was 20 tons.

2. In the Khasi-Jaintia Hills, the chiefs are said to be instruments of governance created by the elders of the clan. Their power is strictly controlled by the assembly or *Durbar*. State formation in these hills is closely knitted with the rising power of dominant clans who are instrumental in the creation of an office of a Chief. This was attested by the fact that the ruling families are not from the Khasi clan as their maternal ancestry is always to fairies and nymphs (Sutnga and Shillong Chiefs) and hence, they are always referred to as 'divine' chiefs.
3. The Neolithic sites of Lawnongthroh has been dated to 1200 BC (C^{14}) and Myrkhan to 1900 BC (C^{14}). These are a part of an ongoing excavation by the author (Mitri *et al.*, 2015).
4. The search for source iron could have pushed the people further west.

REFERENCES

Bareh, A., 1981. Megalithic Culture among the Khasis with special reference to Mawiong Village. M.Phil. Thesis, North Eastern Hill University, Shillong.

Burke, D., 2014. "*Jingkynmaw*: Memories written in stone". In T. Jamir and M. Hazarika (eds.), *50 Years after Daojali-Hading: Emerging Perspective in the Archaeology of North-east India*. New Delhi: Research India Press, pp. 360-75.

Chowdhury, J. N., 1996. *Ki Khun Khasi Khara (The Khasi People)*. Shillong.

Clarke, C.B. 1874. "Stone Monuments of the Khasi Hills". *Journal of the Anthropological Institute*, 3(3): 481-93.

Colani, M., 1935. *Megaliths du Haut-Loas*. Paris: Ecolefrancaise d' Extreme-Orient.

Fürer-Haimendorf, C. von., 1943. "Megalithic Rituals among the Gadabas and Bondos of Orissa". *Journal of Asiatic Society of Bengal*, 9 (4):173.

Godwin-Austin, H.H., 1872. "On the Stone Monuments of the Khasi Hill Tribes and on the Peculiar Rites and Customs of the People". *Journal of Anthropological Institute of Great Britain and Ireland*, I: 122-43.

Gurdon, P.R.T., 1914. *The Khasis*. London: MacMillan & Co.

Hooker, J. D., 1854. *The Himalayan Journals*, Vol. 2, London: John Murray.

Hutton, J. H., 1928. "Prehistory of Assam". *Man in India*, VIII: 228-29.

Kharakor, P., 1988. *Ka Kolshor Khasi kumba paw ha ka Literashor Khasi* (1930-1940). Shillong: Don Bosco Press.

Lyngdoh, H., 1962. *Ka Niam Khasi.* Shillong.

_____. 1964. *Ki Syiem Khasi bad Synteng.* Shillong.

Mawlong, C., 1996. Megalithic Monuments of Khasi-Jaintia Hills: An Ethno-Archaeological Study. Ph.D. Thesis, North Eastern Hill University.

Mills, J.P., 1929. "Ancient Monoliths of North Cachar". *Journal of Asiatic Society of Bengal*, XXV: 295-98.

Mitri, M., 2016. *The Living Megalithic Culture of Khasi-Jaintia Hills, Meghalaya*. Shillong: DBCIC.

Mitri, M.; D. Kharmawphlang and H. Syiemlieh. 2015. "A Preliminary Report on the Excavation of the Neolithic Site at Lawnongthroh (Sohpet Bneng Hill), in Khasi Hills, Meghalaya". *Man and Environment*, 41: 33-42.

Shadap-Sen, N., 1981. *The Origin and Early History of the Khasi-Synteng People.* New Delhi: Firma KLM Private Ltd.

Walters, H., 1832. "Journey Across the Pandua Hills near Sylhet in Bengal". *Asiatic Researches*, XVII: 499-572.

Yule, H., 1842. "Notes on the Iron of the Kasia Hills for the Museum of Economic Geology". *Journal of the Asiatic Society of Bengal,* 11: 853-57.

_____. 1844. "Notes on the Khasi Hills and People". *Journal of Asiatic Society of Bengal*, XII: 612-13.

2
Poumai Megalithic Types and Their Functions

Potshangbam Binodini Devi

Introduction

Megalithic culture is a cultural phenomenon of the dead in different parts of the world. This custom of erecting megaliths on large scale began from Neolithic onwards and it continues till historic period through the Bronze Age. Regarding this culture, it is often claimed that, of all the enigmas in archaeology, it is the most intriguing. It is regarded today by some scholars as the first world-wide movement and by others as a well defined stage of civilization; whereas its existence as an identifiable meaningful cultural entity is denied by many. In archaeology it is a tomb built with big stones in natural forms of roughly or evenly dressed graves marked with prodigious rude stone or pit dug in soft rocks containing human remains. It is also applied to the erection of huge stones either as memorials or for religious purposes. Graves without lithic assemblages but with certain other traits, especially pottery—Red-and-Black Ware—are also commonly classified as megaliths (Devi, 2011). In the following, the megalithic culture of the Poumai Nagas of Manipur will be discussed.

Manipur is one of the smallest hilly states of North East India. It is a cradle of human civilization and creativity which have come under the influence of many cultures of different ethnic groups who came at various times and contributed to the growth of civilization in this region. The present day ethnic groups of Manipur are the descendants of the migrating people which comprise the Meeteis/ Meiteis, the Naga tribes, the Kuki-Chin-Mizo tribes and other Indian communities including the Muslims. The people are predominantly of the Mongoloid elements who speak Tibeto-Burman languages. Compared with other regions of India, the prehistoric archaeology of North East India particularly in the field of megalithic art is still poorly known, because little exploration and excavation has been done so far in this area. It is populated by different communities where various engraving works on megaliths are discovered. The Poumai area described in this chapter lies on the northern part of the state. Two main rivers of this area are the Barak River and the Manipur River (also known as *Turel Achouba*). Both rivers have many tributaries which drain the steep hill slopes and narrow valley of this state.

The Poumais are majorly found in the Senapati district. Every Poumai village is governed by the traditional village council and village authority. The traditional village council is headed by the chief of the village known as *veo*. He is assisted by a number of councillors called *chikumai*. Each councillor is the representative of a clan of the village concerned. They are selected on the basis of seniority. They are equally important and are expected to discharge their respective duties in the village administration.

Poumai Megalithic Types

In every Poumai village, there are a number of monoliths, cairns, and dolmens scattered here and there. They are of different shapes and sizes. Menhirs abound in each of their stone raising place called *Chushebu* of each clan. Dolmens are found in groups, sometimes associated with cairns or raised platforms or stone circles, which serve as seats. This array of stones varies from one site to another in size and shape, where the villagers assemble for rest, gossip, and for formal discussions and also for village council.

Among the Poumais, megalithic culture is a living tradition. They still practise the erection of megaliths of different structures even today. The raising of any structural type of megalith is associated with elaborate sacrificial rituals. In each Poumai village there are 12 structural types of megaliths. The different types of megaliths that exist in the Poumai areas are listed below:

1. *Zaosochu/Zhaosochu/Zhusochu* (menhir/alignment/avenue)
2. *Chukho* (cairn)
3. Smaller *chukho* (smaller cairns)
4. *Raikhubu* (dolmen)
5. *Seibechu* (religious stone)
6. *Chadeichu* (judiciary stone)
7. *Neisha chukho* (religious stone)
8. *Tapu* (a megalith for placing the decapitated heads)
9. *Chuchukho* (a stone circle, related to head-hunting)
10. *Khophochu* (capstone for the grave)
11. *Loupfo* (a cluster/alignment of small stones)
12. *Aro Adu* (village gate and wall)

Zaosochu/Zhaosochu/Zhusochu (Menhir/Alignment/Avenue)

These menhirs are usually raised in the clan's stone raising place known as *Chushebu*. Such menhirs are found singly, or in cluster in the form of alignment or avenues (Figs. 2.1, 2.2). Almost all of them are in or around the terraced fields of their respective clans. Sometimes, they are also found near the intra and inter-village roads, paths leading to their *jhum* or wet fields, and jungles. Some of them are also located inside the residential areas. Each Poumai megalithic structure is erected or constructed after performing a series of feasts of merit. They are *Rasou, Vaove, Moujii, Zhusou*, and *Chiveisou*. These five series of feastings are performed by any intending merit-seeker after getting permission from the traditional village council called *chikumai* or clan elders known as *tsiiko* or both. Once the permission is granted for each merit-seeker, the *chikumai* or *tsiiko* announces the name(s) of the intending merit-seeker(s), who will perform the stone raising ceremony/ceremonies in the next year, while performing the *Zhusou* feasting of the current year of any merit-seeker. Normally on this day all the villagers attend the feasting to know the number of individuals who wish to perform *Zhusou* feasting in the next year's stone raising months called *Donii, Rupii* and *Sapei* (January, February, and March). If the number of intending performer is more than one, the *chikumai/tsiiko* prepares a list of their names and makes it known to the villagers along with the sequence of performance of *Zhusou* by different individuals one after the other.

1. *Rasou*: It is not an elaborate ceremony. The intending merit-seeker along with his family members, guided by the village priest worship the household deity called *Kirakho*. At this time they worship the deity by offering rice-beer to protect them from any suffering during the coming feastings for raising a megalith. It is followed by *Vaove* feasting.
2. *Vaove:* Once the *Rasou* ceremony is performed, the intending merit-seeker sacrifices blameless cattle (cow/bull/buffalo) and offers to their supreme god and goddess known as *Khaliichira* and *Teipfii Khamiru*. The meat of the sacrificed animal is distributed to all the houses of his village. All the clan elders assembled there are served with rice beer.
3. *Moujii:* It is an important feast. No merit-seeker is allowed to perform *Zhusou* feasting without performing the *Moujii* feast. After completing the necessary arrangements, the intending merit-seeker announces the fixed day of *Moujii* feast. Unlike other tribes, in any feast, the Poumais never offer cooked rice to participants except cooked meat and rice beer. Generally it lasts for four consecutive days, but may continue depending on the materials arranged by, the host.
4. *Zhusou:* It is the feast for stone raising ceremony. The first stage for this ceremony is the selection of the stone to be raised. It is followed by the collection of stone dragging creepers (*lirai* and *churai*) and preparation of stone dragging sled (*chukhe*), arrangement of pigs, and cattle to be sacrificed including a small calf, a blameless cow (*khulo*), and a buffalo (*havejii/chahha ahah*), and also a blameless pig (*khaoveophya*), pounding of rice flour for brewing rice beer (*pouyaoh*), preparation of large wooden vats (*tei*) for storing rice beer etc.

After arranging all the required materials, each merit-seeker fixes an auspicious day to drag the stone already selected and raises it. The performer attains the highest status in their social ladder. He is honoured by all. Thereafter, the merit-seeker is allowed to wear a titled cloth. Moreover, he is permitted to hold the fifth stage of feasting series and allowed him to construct a decorated horn-house.

Fig. 2.1: Menhir from a Poumai village

Fig. 2.2: Avenue and Alignment

Chukho (Cairns)

It is a heap of stones piled up one after another to form a raised circular or rectangular structure. On top of such structure (cairn), a series of smaller flat stones are placed to serve as seats. There are various types of cairns constructed on different occasions but having the same function. Some of them are memorials, while others are commemoratives (e.g. village foundation stones). They vary in shapes and sizes, ranging from 97 cm to 250 cm in height above the ground, the circumference being 960 cm to 1420 cm. It is constructed by all the villagers (particularly all the male members of the village of the youths' dormitory and traditional village council). They construct such structure at the courtyard of the village chief concerned, signifying a bond of unity with the village founder.

The erection of such cairn is not accompanied by feast or ceremony. The village chief (*veo*) concerned, who possesses the cairn bears the expenditure for feeding the workers (villagers), while constructing the structure.

Fig. 2.3: A *chukho* (cairn)

Smaller *Chukhos*

It is a rectangular or circular structure made up of smaller and larger flat horizontal stones. Some of them are raised on supporting stones like small dolmens. The largest one is on the central part of the curvature facing the two narrow spaces meant for entrance and exit. Such structures are found in the courtyard of the clan heads of every locality of each clan and different names are given according to the clan to which the smaller cairn belongs. For example, the *Dumai chukho* for *Dumai* clan, the *Papao chukho* for *Paomei* clan, the *Seva chukho* for *Ramai* clan, and the *Pahon chukho* for *Yumai* clan respectively. These structures are not related to any ritualistic feast. Such *chukhos* can be constructed by any wealthy person of the clan concerned (but only after getting permission from his clan elders and village council), by contributing either some amount to meet the expenses, or by offering food and drink while constructing the structure.

Fig. 2.4: Smaller *chukho* (cairn)

Raikhubu (Dolmens)

It is a cluster of dolmens. They are always found inside the settlement areas. They are in most cases associated with a small heap of stones or a raised platform. The smallest dolmen measures 46 cm in height above the ground, while the highest dolmen is 136 cm in height above the ground. The supporting pillars are also formed by piling up a number of small slabs along with an upright stone to serve the purpose. The smallest table stone measures 122 cm × 62cm × 10 cm (length × breadth × thickness), while the largest horizontal slab measures 212 cm × 160 cm × 37.8 cm.

The stone searching, dragging, erecting, along with feasting and the whole process of preparation of the materials required for this ceremony are similar to those of the *zhaosochu*, but the expenditure is more than double of that of *zhaosochu*. Here, the intending merit-seeker will offer the participants food and drink, till the selected stone reaches the village and construction work is completed.

Fig. 2.5: Cluster of dolmens embodying highest social status

Seibechu (Flat Stone)

It is a flat horizontal stone, which is placed on the ground directly. The shape is irregular and measures 435 cm × 163.2 cm × 21.6 cm. It is located in the courtyard of V. Baosil, the chief of Yumai clan. It is a roughly dressed stone. As reported by my informants, this stone was placed there since the time when the Saranamei village was set up. Since that time, they had been using this stone for reading omens by offering a small but blameless calf and sacrificing a full grown young dog with accompanying rituals.

Fig. 2.6: The *seibechu* religious stone

Chadeichu (Cat Stone)

It is an undressed miniature monolith. It measures 78 cm × 82 cm × 60 cm (breadth × length × height). As the name signifies, it is meant for cat's stone (Details given in succeeding pages).

Fig. 2.7: The cat killing stone (*chadeichu*)

Neisha Chukho (Small Cairn with or without a Dolmen)

It is a very small cairn associated with or without a dolmen. It is always found in the courtyard of a Poumai village chief (*veo*). It is formed by piling up undressed blocks of stone or boulders having different shapes and sizes. On the top of it there lays a flat horizontal slab, resting on some supporting stones or placing directly on the raised small cairn.

Fig. 2.8: The religious stone *neisha chukho*

Tapu

It is a huge undressed boulder resting on a flat horizontal stone, supported by some other smaller stones. It is located in the courtyard of the Tungjoy village chief. This monolith is related with head hunting processes. Such type of megalith is confined to the Paomata group of Poumai tribe, particularly to Tunjoy village only.

Fig. 2.9: *Tapu* for keeping the hunted head(s)

Chuchukho (Stone Circle)

It is a circular megalithic structure made up of various sizes. This type of megalithic structure is generally constructed in the courtyard of the head of the clan, or the village chief concerned. The *chuchukho* is related with head hunting.

Fig. 2.10: The stone circle *chuchukho*

Khophochu (Capstone)

It is a horizontal flat stone capping a burial pit directly over the grave (Figure 2.11) or constituted by a number of comparatively lesser but elongated stones for the same purpose. The largest single stone measures 450 cm × 150 cm × 76 cm. In some cases, in modern times, it is remodelled by using cement and concrete to form a larger rectangular flat surface.

No elaborate ceremony regarding the selection and erection of this grave stone is performed. After burying the deceased person along with its grave goods, they simply cover the burial pit with this large flat stone or smaller elongated stones.

Fig. 2.11: Capstone for the grave (*khophochu*)

Loupfo (Cluster/Alignment of Small Stones)

It is small stones arranged in the form of a small alignment. They are always constructed far away from the village settlement areas. They are erected particularly near a river or stream or at the piedmont regions.

Fig. 2.12: A cluster/alignment of small stones

Aro Adu (Village Gate and Wall)

As the name suggests, it is a village gate with or without a wall. They constructed such walls for the entrance and exit of every hamlet of each Poumai village, though they differ in shapes and sizes.

Fig. 2.13: Village gate and wall

Functions of Poumai Megaliths

The different functional features of the megaliths are given in the following:

Zaosochu/Zhaosochu/Zhusochu (Menhir/Alignment/Avenue)

Any wealthy Poumai, who raises or constructs a megalithic structure in his name, after performing all the necessary rituals and feastings, attains a high social status in their society, and honour by all. Thereafter, he is not only allowed to wear a titled cloth called *zhaososa/hrahra*, but also permitted to hold the fifth stage of feasting series called *Chiveisou* and to decorate his house with long-eve boards and also his front wall (showing the number of animals he had hunted or slaughtered during the feast of merit, or the number of heads he had taken during raids) or to construct a new horn-house known as *Chikai* (Fig. 2.14). Hence, each monolith thus raised functions as the menhir of social status.

Fig. 2.14: Poumai horn-house *chikai*

Chukho (Cairn)

This structure functions as village foundation stone, if it was constructed by the whole villagers at the residence of their village chief, when they first settled there. It is also used as the sitting place for the villagers.

Smaller *Chukhos*

These smaller cairns are constructed by each clan members at the residence of every clan heads. Hence, different names are given to each of these smaller cairns. The main function of such megalithic type is to serve as the seats for the clan members concerned.

Raikhubu (Dolmen)

The main function of *raikhubu* is associated with the peace negotiation over head hunting. On the other hand, this structure also serves as sitting or resting place of the villagers, where they gossip and old men do odd jobs there.

Seibechu (Religious Stone)

This stone, since the time of its foundation, had been used for worshipping a small calf with rituals every year. For this the village chief (*veo*) rears a special puppy. When the puppy is fully grown, the *veo* fixes an auspicious day (according to Poumai lunar calendar), and makes it known to the villagers. For this ceremony he procures a calf without any spot of injury. The *veo* on the fixed day sacrifices the young healthy dog and distributes the meat to all his subjects. He then ties ritually the small calf to the specially placed horizontal stone. Thereafter, he observes *genna* during which he does not take any kind of food except rice beer (*pouyaoh*). The whole *genna*/ritual day he sits near the calf and keeps an eye on the animal for it is his duty to observe the direction of the head of the calf when it moos for the first time on the slab. When the calf moos once on the stone and its position is noticed, then *veo* lets the animal free. It is firmly believed that the direction to which the calf turns its head and *moos* once on such ritual slab, gives an indication of the direction from which harmful natural calamities, such as heavy rain or hailstorm or snowfall that can destroy the crops of the year, may come. So, they abandon the area directed by the calf from planting crops for the season. If they neglect this forecast, they may not get a good harvest.

Hence, they consider such ritual stone very essential for confirming the direction for *jhum* cultivation.

Chadeichu (Judiciary Stone)

It is used for performing a ritual annually under the guidance of an expert person. For this they hire an expert from other villages, if there is no such expert in the village.

The main function of this stone is to tie a cat over it and kill the animal ritually by throwing pebbles by all the villagers assembled there. The people think that the thief (if there is any in the village concerned) will surely die in the same way as the cat has and also in the same year. Thus, it is related to judiciary function, which is performed every year till date by the non-Christian Poumais.

Neisha Chukho (Religious Stone)

As the name implies that, it is a shouting stone for the village priest. On the top of this structure, particularly on the flat stone, the village chief climbs up, and shout whenever he wants to make some public announcement. No one is allowed touch it.

Tapu (For placing the decapitated heads)

The main function of this stone is to keep and beat the decapitated head(s) brought from raids by the head hunters, and they formally inform the village chief. The *veo* in turn passes on the news to his councillors through the messengers. Soon all the councillors assemble there to perform the traditional way of beating the hunted head one after another till they feel satisfied. Thereafter, the *veo* asks the hunters to return the head(s) to their respective villages before dawn.

Chuchukho (Stone Circle)

It is also related to head hunting processes, but differ from that of *tapu* in structure and function. Here the function of *chuchukho* is to serve as a site for burying the decapitated head/heads under one of these stones forming the circular structure, which is/are brought to the village by the head hunter(s) on raids. He/They formally inform the village chief about the matter first. The *veo* in turn beats the village war-drum, so that all the village functionaries and male members of boys' dormitory should assemble there in war-dress to perform victory dance and sing victory song. Meanwhile the *veo* asks the head hunter(s) whether he/they would like to keep the head(s) in his/their home(s). If he/they wishes/wish to keep the head(s), he/they should offer a feast next day. If he/they could not offer the feast the *veo* continues to ask each and every person assembled there whether any one wish to keep the hunted head. If nobody wishes to keep the head(s), the *veo* offers the feast and it is his duty to keep the head(s) in his house, and he displays the number of heads by engraving/carving them on the front wall and the front post of his house called *chikai*.

After completing the feast, the village elders along with the *veo* and owner of the head (who can give the feast) dig a hole (under one of those stones constituting the circular structure), and bury the hunted head(s) there till its/their fleshy parts are completely rotten.

After some months or even a year as necessary, the head(s) is/are taken out and washed with water and ritually purified by the village priest (*khaohro*). Thereafter the owner keeps it in his home in a place out of the reach of children and outsiders.

Khophochu (Capstone for the Grave)

These large and smaller elongated stones are used to cover the burial pits. Hence, their main function is to serve as grave stones.

Loupfo (Cluster/Alignment of Small Stones)

These clusters of small stones arranged in a line with some regular interval have some functions. Each miniature stone in the small alignment represents a girl/woman, whom a brave man had won during the prime of his lifetime. Those girls or women were not socially sanctioned or accepted as spouses by the society — and it is equivalent to committing a sin. Therefore, if he erects such structures, they believe, it washes away all the sins, so he can lead a good life after death. Thus the function of this small alignment is to rescue a Poumai sinner.

***Aro Adu* (Village Gate and Wall)**

The main function of this structure is to protect the villagers from their enemies.

Conclusion

The Poumai tribe perform various rites and rituals along with the offering of a series of feasts of merit, which are highly needed, particularly for an intending merit-seeker. After performing all the rituals, the merit-seeker is allowed to select a stone and raise a monolith or construct a megalithic structure in his name. Moreover, the merit-seeker is permitted to wear a special kind of titled cloth. Such permission of wearing the titled cloth is extended up to the grandchildren of the host. Above all, he is allowed to decorate his old/new house with the house-horn called *chikai*, and engraving works on the front wall.

In Poumai areas, the author has come across various types of megalithic structures. They are broadly divided into twelve different types. Some of them have similar structures, but have different functions. Most of the megaliths belong structurally to menhir, alignment, avenue, cairn, dolmen, stone circles, and stone seats. Functionally, the menhir, alignment, avenue, and dolmens are memorials and commemoratives, and monoliths are of social status; the cairns are meant for village foundation stones, resting place, and seats for clan's meeting place; stone circles serve as a group of seats, the small dolmens as well as hiding place for newly hunted head(s); the miniature monoliths, the small dolmens are announcement places for the village chief concerned.

NOTE

This chapter is an outcome of my fieldwork among the Poumai Nagas. Some parts of this chapter have appeared in the following publications given under References.

REFERENCES

Devi, P. B., 1998-99. "Exploration in District Senapati". *Indian Archaeology Review*, pp. 118-120.

______. 2002. "A Live Megalithic Culture found among the Poumais of Manipur". In G. Sengupta and S. Panja (eds.), *Archaeology of Eastern India: A New Perspective*. Kolkata, pp. 363-77.

______. 2011. *The Megalithic Culture of Manipur*. Delhi: Agam Kala Prakashan.

______. 2015. "Living Megalithic Traditions in Manipur". In K.K. Basa, R.K. Mohanty and S.B. Otta (eds.), *The Megalithic Traditions in India: Archaeology and Ethnography*, Vol. II, Bhopal: Indira Gandhi Rashtriya Manav Sangrahalaya, pp. 667-79.

______. 2015. "The Megalithic Rituals of the Poumai tribe of Manipur". Paper presented in the EurASEAA 15 International Conference, Nanterre University, Paris, France.

3
Origin, Affinities and Chronology of Naga Megaliths

Watijungshi Jamir

Introduction

Nagaland, a small state on the North Eastern corner of India, was constituted in 1963 out of a hill district of former undivided Assam. The state, lying between 92°26'–94°30′ E longitude and 23°53'–26°24′ N latitude, is composed of a compact landmass formed by rugged hill ranges of the Patkai Hills on the North East and the Barail range on the south-west forming a watershed of two great rivers of Asia—the Brahmaputra on the north and Chindwin-Irrawady system of Myanmar (Burma) on the South-East as well as deep gorge formed by the rivers—Doyang and Diphu, which flow into the Brahmaputra and the Tizu rivers, which join the Chindwin.

Nagaland is considered to be a place of worldwide fame for its megalithic culture which is of prehistoric origin in other places of the world and have become extinct long ago, but in Nagaland, this prehistoric cultural tradition still persists as a living tradition and offers a rare scope to the archaeologists and anthropologists to study the evolution of Naga society. A person desiring to erect a megalith (monolith) or menhir is required to offer a series of feasts of merit in order to attain the status of pulling a stone pillar or menhir for erecting the same in memory of his dead ancestors or in the name of a living husband and wife.

In order to understand this living prehistoric tradition among the Nagas, I made an attempt to carry out a megalithic survey in the districts, namely Kohima and Phek, where such megalithic remains are available in plenty. Several megalithc sites have been seen in villages like Phekold, Pfutsero, Kikruma, and Khezakenouma in Phek district. The megalithic remains found in Jotsoma, Khonoma, Kohima Village, Jakhama and Viswema areas have also been surveyed in addition to those found in Rengma inhabited areas of Tseminyu sub-division. Almost all the megalithic remains found in these sites are in the form of menhirs, alignment, avenues, dolmens, cist, or burial chambers, cairns, stone seats and platforms over the burial pits, both ancient and modern. I also had a great opportunity to take part and observe an elaborate ceremony of monolith pulling and erection which was organised in the first week of December 1993 in the large playground in Kohima town, when all the traditions, rituals, rites, dances and food were displayed. This offered a unique opportunity to collect data on the rites and rituals connected with the erection of megaliths in Nagaland. In other words, Nagaland offers an opportunity to the archaeologists to study the prehistoric cultural traditions, dating to about 2000–1000 BC in other parts of the world, including south India, where such tradition became extinct more than 2000 years ago, as a living tradition among the Nagas, which is of great interest to the archaeologist for the reconstruction of the evolution of the human society from prehistoric times to the modern.

Origin

As early as 1864, the French archaeologist Alexandre Bertrand argued that the megalithic monument in Europe were all built by one people who spread from the north to the south, and the following year, when the Baron de Bonstetten published his famous *Essaisur les dolmens*, he advocated the same point of view. In 1872, James Fergusson published his *Rude Stone Monument in all Countries*. He had become interested in the megaliths as part of his general study of architecture, and was convinced that they all were part of one stylistic phase of architectural history. Fergusson confessed that up to 1872 no royal road has been discovered, that leads to an explanation of megalithic antiquities but was nevertheless convinced of one thing—that the style of architecture to which these monuments belong is a style like Gothic, Grecian, Egyptian, Buddhists or any other, and that the megalithic monuments of the world were generally erected by partially civilized races after they had come into contact with the Romans, and most of them may be considered as belonging to the first ten century of the Christian era.

Fergusson's dating was not accepted by many archaeologists, but his ideas of architectural style were widely canvassed. De Mortillet, in 1874, at the Stockholm Congress of Prehistoric Archaeology, put forward the view that megalithic monument in different parts of the world were due to the work of different people with different cultures and that was diffused over the world as the custom of building such monuments and not the builders themselves. These ideas of the spread of what may be termed a 'megalithic influence' was widely canvassed at the end of the nineteenth century, most people bringing this influence from the east Mediterranean or Asia while Solomon Reinach reversed it and sent it eastwards from France (*c.f.* Peet, 1912).

In the present century, the problem of the diffusion of megalithic tradition can be seen best against the general study of the diffusion of culture to which archaeologists and anthropologists have given much thought. T. Eric Peet, when he wrote his *Rough Stone Monuments* (1912) forty years after James Fergusson, discussed the megalithic 'influence' or megalithic 'style' idea but rejected it. After very careful consideration, he says, "it thus seems the most probable theory of the origin of the megalithic monuments is that this style of building was brought to the various countries in which we find it by a single race in an immense migration or series of migrations". While advocating this view, Peet was unable to decide when the migrating race came from—the east, the northern Europe, and Africa were all considered and the negative conclusion arrived at, and that it was probable that the problem will never be solved. Sir Grafton Elliot Smith and his pupil W.J. Perry, who between them spent a lifetime in advocating that civilization was due to spread of a master race from Egypt, rapidly and easily incorporated the megalithic monuments of the world in their thesis.

Archaeologists and anthropologists have not unnaturally reacted against the monocentric hyper-diffusionism of the Elliot Smith-Perry School, and there are not many who today regard the megalithic monuments of the world as remains of wandering Egyptians. Nor is it possible to speak of a megalithic race, if the word race is used as it should be, in its strict physical-anthropological connotation of a group of people with heritable physical characteristics in common.

Recently, the problem and this question have been put into fresh perspective by Wheeler's excavation in southern India and by Gordon Childe's discussion of the Indian megaliths in relation to those of Europe and South-West Asia. It is indeed possible, though not proved, that the port-hole cists of the Indian Deccan are derived from those of Western Asia, despite the disparities of time and place; but this does not necessarily imply connection between all megaliths. Others have argued that there is very little in common between the structures in different parts of the world designated as megaliths, save the use of large stones, and that this use of large stones might well have arisen independently in different parts of the world. What is most important, as a student of the theory of material culture is that we should not assume a connection between the two traits formally, constructionally, chronologically and geographically. It is by no means impossible that megaliths originated in southern Europe and spread to India, Indonesia and Japan; but before we can assess the different points of view about the unity or disunity of megaliths, we need careful analysis of the structure in different regions (*c.f.* Daniel, 1963).

Our main problem is the origin and affinities of the megalithic culture of North East India. To trace the origin of the Khasis and Naga megaliths, some scholars have taken recourse to hyper-diffusionist theories. H.N. Ivor Evans (1927) made a comparative study of the megalithic monuments found in Malay Peninsular, with those of Indonesia and North East India. He sees close parallels in the monoliths and the table stones found in all these three regions.

Hutton (1928: 228) speaking on the origin of North East Indian megaliths writes, "the origin of the megalith is of course uncertain, but it appears that it is to be mainly imputed to the Mon-Khmer intrusion from the east. The practice of the disposal of the dead, whether the skull alone as among the Konyaks or the calcined bones as among the Khasis suggests a close cultural link between the tribes of Burma, South-East Asia, Borneo and other islands of the Pacific and those of North Eastern India, Odisha, Chotanagpur and the central India." According to Fürer-Haimendorf (1964), most of the present day practices of the tribes of North East India have close parallel with those of Odisha, the Godabas and the Bondas and South-East Asia. He further observes that the erection of stone monoliths and the use of its substitute in the form of forked 'Y' shaped wooden posts are common among some Naga tribes, the Garos of Meghalaya, the tribe of Indo-China, Oceania, and the Gonds of central India. Basing his judgement on the distribution of common megalithic practices in India, South-East Asia, Indonesia and Pacific Islands, Fürer-Haimendorf (1945) believes that the megalithic culture of South-East Asian type reached peninsular India through North East, Chotanagpur and Odisha from the eastern direction. He argues that this centre of diffusion, though not necessarily origin, lies somewhere in eastern Assam, north Burma or South-West China from where it branched off South-west-ward to India and southward to Indonesia and Oceania.

Affinities

Regarding the origin and affinities of megalithic remains, much has been written in relation with those of Europe and South-West Asia. While discussing about the affinities of North East Indian megaliths, it appears to be fruitful to review some opinion of the experts and scholars on the relation and affinities of North East Indian megaliths with those of South-East Asian countries and Oceania.

To begin with, F.M. Schnitger (1939), who studies the megaliths of Nias in southern Sumatra, notes the common factor of the feast of merit ceremony ardently followed by the Nagas and the megalithic builders of the Nias of Borneo. By way of comparing the two megalithic cultures of the two regions, i.e. Borneo and North Eastern Indian megaliths, he notes that, "even the most superficial consideration teaches us that the cultures of Nias is related to that of the Nagas in Nagaland and also of Manipur and Assam. In both countries, the megalithic institutions largely dominate social life and the necessary feast and ceremonies involved with them. Among the Nias, this is much more true than in Nagaland, for among the Nagas, there are only few tribes such as Angamis, Chakesang, Rengmas who possesses highly evolved megalithic culture. Among the Nagas as well as the Nias, the accompanying assignment of rank assumes a permanent place. In spite of the differences which exists among the Nagas and the Nias, the similarities between their megalithic culture are so striking and so numerous that there can be no doubt of their relation. They must at one time have had a common land of origin and this can have been nowhere, but in the valley of the Irravaddy, and not only ethnologically, but also anthropologically the people appear to be related. I am inclined to include Nagas, Niassins, Dayaks, Philippines and Formosians in one large group" (Schnitger 1939: 145-152).

R. Von Heine-Geldern (1935), who wrote extensively on the relationship of the megalithic cultures of South-Eastern Asia with those of North East India, has pushed the hyper diffusionist theory to its extreme when he suggested that the erection of megaliths was part of a great primitive religious movement which was sometimes undoubtedly carried by migrants, but was often passed from one tribe to another, megalithic culture was promoted by a sort of prehistoric missionary activity.

Fürer-Haimendorf (1946, 1964) recognizes that the megalithic culture of the Naga tribes represents a particularly ancient form of the megalithic complex so widely spread over South-East Asia and a form found only in a similar state of development on a small island of Nias and perhaps on Luzon in Philippine islands. He further draws a close similarity in the carving of a buffalo or mithun horn motif on the megalithic monuments of the Nagas and those found in Indonesia. To him, the carved heads are not merely ornamental, but commemorative of animal sacrifices and thus their value is not only aesthetic, but also definitely symbolic. He agrees with Hein-Geldern (1935) in ascribing the symbolic character to the art of the early megalithic cultures of South-East Asia. As a whole, Fürer-Haimendorf (1964) concludes that the ideas associated with megalithic ritual for gaining prestige for the living and for establishing links with the souls of the dead, are at the root of the megalithic cultures of Indonesia and thus suggests a unity of the megalithic complex extending from the Naga and the Khasi hills over the Nias in Sumatra to Flores Ambon and Ceram. He further observes that the megalithic complex found in Assam and in many part of South-East Asia appeared thus not as an accidental aggregation of various cultural elements, but as well as a coordinated system of customs and beliefs, a philosophy of life and nature.

In a sense, all the megalithic practices are associated in one way or another with the cult of the dead all over the world. That itself is not sufficient ground to establish close relationships between any two megalithic cultures as having a common origin. Fürer-Haimendorf (1945, 1946) admits that there are fundamental differences between the Khasis and the Naga megaliths, in spite of their typological similarities in the menhirs with the table stones in front as they served altogether divergent social and ideological functions.

Archaeological evidence has also been used to trace the origin and distribution of megalithic culture in India and South-East Asia by Hein-Geldern (1935) followed by Fürer-Haimendorf (1945). They identified the spread of the older Neolithic tradition characterised by the shouldered celt type with the Austro-Asiatic and the new or later quadrangular adze type with the Austronesian speaking groups in India. Fürer-Haimendorf agrees that the position of the shouldered celt in the Indian context is not clear, but he agrees with the quadrangular section with the speaker of the Austronesian languages. But so far, there is no archaeological evidence available to support his theory and so it remains hypothetical in nature. So far it has not been possible to distinguish two separate cultural layers characterised by the Neolithic shouldered adze and the late Neolithic quadrangular adze types anywhere in South-Eastern Asia, much less in India (Daniel, 1963; Sharma, 1973-74). So we have to await fresh evidence from these regions to establish relationship between the Neolithic and Megalithic cultures in these regions (Rao, 1977).

The megaliths of India are extensive and peculiar. In the present context it would appear to be justifiable to set aside at once the megaliths of that region, extending from North East India to Bastar on the northern flank of the lower Godavari, where megalithic culture is a more or less a living tradition of the aborigines, but they do in fact differ in general type and concept from most of the south Indian megaliths. C. von Fürer-Haimendorf (1943, 1945, 1946, 1964) observes that they belong essentially to the South-Eastern Asia—Indonesia, Oceania, the Philippines, Formosa—and matches the evidence whatever be the truth of his plausible guess that the Austro-Asiatic immigrants introduced them into North East India. The Bastar Gonds and the Khasis, and the Nagas of Manipur and Nagaland alike erect single standing stones (menhirs) or alignments of stones in honuor of the dead, who are thereby encouraged to help their living kinsman. In Nagaland, as well as Indonesia and Oceania, a forked wooden post of Y-shape is seen as an alternative to the menhirs, and both posts and menhirs are associated with ox-sacrifice. An identical custom occurs in Bastar, the Koyas, and the Raj Gonds of Hyderabad who erect small forked posts carrying the tail of the sacrificed cows on graves or the site of memorial feasts. In all these regions, it is the widespread belief that the soul or 'virtue' of the dead man is attached to the stone or post and benefit his survivors, the village, and crops. Alternatively, the Bondas and the Gadabas of Odisha erect a dolmen (table like cists above the ground), often of small size as the seat of the dead; and this seat may be associated with a stone circle. Generally, the setting up of menhirs, dolmens, and the stone circle links the Odisha tribes both with the Khasis and Nagas of Nagaland and Manipur and with the Gonds of Bastar. The Khasis (though not the Nagas) approach more nearly to the dominant megalithic custom of peninsular India in that they collect periodically the bones of clan members and deposit them in a 'free standing' cist, as big as a small house, built of enormous single slabs. So too do the Mundas of Chota Nagpur who, in addition to setting up memorial stones of North-eastern types, bury calcined bones of members of a family in dolmen like graves consisting of a cover slab, supported by smaller stones. Chotanagpur is geographically well situated for such an interchange, but there remains to discover any equivalent cultural overlap which might explain the Khasi cists.

The problem, then, of interrelationship between megalithic areas and customs is not an easy one. On the whole, however, in spite of occasional and partial analysis, the differences between the megaliths of the tribal area and the ancient tombs of Deccan and Peninsular India are far more impressive than their resemblance. As Fürer-Haimendorf observes, "I have seen the monuments of the Nagas and the Khasis, of Gadabas, Bondos and Gonds, and I have seen many of the prehistoric dolmens and cromlechs of Hyderabad, but was never struck by any resemblance. This alone would, of course, not proof the absence of genetic connection. More important are the differences in function and meaning of the monuments" (*c.f.* Wheeler 1948:150-152).

Among the Angami and the Chakesang Nagas, feasts of merit were considered as the highest social form of accomplishment in the lifetime of a wealthy person to attain high social status. Feasts of merit are also performed by wealthy people in the Chin Hills of Burma, and a pregnant mithun is also sacrificed in one of the feasts as by the Mao Nagas of Manipur. The Chin do not erect stone monuments, but the house of merit seeker is adorned with certain long platform and curved fences. Carved forked planks, to each of which is tied a sacrificial mithun, is erected in the front yard of the house. In the Chin Hills, as among Mao Nagas, feasts are a means of raising the standing of a household, and they focus on the propitiation of the household spirit (Lehman, 1963).

According to H.R. Van Heekeren (1958), megalithic cultures can be grouped into an 'older' and 'younger' phase across Indonesia in prehistoric times. He also believed that the older type has survived in some places up to the present day. In this description of the older megalithic cultures, he included dolmens used as sacrificial altar or as memorials, menhirs, uprights of wood or stones (sometimes in rows or circles), and stone seats consisting of a horizontal stone and one or more vertical ones as back supports, and these seats began to be used for prominent living people and the soul of the dead. Festivals associated with the monuments centred around the sacrifice of cattle, with forked sacrificial poles of wood (and occasionally stone) used to tether buffalos about to be sacrificed. Paved roads and platforms, round dwelling and burial of the dead near dwellings are associated characteristics. The 'younger' megalithic culture of Indonesia also includes dolmens together with stone sarcophagi and cists used as graves, stone statues of ancestors, the art of weaving, beads of glass and carnelians and burials in flexed and extended position.

Megalithic monuments are widely distributed in Indonesia. Dolmens consisting of a flat horizontal stone resting on one or more vertical ones are found in Nias, Sumba and Flores, where they serve as memorial or as sacrificial altars (Van Heekeren, 1958). The stone monuments created connection with the *makimovu* of the Mao Nagas may be compared with these dolmens from Indonesia. The villages on Dmosis Island in North Sumatra also have protective high walls with low narrow entrances. Also a Samosis dolmen are arranged in circles and used as seats for chiefs. The 'Spirit seat' of Java and Bali, which consists of a thick horizontal stone and an upright stone for the support of the back, may also have a similar ideology to the *kathitokhu* of the Mao Naga. Furthermore, the *zhosotu* upright may also be compared with the menhirs erected in Sumatra in honour of wealthy living person or the dead (Singh, 1985).

The megalithic monuments are also found among the Naga ethnic groups living in Manipur where it is also found as a living tradition among them, along with the Feast of Merit. Other rites and rituals associated with the megalithic cultures of the Nagas of Manipur are found to be identical with those found among the Angami, Chakhesang and the Rengma Nagas of Nagaland (Devi, 1993).

To compare the Naga and the Khasi megaliths, the memorial

stones erected in a line by the Khasis (even in number though not always), tallest one in the middle, sometimes from the tallest to the shorter one have a very close resemblance with *tsiese* (menhirs) of the Angami Nagas. Another Khasi megalith, the dolmens, associated with an upright stone may differ in functions but this type of megaliths is very near to the ones found among the Chakhesang Nagas. Burial chambers (tomb) are still constructed by present day Angami Naga megalithic builders by using flat stones as well as modern plastering method. Mortimer Wheeler (1948) observes that the Khasi megalithic culture is closer with those of south Indian megaliths like those of stone cists, table stones or cromlechs and stone circles, but we have not heard anything about feast of merit in these two regions. There appears to be a chain-like occurrence of feasts of merit tradition, starting from Nagaland, Manipur, Burma, Thailand and Indonesia.

Chronology

So far as the chronology of Naga megaliths is concerned, it is very difficult, at this stage to give exact dates of their construction. Wheeler quotes C. Von Fürer-Haimendorf to the effect that the megalithic cists of southern India have Iron Age associated with western analogies and the megalithic memorial stones of Central and North Eastern India have Neolithic association and an Indonesian or South-East Asian orientation (Wheeler, 1948: 183). In the last decade, systematic research in archaeology, particularly the excavation carried out by Mortimer Wheeler in Karnataka, have much enlarged our knowledge by dating them back to the period *c.*200 B.C–AD 50 —the period of the early Iron Age in southern India (Daniel,1963: 23). But Gordon Chide and Fürer-Haimendorf put it back to a period between 1100 and 700 BC, when according to them, the iron using people came to India from the Mediterranean.

Furthermore, in India, some megalithic monuments have been dated firmly on the basis of $Carbon^{14}$ method of reckoning chronology. According to Agarwal and Kusumgar (1974), excavated megaliths from Koria (Allahabad) belong to the Iron Age. A megalith from this site gave a C^{14} date 270±105 BC. Another late date for megalith from Halingali excavated by Soundara is 80±100 B.C. The excavator, however reports that the burial had a later disturbance and the dated charcoal may be later intrusion from the Iron Age settlement. From Payimpalli (Tamil Nadu) we have also two dates giving a range of *c.* 600–200 BC. The earliest dates so far are from the Neolithic-Megalithic overlap phase-I give a central date of *c.* 1000 BC, phase-II date *c.* 1030±105 BC and the overlap phase date *c.* 1105±105 BC gives the high antiquity of Iron Age in the south. Tabalghat have two C^{14} dates from its occupation, which are *c.* 615±105, *c.* 555±1000 BC (Agarwal & Kusumgar, 1974). Thus, if we take into consideration, the early dates of Hallur (*c.* 1000 BC) and the *c.* 600 BC date for Tabalghat and *c.* 300 BC from Kotia (UP) it appears that the megalithism spread from the south to the north (Uttar Pradesh) and not *vice-versa.*

In North East India, so far S.N. Rao obtained one C^{14} date from a post-Neolithic site at Marakdola in Khasi Hills. There is a single cultural horizon that has been noted using cord groove Kaolin pottery in close proximity to the monolith with table stone in front. The carbon sample recovered from this cultural horizon at a depth of 1.3 m from the surface was tested by the Birbal Sahni Institute of Palaeobotany and assigned a date 1292 AD (Rao, 1977).

This last date is applicable to this site of Marakdola alone and the date cannot be extended to the entire Khasi Hills as a chronological marker either for the beginning or for the end of the megalithic culture in this region. It can only indicate that the megalithic culture was flourishing in the Khasi Hills at least in the late thirteen century AD.

So far, very limited sites in Nagaland have been studied and yielded dependable evidence of chronology. In a recent study by Tiatoshi Jamir and others (Jamir *et al.*, 2014) the excavation of Khezhakeno (KNA), Movolomi (MLI) and Khusomi (KSI) and the dates derived reveal the contemporary nature of the sites. Radiocarbon dates for KNA dated Cal. AD 1320-1350 and MLI Cal. AD 1420-1640 appears to support the popular oral tradition of Khezhakeno where villages like Khezhakeno were foci of population growth followed by the establishment of the following villages – Movolomi, Pfulomi and Chichulomi. Around this time a vibrant megalithic culture marked by a mortuary tradition of extended inhumation burials in earth-cut pits topped with capstones and accompanied with grave goods such as terracotta smoking pipes and iron spearheads flourished in the region as evident from the numerous stone monuments and the pit burials encountered from the site.

But the problem of yielding dependable evidence of chronology from sites in Nagaland persists. The problem is of mixing up the recently erected one with those of the ancient period. Megalithism is practiced till today by many ethnic groups inhabiting in different parts of the state. Secondly, the megalithic field in every village under survey is considered as living monuments and they are still protected by the relatives as well as by clan members. Even the most modernised and westernised Christian Naga prefer to keep the tradition living, although they are not allowed under the modern religion to perform the megalithic ritual and feast of merit.

Therefore, it is not possible to provide an absolute date for the megaliths found in Nagaland, however, as most experts and scholars agree, the megalithic culture of Nagaland is undoubtedly of prehistoric origin and has survived as a living tradition performing very significant socio-cultural role amongst the Nagas till today.

REFERENCES

Agarwal, D.P. and S. Kusumgar. 1974. *Prehistoric Chronology and Radiocarbon Dating in India*. New Delhi: Munshiram Manoharlal.

Devi, P.B., 1993. *Studies on the Megalithic Remains of Manipur*. Ph.D. Thesis, Gauhati University, Guwahati, Assam.

Daniel, G.E., 1963. *The Megalithic Builders of Western Europe*. London: Hutchinson.

Evans, I. H. N., 1927. *Papers on the Ethnology and Archaeology of the Malay Peninsula.* London: Cambridge University Press.

Fergusson, J., 1872. *Rude Stone Monuments in all Countries, their Ages and uses*. London: J. Murray.

Fürer-Haimendorf, C. von., 1943. "Megalithic ritual among Gadabas and Bondos of Orissa". *Journal of the Royal Asiatic Society of Bengal*, IX: 149-178.

_____. 1945. "The Problem of Megalithic Culture in Middle India". *Man in India*, XXVI (2): 73-90.

_____. 1946. *The Naked Nagas*. Calcutta: Thacker Spink & Co.

_____. 1964. "The Megalithic Cultures of Assam". In F. M. Schnitger (ed.), *Forgotten Kingdoms in Sumatra*. Leiden: E.J. Brill, pp. 215-22.

Heine-Geldern, R. Von. 1935. *Sumatra the Archaeology and Art of Sumatra*. Verlog Des Institute FurFolkken Des Universal Wein.

Hutton, J.H., 1928. "The Significance of Head Hunting in Assam". *Journal of the Royal Anthropological Institute*, LVIII (2): 399-408.

Jamir, T., D. Tetso, Z. Venuh, V. Mushrif-Tripathy and A.K. Pokharia. 2014. *Archaeology of Naga Ancestral Sites: Recent Archaeological*

Investigations in Phek and Kiphire Districts of Nagaland, Vol. 2. Dimapur: Department of Art and Culture, Government of Nagaland & Heritage Publishing House.

Lehman, F.K., 1963. *The Structure of Chin Society.* Urbana: The University of Illinois Press.

Peet, E., 1912. *Rough Stone Monuments and their Builders.* London/NY: Harper & Bro.

Rao, S.N., 1977. "Continuity and Survival of Neolithic Traditions of North-Eastern India". *Asian Perspectives,* XX (2): 191-205.

Schnitger, F.M., 1939. *Forgotten Kingdoms of Sumatra.* Leiden: E.J. Brill.

Sharma, T.C., 1973-74. "Recent Archaeological Discoveries in North Eastern India". *Puratattva,* 7:17-19.

Singh, O.K., 1985. "A Live Megalithic Culture in Manipur". *Recent Advances in Indo-Pacific Prehistory*: Proceedings of the International Symposium held at Poona, December 19-21, 1978. Ed. V. N. Misra and P. Bellwood, pp. 491-96.

Van Heekeren, H.R., 1958. *The Bronze-Iron Age of Indonesia.* The Hague: Martinus Nijhoff.

Wheeler, R.E.M., 1948. "Brahmagiri and Chandravalli 1947: Megalithic and other Cultures in the Chitaldurg district, Mysore State". *Ancient India,* 4: 181-310.

4

Construction of Megaliths by Karbis of Dimoria

Kalpana Choudhury

Introduction

Dimoria is located on the eastern side of Kamrup (Metro) District of Assam. It is situated at a distance of 38 km on the eastern direction from Guwahati, on the southern bank of river Brahmaputra. North and south sides of Dimoria is hemmed by Morigaon District and Meghalaya, respectively, and on the eastern part by Morigaon and Nagaon District. The western side of Dimoria is bounded by Guwahati Municipal Corporation (GMC). The total geographical area of Dimoria is 26.164 hectares. The region has a varied physiographic feature from low lying flood plains through mountainous plains to the hilly areas. In fact, the topography of Dimoria reveals that more than three-fourths of the area is covered by hills; and rest of the area is encompassed by rivers, *beels*, marshes, swamps and forests. The hills of Dimoria stretch almost from the bank of the Brahmaputra river and merges with the ranges of Shillong or Meghalaya plateau. The major communities inhabiting Dimoria are the Assamese caste Hindus, Bodos, Garos, Karbis, Nepalis, Rabhas, Tea Garden Community, Tiwas etc.

During the medieval period Dimoria was a Karbi Kingdom, and was known as Dimorua. Though not well recorded and preserved, yet history mentioned that there was an ancient Kingdom on the eastern side of present Kamrup district, on the southern bank of Brahmaputra river. Subsequently, the name Dimorua became Dimoria, but no one knows how and when the name of the kingdom was changed. The local folktales and legends supported the view that the kingdom was managed by a king who belonged to the Karbi tribe.

The Karbis, also earlier known as Mikirs in the Constitution Order of the Government of India, constitute an important populous Scheduled Tribe, principally inhabiting the Karbi Anglong District of Assam. They consider the term 'Mikir' to be given by the neighbouring Assamese people. Stack and Lyall (1904:3) stated "The name Mikir is given to the race by the Assamese, its origin in unknown". Barkakati (1981) also supports their view and opined that the 'Mikir' is a name given to the tribe by the Assamese. They call themselves 'Arleng' which means 'Man'.

It is a popular belief among the Karbis that they came to their present abode, especially to the district of Karbi Anglong, from the east. This migration must have been during the first and the second millennia before Christ. They belong to the Tibeto-Burman ethno-linguistic family. From the point of view of habitation, the Karbis are divided into three groups, namely Chinthang, Ranghang and Amri. The Ranghangs and the Amri are also referred to as Nilip Ranghang and Dumurali, respectively. The Chingthongs live in the Mikir Hills of the former Golaghat and North Cachar Hill Sub-Divisions, and the Ronghangs in the plains of the Nagaon District. The rest who live in the plain districts are called Amri in North East India, particularly in Assam, Manipur, Meghalaya and Nagaland.

Megalithic culture is still practiced by different tribal communities in the same pristine way, or in a modified form. A few tribes of Assam, especially the Karbi is a major tribe in Dimoria and they practice this culture since time immemorial. As regards the erection of megaliths, some differences are observed among the hill and the plain Karbis, but feast of merit is a common feature integral to both the situations. This feast is a kind of entertainment offered to the villagers at the time of erection of the megaliths by the deceased's kith and kin. The nature of the feast determines the nature, power, property and position of the deceased in the society.

Generally, a megalith is erected among the Karbis only following a natural death. Unnatural deaths like committing suicide, killed by animals, like buffalo, elephant, tiger etc. are all considered inauspicious, and hence, such deaths are not oriented as equivalent to a natural death. In fact, such dead bodies are not cremated; and in such a situation, megaliths cannot be erected in the memory of the victims of unnatural death.

The megaliths in Dimoria are mostly concentrated in the hilly region. This includes by far, the most antiquated megaliths. This does not mean that the huge clusters of megaliths in the foot-hills and the plain region are of recent origin. Even in the plains and foot-hills, age-old megalithic structures are found. There are more than 2000 megaliths distributed over twenty villages in the Dimoria area.

Categories of Megaliths

On the basis of their structure, entire megalithic assemblages could be divided broadly into two categories — (i) Memorial or Commemorative, and (ii) Funerary or Ritualistic.

Memorial or Commemorative Megaliths

This type of megalith is erected to commemorate the death of an individual or for the members of a clan. This signifies the status, prestige or social eminence of a person. Sometimes, it is also erected to commemorate some events of public interest — social, political, ideological or the events of such categories. This is mostly represented by the construction of a menhir which the Karbis refer to as *long-e*. Typologically, this memorial or commemorative megalith could be identified as menhir. These are erected vertically on the ground selected for the purpose. The size of these may vary occasionally in height, ranging from 1.57 m to 2.57 m, with a common height ranging between 1.20 m to 1.80 m. They are essentially either memorials or commemorative pillars planted near the village path leading to habitation areas or *jhum* fields.

When a new village headman is selected, he should raise a menhir with a table stone in front in the memory of his selection as a village head. Locally this is known as *long-e-sarthe* (stone of the *sarthe*, head man). A great menhir is found in Magursila village of Dimoria with an alignment of other megaliths. It is a menhir raised after the death of the *sarthe*, who was the headman of 13 villages and was said to be very powerful.

Funerary and Ritualistic Megaliths

The Karbis of Dimoria erect a series of stones which are connected with funerary and ritualistic practices. These are mostly represented either by menhir or dolmen. The Karbi name of the menhir, as has been already referred to, is *long-e,* and for the dolmen they use the term *cheng-e*.

The menhirs of this category are usually big, thick and roughly shaped slabs of granite. The common size of a menhir is 1.20 m × 0.85 m × 0.20 m (length × breadth × thickness), respectively.

The flat table stone known as *cheng-e*, are usually of the size 1.65 m × 1.09 m × 0.76 m.

In the following the funerary aspect is discussed. Funeral system is integral to each society of the world. The Karbis also have a pristine set of funeral system. Funeral system prevalent among the Karbis could broadly be divided into two categories. These are — (a) *Pafolosok* (to burn), and (b) *Lungle abhar kibi* (to bury).

Pafolosok is connected to the cremation of the dead body. It is of two types. In the first case, the dead body is cremated, but in such case they never erect memorial stone or *long-e.* In fact, they offer a feast to the co-villagers for the welfare and peace of the soul of the deceased. In terms of the second they erected a menhir (*long-e)* after the cremation of the dead body. In this case also a feast is offered to the co-villagers for the well being of the soul by the family members of the deceased.

In the *Lungle Abhar Kibi* process the dead body is buried. Generally, this is observed in the case of the death of a small boy or a girl. The Karbis refer to this as *lungle abhar kibi*.

If some people die unnaturally, i.e. due to the attack of elephant, tiger, snake etc., falling from the tree, drowning in water and so on, they believe that the deceased committed sins, due to which he or she is punished by god through accidental death. They believe that, if someone has not committed any sin, he or she never die untimely or unnaturally. Memorial stones are erected in the name of those persons, but separately, far from the general megalithic burial site (*long-e-an*). No rituals are performed in case of those people, who are the victims of unnatural death. After the erection of the stone, the family members should be sanctified by sacrificing a fowl and arranging a feast in the name of the dead, in which co-villagers should be entertained.

Construction of Megaliths

For the construction of megaliths, hard, consistent, harmonious, and durable rocks are essentially preferred. As a matter of fact, rock type used for the monuments varies from village to village and region to region, as the same type of rock is not always available in all places. The type of rock to be used for the above purposes must be locally available, since it would be difficult to transport these massive rocks from a place to a desired distant place. However, it is observed that mostly two types of rocks are being selected by the people of Dimoria for construction of megaliths. These are igneous and sandstone or their metamorphic types. Generally, granite and its metamorphic variety, the gneiss, are the most commonly available rock in the area, which are primarily used. Sometimes, sandstone is also found, but quartzite is seldom used by the Karbis. This may be because of the fact that the latter type is not readily available in the vicinity. The granite stone, which is generally selected for making the megaliths, is called *long-ki-e* by the Karbis.

The Karbi process of erection of a megalith is a complicated one. Erection of a megalith has different stages, which are briefly described below.

Selection of Stone

It has been already discussed that primarily one type of rock is selected by the Karbis of the study area. In fact, the selection of rock depends on its availability as well as its proximity to the village. Primarily, they look for strong, durable rock of required shape and size irrespective of the type and variety. When a person dies, a few villagers go up the hill in search of the rock to be erected as megalith. They carry a pair of betel-nut, a pair of betel vine leaf, a handful of rice, and a potful of *harbong* (rice beer) along with a few machetes and a big hammer. Usually, they select a rock of 0.90 m × 0.15 m × 0.30 m. However, if they do not find a stone of aforesaid measurement, then they have to break a bigger stone with the help of the hammer, till it acquires the expected shape. According to the Karbis, only the 'living stone' (i.e. unweathered, uneroded and fresh) can be used for megaliths. In order to know whether the stone is living or dead, they strike the stone with a hammer. If the stone is hard enough and produces sparks during hammering, then they take it for granted that it has a life. If the stone is not sparking and easily breaks into pieces after hammering, then they consider it to be a dead stone, and abandon it.

After finalization of the stone selection, they start the ritual. First of all they offer betel-nut and betel vine leaf, throw rice and pour rice beer on the stone by uttering the following hymn[1]:

> "High mountain, wide mountain,
> This stone is neither yours nor ours,
> From today the stone is no more your child,
> And now onwards it becomes a man's soul.
> We are paying homage to you
> By offering rice beer, rice, betel nut and betel vine leaf.
> Look, we are carrying your child on the back
> To erect it as the dead man's soul."

Transportation and Erection of Stone

There are two methods of collection and transportation of the stone blocks from the hills. These are – (a) *Arjan kibi* (to carry on pole), and (b) *Kithi karhi* (to carry in a trolley).

In the first method, i.e. the *arjan kibi*, a group of persons carry the stone to be erected as megalith by hanging with the rope or jungle creeper on a carrying pole, made of bamboo. In the second method, i.e. the *kithi karhi,* the stone is put on a wooden trolley, and it is carried down to the village from the hill top by pushing and pulling the trolley. However, in all the villages of the study area the first method is followed to fetch the required stone and the second method is very rarely used by them.

After transportation of the stone to the village they perform some rituals. At the beginning of the ritual the priest *(karkun)* purify the place (where the stone is to be raised) by sprinkling water in which a few leaves of sweet basil are dipped. With the mentioned holy water the stone is washed. After the purification of place and the stone the priest starts the incantation addressing the stone:

> "O' great stone,
> You are the child of rock-cave.
> As real stone remains static,
> You too will also remain in the same.

O' (calling by name the dead man),
We have erected this stone in your memory."

A flat stone (dolmen) is also placed on the same day in front of the menhir of burying the dead. No elaborate and separate feast is offered for placing these structures. These are used for offering food to the deceased.

Fig. 4.1: Menhir at Chenimur village

Fig. 4.2: Dolmens at Batakuchi village

Fig. 4.3: A ritual procession for menhir transportation

Post-Construction Ceremonies

Post-Erection Ritual

After the megalith is erected, pigs or hens are sacrificed and the blood of the sacrificed animal is sprinkled over the megalith. During the process of sacrifice, the following hymn is chanted.

> "O' the child of the birds' king and the king of pigs,
> You are bestowed with blessings from sun and moon;
> Like this the Karbis will save you
> From kites and other enemies,
> And they will also provide you food grains.
> Therefore, you have to sacrifice yourself at the edge of *long-e*.
> Man will not be responsible for that sin."

After the erection, the exposed portion of the megalith is enfolded. If the deceased is male, the stone is wrapped with a cloth called *fali* (loin cloth) or *gamocha* (hand woven towel), and in case of a female, the stone is wrapped with a cotton thread which is not hardened by adding starch. Only on the last day of the funeral, the cloth or thread is taken away from the stone.

A feast is then arranged, in which boiled rice and curries of sacrificed pigs and chickens' meat are served to the co-villagers. A share of the meal is offered to the deceased's soul on the flat stone (*cheng-e)* kept along with the *long-e.* All the people present there are entertained in the feast and all of them proceed to the deceased's house after completion of the feast. There they sit in the courtyard to console the bereaved family.

Thereafter, they leave the place without uttering a customary word of parting. It is believed that it is inauspicious to pronounce parting words, which may bring hazards and disasters to the deceased's family. In the evening the village youths gather in the deceased's house. They sing and dance throughout the night, with an intention to console the grieved family and to help the family members to cope with the situation. From the day of the person's death till the last day of the funeral, the deceased's family members neither can eat any bitter food, nor can prepare rice beer.

Bidding Farewell

The farewell to the deceased's soul is known as *kasirdam* among the Karbis. This ritual is performed on the tenth day after the erection of the menhir. At dawn of that day, five respectable members proceed towards the megalithic site and stop near it. The group is generally composed of male members from the deceased's family, a priest, an assistant of the priest (*bangthai*), and a ritual advisor (*bichar-hojer*). In some of the Karbi villages, a village king (*raja*) is present. In those villages, the king is the integral part of the farewell group.

Females are strictly prohibited from joining the group. This group takes a pig, a pot of rice beer and some quantity of unboiled rice to the place where the megalith is erected. There a pig is sacrificed, and a little meat is cooked, and offered in the name of the deceased on the flat stone (*cheng-e*) along with rice and rice beer. Then the cloth/thread which was wrapped round the stone is removed by any member of the group.

In the afternoon, the family members and kins of the deceased, along with the clan members and neighbours, assemble near the megalith to bid farewell to the deceased. They carry rice beer, meat and fruits with them and offer these in the name of the dead on the table stone (dolmen) and then sit around the megalith. Then one of them prepare a paste of boiled egg (*kiup-o'ari*) and roasted *lata* fish (z.*Ophicephalus punctatus*) and distributes it to all the people present there in *lathenghararang* (a kind of leaf). They do not eat it; instead, they smell it and keep the sacred food aside.

Then they come back to the deceased's house and arrange a feast with the meat of the sacrificed pig on the following morning. All the young boys and girls of the deceased's clan assemble in the deceased's house, sing songs, beat drums, dance and relish the food of the feast. It should be noted here that this ritual is integral to the mortuary rite and is not only an indispensable custom of the animist Karbis, but performed by the Christian Karbis too.

Purificatory Ritual

Purification is an essential ritual, observed at any time of the year as and when the family is supposed to be ready for the process of purification. This, in fact, is another set of ritual, which is not only a purificatory function, but also has a close connection with the deceased. This is a household ritual and is confined to the family members of the deceased only. They select a convenient date for this ritual. The process of purification is described below.

A priest is invited to conduct the ritual. He collects the following items for the purification ritual.

(a) A kind of reed like grass (*tibong*)
(b) Bamboo basket (*iring suway*)
(c) Bamboo split (*tamal*)
(d) A few fowl (*nangwba*), and
(e) One pair of egg (*dimwba*)

Two cross structures are made by inserting four *tibong* grass in soil under the water of a spring in upright position. The apexes of all the grass are put together and tied with slender bamboo split, to form a semi-circle, through which the men can proceed. Then each member of the deceased's family equipped with a bamboo basket and a hen in hand passes through the grass structure. While passing through the structure, water is sprinkled over the body of the person by the bamboo leaves and the following hymn is recited:

O' Hemphu[2], we are not inebriated.
Death has brought defilement to our house and main post
And also to Lakshmi[2]
On this auspicious day,
We prepare wine and invite a priest to purify.
We have collected bamboo baskets,
and planted on the river bank.
After sanctifying the impure house,
May there be no disaster,
From attack of insects, death, diseases.
Children be free and blessed by the *Burhagohairr*[2].

After completion of this purificatory ritual, they return back to the megalithic burial place. There they offer rice to *Yama* or *Yambang an kibak* (the god of death). The priest wears *niopniton* (sleeveless jacket) and advices one of the male family members to welcome the soul of the dead to the home by holding a yellow hen in his hand. The priest also advices him to offer rice beer, betel nuts and betel vine leaves to the soul of the deceased and recites the following hymn.

O' Kur (name of the deceased),

Do not lie on the river bank, hills and forest.
Do not wet yourself with dew and rain.
You have your house with main post and forefathers.
Come, and stay with your forefathers,
and take part in the remembrance of your forefathers,
and cast a glance for the welfare
and prosperity of our children and grandchild.
Come, come, let us go to our own house.

This way the soul is welcomed and commended to the yellow hen. Coming home the hen is tied to the main post of the house. The bird is then sacrificed and its meat is offered to the gods. After the soul of the deceased is placed at the bottom of the main post of the residential house of the deceased, the funeral rituals come to an end.

Concluding Notes

Thus, among the Plains Karbis of Dimoria, erection of megalith is an integral trait of their culture, especially mortuary rites. These are integral to the religious system of the Karbi inhabitants of Dimoria, which are linked with innumerable beliefs, taboos, rites and observances. These monuments are not only erected for funerary purposes, but also to commemorate the feast of merit and other events coupled with various beliefs and faiths.

In Khamar village of Dimoria, a good number of megaliths were found. Out of those, four belonged to the royal family of the Dimoria kingdom, easily identifiable on the basis of their structural variations and engravings. A grand feast was offered to the villagers and neighbouring villages when Sher Sing, the last king of Dimoria died. In that remarkable feast, 15 pigs and a good number of fowls were sacrificed. One quintal of rice was prepared along with curry prepared from plenty of vegetables. Around 100 litres of rice beer was used to entertain the guests. Besides, plenty of area nuts and betel vine leaves were offered to the guests.

Due to forces of modernisation, industrialisation etc., some changes have occurred in Dimoria. Much of the megaliths are in disarray, and people are using modern material (like cement and mortar) instead of stone. What is interesting is that despite all these, the inner meaning of the stones is still being followed.

NOTES

1. These chanting hymns are literal translations of the Karbi hymns in original.
2. These are various gods and goddesses which the Karbis revere. Hemphu is the supreme power of all the rules and regulations; Lakshmi is the goddess of wealth and prosperity; and Burhagohairr refers to the old benevolent god.

REFERENCES

Barkakati, S., 1981. *Tribes of Assam.* New Delhi: National Book Trust.

Stack, E. and C. Lyall. 1904. *The Mikirs*. Guwahati: Lawyers Book Stall.

5
Ideological Basis of Megaliths in Mizo Society

Malsawmliana

Introduction

The Mizos raise megaliths to mark various events of significance in society such as the commemoration of the achievements of chiefs, the *thangchhuahpa* (warriors), and also the foundation of villages, settlements etc. Memorials were not only raised for the living but for the dead as well. Irrespective of the event, megaliths are primarily commemorative in nature, serving as a link between the world of the living and that of the dead. Memorials may be of wood or stone, sometimes both, on which the figures of human, animals and other prestige goods were carved. These carvings provide valuable insights into several aspects of early Mizo society. In this chapter, attempt will be made to understand some ideological basis of the megaliths in Mizo society.

Traditionally, the Mizos preferred the use of stones as memorials to the dead. However, wooden planks were also sometimes used for the purpose of commemoration. It may be noted that stone and wooden planks were erected not only to mark the grave, but also to bridge the world of the living with that of the dead. The Mizo believe that memorials raised in memory of departed souls would make the latter happy and that they would use such memorial stones as resting places whenever their spirits visited the village. Thus, megaliths served the purpose of linking the dead with the living. It ensured an uninterrupted flow of life from the distant past into the distant future. In this sense, the eschatological implication of planting a stone is that man's position in life after death is largely dependent on his personal achievements in his earthly life (Darchawna, 2005).

Death as Honour

The early Mizos believed in the existence of the two final abodes of the dead, *Mitthi Khua* and *Pialral. Mitthi Khua* was a resting place for ordinary and common people who have not performed feasts of merit during their lifetime. Life there was supposed to be full of misery and anxiety. On the other hand, the second abode of the dead, *Pialral,* was located on the banks of the river *Pial* where life was different from that in *Mitthi Khua. Pialral* was regarded as the most pleasant place where one did not have to work. Here the soul is completely free from suffering, hardship and pain. It is a place where only the *thangchhuahpa*, i.e. the warriors and their families were permitted to live in.

The proud title of *thangchhuah*, which carries with it much honour in the living world as well as the right of admission to *Pialral,* was much coveted by all who aspired for status in society and a secure place in the world hereafter. Two types of *thangchhuah* were recognized – (a) the *Inlama Thangchhuah*, and (b) the *Ram Lama Thangchhuah*.

To gain the title of *Inlama Thangchhuah*, one must have enough wealth to perform a series of feasts and ceremonies, and to do that, one must possess enough domestic animals that were required to be slaughtered in the course of the feasts (Fig. 5.1). These are indicated below (after Liangkhaia, 1938: 46-49):

(a) *Sakung* – This is performed by killing a big male pig (*vawkpasutnghak*);
(b) *Chawng* – This is performed by killing three pigs – two males and one female; and a large quantity of rice beer is prepared by the performer;
(c) *Dawino chhui* – One must perform five religious sacrifices such as *Hnuaite*[1], *Lasi*, *Chung*, *Vansen* and *Hnuaipui*, and slaughter a female pig and a hen for sacrificial offerings;
(d) *Sedawi Chhun* – This is performed by the killing of one

mithun, one big pig and two small pigs; a large quantity of rice beer;

(e) *Sekhuan/Zankhuang* and *Mitthirawp lam* – This is performed by killing a mithun, small pigs and serving a large quantity of rice beer; and

(f) *Khuangchawi* – This is the greatest of all the ceremonies and represents the final feast in the prescribed series. It is performed for three days, and on the evening of the third and final day, the couple, who holds the feast, throws to the crowd cotton, hens, brass pots, clothes and sometimes guns and gongs, and members of the village scramble for these gifts.

After the feasts for *Inlama Thangchhuah* are over, the performer is given the title *Thangchhuahpa* and is also dubbed as *Zawhzawzo* meaning "one who has completed everything". Automatically, his wife also shared the coveted title of her husband and she was given recognition as *thangchhuahnu* ('*nu*' means 'woman'). The *thangchhuahpa* was entitled to open the windows in his house as wide as he wished and to make a verandah (*vanlung*) in his house. He was also entitled to wear specially designed clothes with red and black stripes called *thangchhuah puan*.

The other title, *Ramlama Thangchhuah* can only be obtained after killing animals like bears, sambar deer, barking deer, wild mithun, stags, wild boars, viper snakes and hawks. If a man killed all these animals, he qualified for the coveted title of '*Thangchhuah*'. An account of the journey of *Ramlama Thangchhuah* to *Pialral* by Shakespeare (1988: 63) indicates how the killing of the above mentioned animals guarantees the warrior entry into *Pialral*:

> "... after death, man (*thangchhuah*) holds the horns of the sambar deer while sitting on its head, the *rulngan* (viper) will wind itself round him and the horns, the *muvanlai* (hawk) will try to seize the *rulgan*, but the *thangchhuah* can drive them off. That is why they always fly screaming so high in the sky. The *vahluk* or hawk shade him by flying above him and also hide him from *Pawla*[2], and thus the *thangchhuah* is carried to *Pialral*."

Thangchhuahs were honoured in public by being given seats next to the chief on every festive occasion. Beside the above entitlements, the *Thangchhuah* ceremonies also ensured the following (Sangkima, 1992: 59):

(a) Achievement of eternal bliss at *Pialral*;
(b) Avoidance of the pellets of *Pawla*; and
(c) Gaining respect and honour during one's life time.

Given the honour and prestige that comes with the titles, they represented the ideal towards which the Mizo strive for, in life.

The *thangchhuahpa* usually erects his memorial stones at the entrance of the village during his life time, on which carvings of humans, animals, gongs etc; are depicted. The engraving of such figures demonstrates the material achievements and status of the person in the society. Sometimes, the picture of the *inlama thangchhuahpa* is engraved on stone in which he is shown wearing the feathers of a horn-bill (*vapual*) in his head while the *ramlama thangchhuahpa* was depicted wearing a head dress made of goats' hair (*thanchhawn)* spearing the head of a slave with one hand and carrying a metal spiked spear in his other.

Fig. 5.1: Slaughtering of a mithun for feast

Memorials for Honouring Death

Stone Menhirs

The Mara clans living in southern Mizoram believe that the spirit of the deceased visit their home for the last time before going off to their final abode. Accordingly, a ceremony called *Athiteukhei* which means "sitting with the dead" is performed during the course of erection of memorial stones to dead relatives (Parry, 1976: 414). N.E. Parry (1976) provides details about the ceremony. He states,

> "On the day fixed for the *Athiteukhei* feast, all the deceased's relations and friends are invited. Mithun or pigs are killed, *sahma* is made, and a feast is prepared. Against the wall of the house which faces down the slope a tray is placed, covered with every sort of edible and drink; this is for the spirit of the deceased, who is supposed to come and sit with his friends and to partake of the good things provided. In the course of the day the memorials are finished, and then the women all have their feast inside the house and the men on the verandah. When the food is all consumed, the men join the women inside the house and they drink *sahma* together. In the evening after sunset all the edibles on the tray are collected in a small basket and hung on a forked stick on the grave near the *thangri*; this is to show the final separation of the dead man's spirit from the living. The next day the whole village holds an *aoh* called *viachawpana;* no one may do any work, and the women may neither spin nor weave; it is believed that unless this *aoh* is observed, the dead man's spirit will carry off with it to *Athikhi* the spirits of rice and of all the other kinds of edibles and there will be a famine. The *aoh* need not be held on every occasion that a memorial post is erected, but only on the occasion of erection of the first memorial posts between the harvest and the burning of the new *jhums*. Memorials are erected by the deceased's heir. If the latter is very poor and cannot afford to pay for the sacrifice and feast required, a little of every kind of available edible is collected in a basket and hung up on a forked post over the grave…" (p. 414).

The above observation clearly indicates the ritual connection between the memorials and agricultural practices in Mara society. It may also be mentioned that the above observation made by Parry, refers to a funerary ritual that cuts across all sections of society, since *Athikhi* is a common place where the spirits of the dead reside. However, it is worth noting that the spirit of a chief remains that of the chief and so thus that of a warrior and an ordinary person. This suggests that personal achievements, position and status in one's earthly life has a direct bearing on the life hereafter. In other words power and prestige earned by an individual on earth is carried over into the life hereafter.

Wooden Memorials

The Mizos sometimes use wooden posts instead of stones as memorials to the dead. They used a thick plank of hard wood, sometimes accompanied by a long pole of about 5 metres high as a memorial to the dead. Figures of human, animals, weapons etc. were carved on the plank. For instance, the Tlaisun (Tashons) clan while living in the Chin Hills of Burma set up wooden memorials to dead chiefs which are accompanied by a long pole of about 4.58 metres high. It is said that the bottom 1.52 metres of the pole is carved to represent the chief and the remaining 3.04 metres of the pole is carved to represent the turban of the chief, who is thus represented with 1.52 metres of the body and 3.04 metres of turban. Bertram S. Carey further states that there are other smaller wooden memorials representing the wives and children of the deceased chiefs (Carey & Tuck, 2008).

The Mara also erect wooden posts called *thangri* along with a stone monument (*lophei*), over the grave of every individual (Parry, 1976; Hlychho, 2007). The *thangri* was made from a well grown *khaimei* tree (b. *Schima wallichii*). After cutting off all of its branches it was roughly hewn into shape having four sides. The lower part of the post represents a human body surmounted by a head. A man's *thangri* has no neck and the body runs straight up to the head while a woman's *thangri* has a sort of lozenge-shaped neck. The horns on the top of the *thangri* represent hair. A man's *thangri* has one horn while a woman's has two (Fig. 5.2). Conventional ornaments such as beads, necklaces etc. were carved on the body of the *thangri* using chisels. Carvings depicted on the *thangris* vary from village to village and also depends on the status of the deceased person. The carvings are dyed a dark colour consisting of a mixture of pig's blood pounded with ashes from the leaves of the *bahru* palm (b. *Calamus erectus*) or the *thiahra* palm (b. *Borassus flabellifer*). The carvings on the post generally convey the prosperity and status of the deceased in the society.

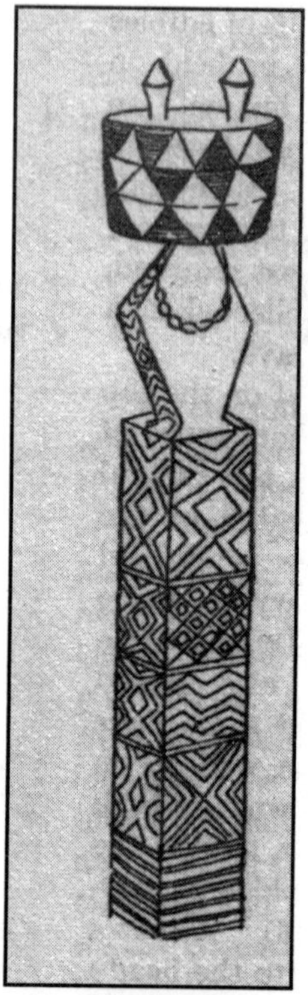

Fig. 5.2: *Thangri*, a wooden post of the Mara

The *thangri* of the chiefs and nobles were also adorned with a plume of red goat's hair or horse hair. In case of a warrior, another wooden post which was about three feet high was erected by the side of his *thangri.* On such a post, a number of holes are made and a peg is inserted through each hole to represent a human head and slave captured. Thus, the numbers of holes depend upon the number of human heads a warrior has taken and slaves captured in a war or raid. For example, the wooden post of a warrior who had taken four human heads and captured five slaves would have nine pegs run through the top. Besides, if he possessed a gun, its representation was carved on the post. It is also said that if such a person had succeeded in seducing another man's wife, a plume of white cock's feathers is tied to his *thangri*. In case of women, the possession of the highly valued necklace (*pumtek*), would be carved around the neck of the woman's *thangri,* and if she possessed a metal belt, a band would be carved at the bottom of the *thangri*. Later, when the Lushai Hills established links with their neighbours through trade in and around the eighteenth century AD, they began to use ornaments like looking glass and other imported items. These changes are reflected in *thangri* of the period which have pieces of looking glass and coins inserted on the neck of the *thangri* of both young men and women. The decorations or carved figures on such memorial posts all have specific terms.

Each of the terms used for decorations on *thangri* are explained by N.E. Parry (1976: 416) who states –

> "In a woman's *thangri*, the horns on the top represent the hair and are called *hrong*. The lozenges on the head are called *athei hmong*, meaning cucumber seeds. The circle hanging round the neck is *sisari,* the pumtek necklaces; the lozenges and triangles of the upper part of the body are *kei ongpa.* The small lozenges inside large lozenges are *athei hmong* (cucumber seeds); below these come zig-zags (*kiameichei*), and again lower come triangles enhanced by internal repetitions, all those on one side having the same base, called *keiongva khangpi*, and lasts of all bands *ahra*, to represent a woman's belts."

Forked Posts

Aside from the memorial posts, the Mizo also planted the *seluphan,* a forked or Y-shaped post for commemorative purposes during the *Sedawi* ceremony, at the courtyard of the performer (Fig. 5.3). The word *seluphan* is a combination of two words, *selu* meaning 'head of mithun' and *phan* meaning 'wooden post'. Thus, it is a wooden Y-shaped post on which the skull of a mithun was attached. It was a status symbol and it was the ambition of every Mizo to have a long line of such posts in front of his house. The *seluphan* was erected during the performance of *Sedawi*, one of the series of feasts of merit to attain the title of *thangchhuah*. A day before the feast, a group of men, one of which should be the close relative of the performer, led by the village priest (*sadawt*) would go into the forest in search of a suitable wooden post which would preferably be the *thingsia* tree (b. *Castanopsis tribuloides*) (Zawla, 1964: 23-24).

Fig. 5.3: *Seluphan*, a wooden Y-post of the Mizo

They take with them a sacrificial cock, food and rice beer (*zu*) into the forest. When they find the tree, the *sadawt* would spit *zu* three times over the tree chanting a hymn. Then he throws a pellet three times towards the upper end of the tree and when the pellet flies over the tree, others would utter the words "*a khum e, a khum e*" which means "the pellet flew over the tree". Then, they would cut down the tree with a *dao*, with the *sadawt* saying "*ka ar hlui khuangin a thai thluk e*" meaning "the fall was caused by my crowing cock". The wooden post is then erected at the courtyard of the feast-giver or performer in the evening of the first day of the ceremony. In the course of the ceremony the *sadawt* draws a circle on the ground using a porcupine quill and chants the following verse before the setting up of the post (Lalthangliana, 2001: 341): "*Mu chhepa fuk nan ka ti lo, Sa chhepa fuk nan ka ti lo, Chalvawma lu chuan nan ka ti e*" meaning "The post was not meant for birds and other animals, but for the head of the mithun".

The *sadawt* then keeps one boiled egg fixed to one end of the post in the belief that it would ensure greater abundance for the family of the performer. The *sedawi* ceremony lasts for seven days and is the first feast celebrated by the killing of a mithun. On the last day of the feast, the skull of a mithun is placed on a higher spike of the *seluphan.* Thus, the erection of the sacrificial post, *seluphan*, during the *Sedawi* feast involves the sacrifice of mithun. The *seluphan* was generally about 8 to10 feet high.

Shakespeare (1988: 90) details the setting up of the *seluphan* thus,

> "The skulls of mithun killed on these occasions are placed on posts to one side of the entrance of the house of the giver of the feast, and it is the highest ambition of the Lushai to have a long line of such posts in front of his house. Each post is cut out of a tree of considerable size, which is dressed until the lower 7 or 8 feet are only some 8 or 9 inches thick. Above this, the tree is roughly cut into a plank some 8 or 9 inches thick, forming an irregular quadrilateral, the lower side being a foot or so long and the upper from 2 to 3 feet, while one side may be 18 inches and the other 2 feet or a little more; at each of the upper corners there is a perpendicular projection some 12 inches long terminating in a spike, a short distance below which a ring of wood is left. The skull is placed on the higher spike, while on the lower an egg is affixed by a thin peg of fir wood."

Concluding Notes

Thus megaliths and feasts go hand in hand and are an indispensable and distinctive feature of the megalithic tradition of the Mizos. The performance of feasts, especially the series of feasts of merit as cited above were intended to enhance the prestige and status of the donor in his earthly existence as well as to ensure a path to paradise (*Pialral*) in the world of the dead. So, the erection of megaliths through which the donor illustrates his social accomplishment, was always accompanied by the performance of feasts. Such feasts and erection of megaliths normally involve the whole community who take an active role in the harvesting of paddy, pounding and brewing of rice, the collection of firewood and preparation for the feast, and in return, they were given food and rice-beer (*zu*). The performer during such occasions was able to share his prosperity with the community which in return ensures his prestige in the society.

One important consideration in putting up megalithic monuments was the economic stability of the individual. To undertake a feast of merit, one must be rich and prosperous enough, as the erection of stones involved feasts in which huge quantities of rice beer were consumed during the course. The expensive nature of the feasts makes it almost impossible for the common people to undertake such an exercise. However, the lavishness of the ceremony and the feasts depends upon the prosperity of the performer. He should possess at least a fair amount of paddy for making rice beer and a number of domesticated animals that must be slaughtered. Being the staple food of the Mizos, rice is cultivated in *jhum* land. Other than rice, maize, millet, peas, jobs tears, chillies, cotton, and fruits like cucumber, watermelon, melons etc. were also produced.

The Mizos are primarily food producers taking recourse to shifting cultivation after a period of one year and substantially depend upon hunting and domestication of animals to supplement agriculture. The domesticated animals include mithun, pigs, dogs, fowls or hens, and goats. Mithun is the most valued domesticated animal and wealth is measured on the possession of mithun. Every family also rears pigs as they play a significant part in sacrificial performances. The meat of pig (pork) is a popular dish for both men and women, while goat is domesticated not only for food, but also for sacrificial offerings. Goats are also essential as offerings in almost every sacrificial performance of the Mizos. Dog is another favourite domestic animal used commonly for hunting wild animals and sometimes as sacrificial offerings. Poultry occupied an important place in the traditional life of the Mizos, and hens and cocks were domesticated for food and sacrificial offerings in every home.

The link between the megaliths and the feasts of merit are also brought out during the course of the *Sikpui Roui* festival of the Hmar clans. The *Sikpui Roui* is a thanks giving festival of the Hmar clan, which is observed during the winter season. The festival signifies peace, health, success and abundance in the village. Whenever organised, they forget all past troubles and sufferings (Bapui, 2016). If there was any serious sickness or bereavement in the village during the year, the festival was postponed to the following year. During the course of the feast, people try their best to settle disputes and to be at peace with all members of the community. Flat stones to be erected during the course of the feasts were first carefully selected. The stones should be blemish free and unmarked by humans. The flat stone thus erected as stone seats, become a sacred place. The *Sikpui* dance is performed during the feasts.

Fig. 5.4: *Sikpui Lung*, a sacred stone seat of the Hmar

Thus, there may be some driving forces that led to the raising of megaliths among the Mizos which cannot be mentioned in this chapter. However, megaliths are a material expression of ideas concerning the place of humans in nature and society. For the individual and groups with common interests, rituals and monuments which assured the souls of continuous life after death and which were thought to promote fertility and the satisfaction of personal ambitions implicit in the various feasts of merit; which served to link the world of living with the world of the dead, thereby ensuring not only social continuity, but also a passage into paradise, are essentially a society's response to the material realities of life.

NOTES

1. These are rituals and sacrifices – *Hnuaite* is a sacrifice in which a female piglet is offered to *Lasi*, a spirit that stays around the house. *Lasi* is also the fabled creator of animals and the spirit of hunting which was believed to have control over animals. *Chung* sacrifice is performed to appease the spirit who had a power over the sun and the rain. In *Vansen* sacrifice a red cock is offered to worship the spirit who was believed to live in the clouds and a giver of abundant blessing. In *Hnuaipui*, a full grown female pig was sacrifice to worship the spirit who inhabited the lower region of earth.
2. *Pawla* is the name of a mythical being who lives at the junction of the roads leading to *Mitthi khua* and shoots with his pellet-bow at the souls of the departed as they pass on their way thither.
3. *Sedawi* is the fourth stage of the series of feasts of merit of the Mizo during which the skull of mithun slaughtered is attached on top of the sacrificial post i.e., *seluphan*.

REFERENCES

Bapui, V.T., 2016. "Festival of the Hmars". http://diprnchiils.gov.in / festival.htm#festival_ of_the_hmar.

Carey, B.S., and H.N. Tuck. 2008. *The Chin Hills*, Vol. I. Kolkata: Firma KLM Private Ltd.

Darchawna. 2005. "Monoliths of Mizoram". In Sangkima (ed.), *A Modern History of Mizoram*. Guwahati: Spectrum.

Hlychho, P.T., 2007. *Maraland: Yesterday and Today*. Shillong: Hlychho.

Lalthangliana, B., 2001. *Mizo Chanchin*. Aizawl: Remkungi.

Liangkhaia. [1938] 2002. *Mizo Chanchin*. Aizawl: Mizoram Publication Board.

Parry, N.E., 1976. *The Lakhers*. Calcutta: Firma KLM Private Ltd.

Sangkima. 1992. *Society and Social Change I.* Guwahati: Spectrum.

Shakespeare, J., 1988. *The Lushei-Kuki Clans*. Aizawl: TRI.

Zawla, K., 1964. *Mizo Pipute leh an thlahte chanchin*. Aizawl: Zawla.

6
Longtsaok Tradition of Lepchas in Sikkim

Charisma K. Lepcha

Introduction

Lepchas are the oldest inhabitants of Sikkim. They call themselves *Rong* from the Lepcha word *Rongkup* or *Rumkup* meaning the children of snowy peak/the children of God. Tradition has it that their creator God, *Itbumu,* created their progenitors Fudongthing and Nazongnyu from the pure virgin snows of Mt. Kanchenjunga, the third highest peak in the world and the guardian deity of Sikkim. But before these grand acclamations, that is more popular today, Kanchenjunga was known as *Konchen Kongchlo* for the Lepchas. It was their source of origin, and believed to be the 'original big stone' (Foning, 1987; Wangchuk & Zulca, 2007).

Stones have always been important to Lepchas. Their culture of erecting upright stones known as *longtsaok*s on various occasions is of particular interest because it is in line with the widespread megalithic culture that exists in North East India. It allows us to study and compare the similarities and differences of these stone structures and its significance across the region.

Archaeological findings of stone tools in Sikkim show Neolithic assemblages that can be categorized firstly with those that share the South-East Asian Hoabinian culture dating around 10,000–8,000 BC and secondly, the polished tools that resemble the Sichuan and south

China cultural assemblage of 8,000–4,000 BC (Mullard, 2011). According to Lepcha tradition, these Neolithic celts were revered as *sadaer long*, charms from the thunder God, to protect their homes from lightning. "A house without one of these objects is not a complete house at all" (Foning, 1987: 30) as each house would be required to have one.

Lepchas lived at a time in geological history where pronounced geological and environmental changes had occurred, and stones — boulders — were the most easily available resources for them. They would erect upright stones as markers to commemorate a special occasion or an event. It was known to Lepchas as *longtsaoks* – a derivation of two Lepcha words, *long* meaning 'stone', and *tsaok* meaning 'hard'. It is defined as "an upright monumental stone standing either alone or with others, erected in memory of some important event" (Tamsang, 2009: 764). It was a megalithic tradition among Lepchas that is only remembered by the old and the few. It is believed to be sacred symbols of the Lepchas.

> "To understand the true significance of our belief in the divinity of the 'Long Chok' or the upright stones which we use in every act of venerating, worshipping, and invoking the gods, in appeasing devils and demons, and in sanctifying our worldly acts, one has to understand the base of our Lepcha culture. It has emanated from the original 'Big Stone,' the Kongchen-Kongchlo or Mount Kanchenjunga, the eternally pure white, awe-inspiring, inexplicable structure that we see constantly standing before us."
>
> (Foning, 1987: 43)

The above passage is an excerpt from *Lepcha, My Vanishing Tribe* (1987) — an important text on Lepcha research covering Lepcha culture, religion, social institutions and also dedicating a chapter to 'the stones'. Narrated from a native perspective, Foning gives the first insight into the symbolic understanding of why Kanchenjunga is known as the big stone and the importance of stones in the Kanchenjunga landscape. *Longtsaoks* are what we understand as megaliths in archaeology. It is often referred to as "a large stone structure or monument standing either alone or with other stones" (Marak, 2012: 34). At first glance, it may seem like Sikkim has no megalithic history because the monasteries and the temples often overshadow the long existing tradition of megaliths in the state. Also, there has hardly been any study on the megaliths of Sikkim, but it is to be remembered that the history of Sikkim actually begins with the megalithic tradition of erecting stones at a place called Kabi Longtsaok, 17 kilometres north of Gangtok.

History speaks of a time when the Tibetan noble Khye Bumsa travelled to Sikkim to seek blessings from Thikung Tek, a Lepcha chief for his barren wife. The chief blesses them with three sons as the Tibetan couple return to thank the Lepcha chief. Legend has it that when Thikung Tek lifted one of the sons, the child's feet touched him on his forehead. The Lepcha chief took this as a sign that this child's descendants would rule Sikkim someday so he called on Khye Bumsa to swear a blood brotherhood between the Lepchas and Bhutias as equals.

> "The blood brotherhood ceremony was consecrated at Kabi Longstok with the two sitting on animal hides and surrounded by blood of sacrificed animals. Khangchendzonga was invoked as witness to solemnize the undertaking of blood brotherhood by the two communities and stones [*longstok*] were then erected at the spot to mark the event."
>
> (Wangchuk & Zulca, 2007: 54)

This event in Kabi took place at a site of standing stones which can still be seen today. It appears to be a site of "megalithic structures of some antiquity" (Mullard, 2011: 41) and has become a "historic landmark" (Foning, 1987: 34) commemorating the sacred covenant between two communities. It would also be the first documentation of a megalithic structure in Sikkim.

Types of Megaliths in Sikkim

Sikkim has a number of stone sites like the one in Kabi where certain stone structures have been erected. It is usually side-lined just as some site of "ritual importance" (Mullard, 2011: 136). But a closer study reveals the different varieties and significance of these stone structures. While we have established that megaliths are large stones, it is also argued that megaliths could be smaller stones too (Yondri, 2006; Marak, 2012). These megaliths, however, need to be understood in the cultural and religious context of the place. This chapter is a nascent attempt to identify the megaliths that the author has come across during her fieldwork in Sikkim.

Fig. 6.1: Megaliths in Dzongu, North Sikkim

Morphological Types

Morphological types, based on the physical appearance of the stone with regard to their size, shape and structure, of the megaliths are discussed in the following.

(1) *Menhirs and Alignments*: Menhirs are the most popular megaliths of our imagination. These are upright stones usually standing alone or in an alignment — where more than two tall stones stand side by side. Menhirs can be found in various places — near settlements, monasteries and in the forest too. It is believed that the size of a menhir in the region used to be as tall as "ten-feet high" (Foning, 1987 : 48), but today we mostly see only the smaller kind.

One of the most prominent menhir is found in the premises of Dupdi monastery, the oldest monastery of Sikkim. It stands tall and upright — unmistakably a menhir next to a smaller stone as seen in Fig. 6.2. When asked about the menhir, the head monk mentioned that the stone was the place to tie the horse of Guru Rinpoche, the founder of Buddhism in Tibet who is believed to have passed through Sikkim on the way to Tibet in the eight century BC. But if you examine this menhir, it is more than just a tall stone to tie the horse. Today, there is a stone circle around the menhir. but it is probably a recent addition to separate the menhir from the monastic structures.

Fig. 6.2: Menhir with a stone circle at Dupdi monastery, West Sikkim

On the other hand, smaller menhirs and alignments in Sikkim are also raised in honour of a legend or a historic personality. Thikung Men Salong, the person who is believed to have invented the Lepcha script was commemorated (Fig. 6.3) and stones were erected in Namprikdang, North Sikkim.

Fig. 6.3: Commemorating Thikung Men Salong in Namprikdang, North Sikkim

At other times, the reason could also be during some Lepcha festival as the menhirs in Fig. 6.4 that was erected during the Tendong Hlo Rum Faat festival of the Lepchas about a decade ago.

Fig. 6.4: Alignment in Tintek, East Sikkim

(2) *Cairns*: These are human made pile of stones and probably the most popular kind found in Sikkim. Cairns could either be "a heap of stones or rubbles of smaller but somewhat regular slabs either enclosed within a circle of small or considerable sized boulders" (Marak, 2010: 43). Lepchas practiced this rough assemblage of stones for burial purposes as shown in Fig. 6.5.

Fig. 6.5: Cairns in Dzongu, North Sikkim

Another explanation of cairns is the "piling up of stones one above the other without any enclosure" (*ibid.*); and these are commonly seen around sacred lakes and monasteries of the state. From being used as burial marks to trail markers, today it has become a religious marker in Sikkim. People generally assume that cairns are of Buddhist significance, but they are pre-Buddhist material culture that still exists today.

Fig. 6.6: Cairns in Khelchopari lake, West Sikkim

(3) *Stone Seats*: These are large oblong boulders placed horizontally in jungle trails or nearby paths. It could be of various shapes and sizes. Figure 6.7 shows a rectangular slab of large stone placed on an uphill way to Tholung, North Sikkim.

Fig. 6.7: Stone Seat on the way to Tholung, North Sikkim

Functional Types

The following paragraphs will discuss the function of these megaliths under various sub-themes:

(1) *Burial Stones*: Traditionally, Lepchas buried their dead, and the burial ground is called *chyokbum.* Graves are dug of different sizes and shapes with the spherical mound being the most common type.

> "Over the grave, flat stones are used as cover. With the earth around, a low spherical mound is raised, on top of which, normally, four longish stones are planted. On top of these uprights, two of more longish flat stones are balanced; this is considered the normal outside arrangements of a grave" (Foning, 1987: 40).

While burying the body, the head would be slightly raised with the help of stone pillows, so to give an appearance of facing Mt. Kanchenjunga. There may be slight variations but right above the head, an upright stone would again be erected to complete the burial.

(2) *Memorial Stones*: These stones are erected mostly in the memory of the dead. Figure 6.3 is an example of the memorial stone that has been erected in North Sikkim in memory of Thekong Men Salong. Since Lepchas believe that their souls return to the peak of origin when they die, the stones are erected in the shape of mountain peaks as memorial stones too. There is no practice of erecting memorial stones when a person is still alive.

(3) *Resting Stones*: These stones are placed at areas where people can rest and be refreshed. They look like stone seats and could sometimes have a stack of stones atop as well. These could be cairns as seen in Fig. 6.5 or without any stones as seen in Fig. 6.7.

(4) *Watch Towers*: Watch tower-*cum*-fort remains are found scattered over Sikkim and its neighbouring areas in strategic locations. They would stack layers of stones that would serve as their purpose during the time of war and invasion as big boulders are found to be chiselled and polished suiting the needs of a watch tower.

(5) *Religious Stones*: These stones are erected during a ritual or a festival and could be of different types. Lepchas do not have a permanent place of worship hence they worship anywhere their *mun* or *bongthing* (priestess and priest respectively) considers appropriate. Sacrifices and offerings are made of flowers, fruits and by erecting stones that represent different deities. Most stones erected during rituals are shaped like mountains.

One of the main reasons for these stones to be shaped like mountains is for the fact that Kanchenjunga still holds supreme in Lepcha cosmology. It occupies the central place of worship and the erecting of a stone representing Kanchenjunga is deemed important. Another point dwells on the belief that Lepcha clan origin is found in the different peaks on the Kanchenjunga range. Each clan has their own mountain peak so when somebody dies, their souls return to their peak of origin and these *longtsaok*s are erected to represent the same.

Longtsaok Legacy

Though *longtsaok*s were an important tradition among Lepchas, changes occurred in due course because of the culture contact with other religions and cultures. In that, the coming of Buddhism with the establishment of Namgyal dynasty was to alter their belief system and the megalithic culture of Lepchas in profound ways, especially in terms of death rites.

"Megaliths are ancient tombs" (Marak, 2012: 48), and stones have been associated with graves. But the acceptance of Buddhism meant that the dead was not to be buried anymore. Buddhists cremate their dead so when Lepchas converted to Buddhism, there was no need for these burial tombs and stones that was deemed important at some point of history. Later in history, Lepchas also converted to Christianity, but the Christian burial was different with its own set of rules, so the practice of erecting *longtsaoks* became a thing of the past. "These big upright stones, or Long Choks, which were obligatory in the long past, as being the replicas of the all important Kongchen and other Chyu Rums or gods, have now become miniatures" (Foning, 1987: 48).

Indeed, the bigger *longtsaok*s are rare and the ritual specialists also opt for the smaller ones as Foning laments,

> "The size of these replica stones has gone down considerably and… a renowned *bongthing* used stones about half a metre in height. And now, one of his sons, who is a *bongthing* is satisfied with only small ones. It seems that at this rate, by the turn of the century maybe only pebbles will serve the purpose; and eventually, the whole thing is sure to fade out" (*ibid.*).

In reading the above passage, we have to remember that Foning was a bit of hypochondriac like Malinoswki who thought that everything about Lepchas was dying out or fading away, but in some ways he was right and foretold the future of *longstaok*s in Sikkim. It is true that smaller stones are raised in contemporary times and bigger *longtsaok*s are nowhere to find. There are various external factors which have challenged this cultural tradition of megaliths in Sikkim which shall be discussed below.

Challenges

Since the traditional Lepcha religion practitioners are few, the raising of *longtsaok*s have naturally decreased. The introduction of Buddhism meant Lepchas were brought under the Buddhist fold and Buddhist ideas were incorporated into their traditional beliefs. For instance, Kanchenjunga, the source of Lepcha origin was made a Buddhist god and a "double-layered religious system" (Torri, 2010 : 149) prevailed. And when two religions come together, there is always a more dominant force. In that the indigenous religion was bound to be side-lined as we can see from the menhir that is found in the oldest monastery of Sikkim (refer Fig. 6.2). The menhir is undoubtedly older than the monastery but today it finds itself in a side corner of the monastery premises with stories of Guru Padmasambhava's horse attached to it instead.

Likewise, the syncretism with Buddhism meant that these *longtsaoks* would always be adorned with the Tibetan-Buddhist white silk scarf called the *kahatag*. It is rare that you find megaliths in Sikkim without the *khatag* or surrounded by colourful (*lungta*) prayer flags as seen in Fig. 6.9. The tradition of the *khatag*s and the *lungta*s sometimes undermine the importance and significance of these megaliths that have withstood time.

Fig. 6.9: *Longtsaok* in coronation throne in Norbugang, West Sikkim

But it is not just the Buddhist faith that has overtaken the *longtsaok* space. Hindu Brahmins are conducting the ceremonies there and "in place of bathing the Long-choks with the blood of sacrificed animals, they use vermillion powder and pour milk over them, the Hinduised Aryan version of the offerings to the gods. The devotees who happen to pass that way offer flowers and coins" (Foning, 1987: 48). These instances tell us of the religious appropriation taking place as Lepchas themselves have stopped paying attention to their sacred stones.

The second challenge comes from the lack of interest and support in the study of megaliths by both government and academics. Well trained archaeologists are required to identify, study and excavate the archaeological sites in Sikkim if we are to study these stones in a scientific manner.

Thirdly, this megalithic tradition (even if it is erecting smaller stones) is a living tradition among Lepchas. 'Living megalithism' is the term used for the cultural practice of erecting megaliths by living people (Marak, 2012: 42) and we can see that this tradition will soon be out of practice in due time. It, therefore, becomes our imperative to study the existing *longstaok*s and take a deeper look into the socio-cultural dynamics of this dying tradition.

REFERENCES

Foning, A., 1987. *Lepcha, My Vanishing Tribe*. New Delhi: Sterling Publishers.

Wangchuk, P. and M. Zulca. 2007. *Khangchendzonga: Sacred Summit*. Kathmandu: Hillside Press.

Mullard, S., 2011. Opening the Hidden Land: State Formation and the Construction of Sikkimese History. Leiden: Brill.

Gorer, G. [1938] 2005. *Himalayan Village: An Account of the Lepchas of Sikkim*. Kathmandu: Pilgrims Publishing.

Marak, Q., 2012. "Megaliths of North East India". In T.B. Subba (ed.), *North East India: A Handbook of Anthropology*. New Delhi: Orient Blackswan, 34-53.

Tamsang, L.S. [1980] 2009. *The Lepcha-English Encyclopaedic Dictionary:* Second Edition. Kalimpong: Mrs. Mayel Clymit Tamsang.

Torri, D., 2010. "In the shadow of the devil: Traditional patterns of Lepcha culture reinterpreted". In F. Ferrari (ed.), *Health and Religious Rituals in South Asia: Disease, Possession and Healing*. New Delhi: Routledge, Kegan and Paul Ltd., pp. 148-165.

Yondri, L., 2006. "A Short Review of the Megalithic Functions in Indonesia". In T. Simanjuntak, M. Hisyam, B. Prasetyo and T.S. Nastiti (eds.) *Archaeology: Indonesian Perspective*. Jakarta: LIPI Press, pp. 295-302.

Section-II

Symbolic Nature of Megaliths

7
Megaliths, Materiality and Meaning

Mayanglambam ManiBabu

Introduction

The present trend in archaeological research goes beyond merely identifying and describing the material remains of the past, which focuses on constructing and understanding their identities, experiences, and meaning to the *authors* who made and used them. This, however, refers at expanding to their non-material domains, which are not immediately visible in the archaeological record. Many studies of meaning have focused artifacts as material symbols and their meaning is embedded throughout their process of manufacture as well as their use and final deposition. Hence "archaeologists generate tacit experiences with the things of the past" the commitment of which "is borne out in archaeology's diversity as a bridging field connecting diverse ways of working with remains" (Rathje *et al.*, 2013: 5). The first ever known material objects, the artifacts, happen to be made with the naturally-occurring stones that are readily available to the people in their surroundings. It is a fact that making of stone artifacts required in daily activities of humans dates back to the early-middle part of Pleistocene approximately 2.7 to 2.5 mya (Semaw, 2000). Subsequently, in the later part of human prehistory, the Neolithic or earlier, large stone monuments were built. Hence, the issue with stones as important raw material, their management and treatment has been more significant in cognizing prehistoric knowledge systems. Use of large stone blocks as a representation of symbols also had a long history world-wide. Undoubtedly stone monuments are the material manifestation of the users' behaviour that can be monitored archaeologically. This agenda of material culture comes within the larger socio-cultural horizon of the people who made and used them.

Relational ontology, as a theoretical movement, tries to structure the past through different theoretical perspectives to the interpretations of archaeological materials, places, and persons that constitute multiple social worlds. This aspect, having both opportunities and challenges to archaeologists, is most fascinating for all archaeological record throughout its history. Though functional explanation is the heart of processual archaeologists, putting stress more on 'scientific' and 'anthropological' underpinnings to archaeological items to understand the causes of culture change (process) in varying environmental and cultural settings (Sabloff, 2005), they are unable to give proper orientations towards interpreting relationship between material culture and social system. This eventually gave rise to the emergence of post-processual archaeology of 1980s and later, aiming to pursue archaeological data in terms of their meaning or symbolism, history, agency etc. Such social interpretations of material culture become the heart of this school of archaeological thought (VanPool & VanPool, 1999) against the processualists' scientific framework (Hodder, 1982a, 1982b; Shanks & Tilley, 1987a; Miller & Tilley, 1984, Leone, 1982). Material culture studies, however bridge the processual and post-processual schools, not on their own premises, but as an acknowledgement of the role that materiality plays in the construction and constitution of humans and societies (Oestigaard, 2004). With a number of initial works (Friedman & Rowlands, 1978; Hodder, 1982a,1982b; Miller & Tilley, 1984) there seem to rise contention of post-processualists against processualists, humanists against scientists, history against evolutionary theory, and an interest in the particular against an interest in generalisation (Preucel, 1991; Yoffee & Sherratt, 1993). These works could enable us to go to an important departure in material culture studies establishing relationship between social practices and material culture patterning. In reality, post-processualists' humanists mentation has its base on the postmodern thought in the social sciences (Watson, 1990; Bintliff, 1991, Duke, 1995; Knapp, 1996) and hence shares many elements with critical theory, feminist theory, hermeneutics, neo-Marxism, poststructuralism and so on (Rosenau, 1992). Post-processualists' argument to the peoples' relations with the material world are to give meaning within larger socio-economic relations and political system of the past on the argument that *material culture is active,* not in terms of "their initiating and modifying agency, but rather about their presumed symbolic function" (Fahlander & Oestidaard, 2008:4) which is "meaningfully constituted" (Hodder, 1982a:75; Hodder, 1992:15). Many post-processualists (Hodder, 1982a; Leone 1986; Bawden, 1996; Thomas, 1996) view material culture within a contextual agenda of human activity, and even put its analogy with structural component of human language, its ability to order human life. "The ordering of objects through action can be used to communicate meanings in the same way that words, which also are symbols with a multitude of meanings, can" (VanPool & VanPool, 1999: 39). To Ian Hodder (1992) material culture in the archaeological record is more like a 'text' waiting to be read.

Material Culture, Materiality and Megaliths

Human cognition, mind and meaning are indispensable areas in material culture studies, and archaeologists are quite cognizant to what Merlin Donald remarked — "we cannot have a science of mind that disregards material culture as we cannot have an adequate science of material culture that leaves out cognition" (Donald, 1998: 186). Material culture, in its strict sense, is the object manipulated or manufactured by humans, comprising the results or leftovers from intentional and unintentional human practice, and its studies are based on the idea that "materiality is an integral dimension of culture" (Tilley, 2006:1). Sixty years ago, Vere Gordon Childe (1956:1), following Marx's ideas, suggested that objects are always and exclusively "concrete expressions and embodiments of human thought and ideas". Julian Thomas (2007:15) refers to material culture as representing "ideas that have been made material, and natural substance that has been rendered cultural." In a given society material culture may "facilitate interventions in the natural and social world as technology, provide a communicative medium of symbolic significance in a structure of difference and signification, (and) provide a medium for social domination as an expression of power and ideology" (Shanks & Tilley, 1987b: 131). Material culture studies are based on the idea that "materiality is an integral dimension of culture" (Tilley, 2006:1), which is all about the relational matrix of persons, bodies, things and cognition. Pfaffenberger (1992) rightly commented that technology and material culture form the primary means by which people establish their viability, given the constraints imposed upon them by their environment and the demands of social integration. Of the two dimensions of artifact (Binford, 1965), the *primary* and *secondary*, the first refers to the instrumental dimension related to the artifact's function; and the *secondary* to the artifact's social meaning and symbolism (Pfaffenberger, 1992). A similar category to this is James Sackett's (1982: 70) functional class of *utilitarian* and *non-utilitarian* — the first include those in their material realms, and the latter the socio-religious context. Ian Hodder (1992) also sensed the dual nature of material culture, and remarked that the underlying reason for archaeology's most fascinating aspect of linking together the 'softer' humanities and social sciences with the 'harder' physical and natural sciences, is due to the dual character of material culture. He further reiterated that material culture is both the product of human purpose and yet it is material following the laws of the non-human world. The term itself captures the duality of 'material' and 'culture' (*ibid.*). Daniel Miller (1985, 1987) first broached that there is an interactive relationship of material culture with social system, social strategies and artifactual variability; and bespoke of an independent discipline of material culture. His approach paved the foundation to the development of the well-established field of material culture studies. Miller and Tilley's (1996:5) anteceding definition of material culture study is "the investigation of the relationship between people and things irrespective of time and space (and)... (T)he perspective adopted may be global or local, concerned with the past or present, or the mediation between the two."

In order to see the intrinsic relations that stone artifacts (including other man-made objects and features) have in the larger respective social network, one needs to emphasize materiality in many facets. The concept of materiality in archaeology is of recent development (DeMarrais *et al.*, 2004, Tilley 2004, Fahlander & Oestigaard, 2004; Miller, 2005; Meskell, 2005; Tilley *et al.*, 2006; Ingold, 2007). In terms of the conceptual meaning, materiality[1] and material culture are not synonymous though the two "share some similarities, but also some important differences" (Fahlander & Oestigaard, 2008: 4). The term materiality "is just not a substitution for material culture, but embraces a greater variety of things and substances" and its "active role... in the social process seems not to be about their initiating and modifying agency, but rather about their presumed symbolic function" (*ibid.*). Its main characteristic is its physicality, and "to study material culture is to consider the implications of the materiality of form for the cultural process" (Miller, 1994: 400). Conceptually expansion of materiality, hence include a wider perspective of how objects are integrated in the social realm (Fahlander & Oestigaard, 2008). "Materiality … constrains and creates human behaviour, and since all materiality has various time dimensions, archaeology as material culture studies is independent of the temporal depth of the artefacts or manifestations of materiality which are the objects of study" (Oestigaard, 2004: 85).

It is natural to find two sides of materiality (Ingold, 2012) – one side being represented by the material character, the brute materiality [which Oslen (2003:88) referred to as 'hard physicality'] and the other side the socially and historically situated agency of human beings who, in appropriating (this) physicality for their purposes, project on it both design and meaning in the conversion of naturally given raw material into the finished forms of artifacts (*loc. cit.*). A stone is simply a formless lump of rock in its state of hard physicality or brute materiality (Tilley, 2007:17) which needs another concept of materiality to understand how particular pieces of stone are given form and meaning within specific social and historical contexts (Tilley, 2004). To perceive this latter aspect, *secondary* dimensions rather than *primary* are necessary. The physicality of artifact in the form of erected monument, for instance, is hence materialized, projecting meaning and message to the viewers as an organism. Such materiality encompasses the material or physical component of the environment and emphasises how those material properties are enrolled in the life projects of humans (Jones, 2004). In order to see the intrinsic relations that material cultures have in the larger respective social network, one needs to emphasise materiality in many facets. Imagery of monumentality of megaliths results with an attachment of contextually inferred meanings set within hermeneutic, phenomenological or landscape frameworks — all belonging to post-processual paradigm. One of the main concepts of materiality is to understand how particular pieces of stone are given form and meaning within specific social and historical contexts (Tilley, 2004) and materiality, in fact, is to emphasize the physicality of the material world (Boivin, 2008). The importance of knowing cultural context of monuments is concerned with their placid mundane *chaine operatoire* of technology involving procurement, quarrying, carving, transportation and erection, but also the normative gestures relating to their materiality and monumentality. The location of megalithic monument is not merely a setting or background, it is indeed a *context* in its etymological meaning; it is the *fabric* of their formation and a *space* of cultural intervention to the natural landscape.

The present chapter aims at exposing the nature and extent as well as array on how large stones are exploited, materialized and used as *external symbolic storage* by the indigenous Naga tribes of Manipur. The present discussion is mainly on the megalithic monuments erected in conjunction with gaining status and prestige of an individual in the society. Megalithic monuments in Manipur, first reported as early as 1887 (Watt–1887), are found in profusion in all the Naga inhabited areas, especially in the Senapati District (24°37'–25°37', N latitude and 93°40'–94°29' E longitude), bordering Phek District of Nagaland to the north, Tamenglong to the west, Ukhrul to the East and Imphal (West and East districts) to its south. And it is a fact that among some of the Naga tribal populations, such as the Mao, Maram, Liangmei and Poumai, megalithism is a continuing cultural tradition. These tribes share a more or less similar economic adaptation pattern as well as socio-cultural setups. They have a traditional male-oriented social system, where the principle of organization, fundamentally, is to the agnation who governed residence, descent, access to economic resources, political affiliation and linkages through marriage etc. Their land is bestowed with rich natural resources of vegetation, wild fauna and land. Terrace farming and swidden cultivation (practiced rarely at present), and pig and cattle husbandry provide the means of livelihood of the people. Pigs and cattle are the universal domestic animals that furnish sacrificial victims for many rites and ceremonies.

The Naga villages nestle strategically either on hilltops or the highest possible points along a hill slope. Usually traditional villages were defended by ditches, stone walls, spiked bamboo palisades, or thorny fences, for reasons of security. The old practice of head-hunting, and inter-clan/village feuds were the main contributing factors to the fortification of villages (Hodson, 1911; Shimray, 1985; West, 1985). Owing to these factors, "the Nagas were so disunited" (Longchar, 2000:126), hence giving rise to diverse dialects, and make the people of one village unable to put across with those of the same tribal group. Another reason of diverse linguistic variations, according to Hutton (1965: 25) is due to "the isolation of village communities, cut off from their neighbours by forest, mountain, and river". Of the Western Rengma Naga tribe, J.P. Mills (1937: 285) noted that in "a small tribe of some seven villages, two languages were spoken, different wards of the same village, or even opposite sides of the same street, using mutually irreconcilable languages." Naga villages are administered by the Village Council, comprising a head and other subordinate dignitaries, through the indigenous customary laws and also according to the collective mandate. Each Naga village is a highly organised social, political and cultural unit enjoying sovereign and democratic practice (Hodson, 1911; Horam, 1977; Venuh, 2004). One of the most intriguing characters of Naga villages is their territorial segmentation into different sects, called *khel* (locality) occupied by a particular clan or otherwise. Every *khel* have well defined lands with boundaries, which are well guarded, and any encroachment or dispute related to land is strictly dealt with. In reality, the relationship between the land and the people is intimate and foundational. Land is categorised on the basis of its usage and ownership – all its categories and management are central to the organisation of the society. At least three categories of land are known to the people such as – (a) individual homestead/settlement area; (b) cultivable/terrace field; and (c) family/clan forest land. In all these categories of land, amidst the vast hilly terrain, deserted villages and untrodden spaces are littered with sporadic clusters of large stone monuments, the megaliths, the stone walls/fences, stone terraces etc. Exploitation of the naturally-occurring large blocks of stone is of both utilitarian and non-utilitarian in character. Under the first category, stone boulders are utilized – (i) as either perimeter of one's habitation boundary area/forest land; or (ii) as a device to make a sloppy habitation site into a plain level so as to make them easier to make shelter; or (iii) as flight of steps to make access to climb up the steep slopes; or (iv) as stone wall/gate constructed by way of pilling up flat stone blocks/slabs on opposite sides of a village gate etc. Such utilization (of stone boulders) is related with the *practical technology* where objects are used "to perform satisfactorily tasks in an efficient and effective way" (Hayden, 1998: 27). Practical technology is meant to solve practical problems of survival and basic comfort (Hayden, 1993: 203) and is logically and empirically a response to stresses in the environment, hence, it can be directly related to real survival benefits (*loc. cit.*). And these may be perceived as an adaptation strategy to their natural environment being promoted by human and agricultural intensification. A good number of stone walls and fences often provide a 'skeleton' to the landscape, giving a coherent structure and perspective to the village. Individual walls may include particular features forming unique architectural monumentality, which add meanings to the cultural landscape. Methods of walling and fencing one's residential perimeter, and their vernacular styles by individual families do not vary significantly across the Naga villages. These are generally of not so much of height. Some of the features that are generally common to the walls include —(a) consisting of two faces of large stones ('the double'), which gradually taper towards the top; (b) the cavity between the double is filled with small stones; (c) longer stones link the two sides of the wall together at intervals, often placed half-way up the wall and; (d) larger stones are generally used in the lower levels of a wall, with slightly smaller ones on the above towards the top (Manibabu, 2014). These features provide collectively a subsequent character of land use patterns of the people, making a unifying feature of the landscapes. The way in which a stone fence and wall is constructed and the vernacular features that it has contributed obviously provide a "sense of place" and "a sense of stone".

The second domain is related with immediate use of large stone blocks as monumental structures, erected to commemorate persons or events, funerary or ritualistic. These comprise the single standing stones, alignments, avenues, dolmen, capstones or flat stones, stone seats, stone circles etc. which make every Naga village of intriguing character. Erection and management of such large stone blocks towards their realm of materiality have varied typological variants, which are attached duly with their myriad functions. Each of the monuments has its own active, ongoing process of creating and negotiating symbolic meaning. Materializing stone blocks into monuments is none other than the transformation of ideas and values, and propagation of meaning of a system into a physical reality as a symbolic object—sharing and participating with the viewers. It is strongly augmented that there is a dialectic relationship between the ways the large stone blocks are materially produced and the ways these are experienced and conceptualised, reflecting an ontological category of Naga social matrix. By advocating a relational approach to find monumentality in the ongoing relationship between material object (the megaliths) and persons (the agents), this chapter offers an opportunity to uniting these varied areas into a unified discourse. Every Naga village possesses megaliths of such monument categories, which are meant to intend as – (i) *resting stones* (comprising a single or composite flat stones meant for the purpose of sitting or resting, which are usually seen by the side of an intra-village lane leading to the terrace fields, water sources or neighbouring villages), (ii) *recreational* or *gambol stones* (related with gay, light-hearted recreational activity or indigenous games for amusement), (iii) *judiciary or omen avowing stones* (connected with oath taking by an alleged offender of his commitment to tell the truth), (iv) *fertility* or *prognostication stones*[2] (related with the prediction of one's likely accomplishment), (v) *memorial or commemorative stones* (the single standing stones commemorating important social occasions or individual events of social significances), and many more. Of these, large single standing stones (menhirs) to memorialise a man's social prestige and status configure as the most absorbing item in terms of their metaphorical perspective as external symbolic storage of the peoples' world view. Among the people, the physicality of such stone monuments that are being materialised duly with symbolic meaning owes to their indigenous system of exposing ability to throw one's wealth by way of giving feast to the fellow members at the cost of gaining a position in the society and this very tradition is a part of their social life. Physicality of artifact in the form of erected monument is, thus materialized, projecting meaning and message to the viewers. In one's lifetime a male individual can initiate to erect such stone monoliths whenever he is sufficiently affluent to do so, that is, if he could bear the huge expenditure to be incurred during the erecting procedure. In the bygone years, the Naga efficacies of prestige ideology were tied with the prowess in warfare, head hunting, and megalithic implantations. The last two domains "seem central to understanding the values and beliefs of Naga society" (West, 1985: 25). Of these only the last tradition exists as the Naga signal of manifesting ultimate status, which has immense ethno-archaeological significances in deriving a good number of ethno-graphic postulates that persuade relevancies to the prehistoric megaliths of the region and beyond. This can, however, be proceeded with either processualists' perspective of *middle range theory* (Binford, 1983) or with post-processualists' issue of *context* that aims at "exploring the symbolic dimensions of material culture" (David & Kramer, 2001: 54) towards understanding 'meaning' (Conkey, 1989; Cunningham, 2003; Hodder, 1986; Miller, 1985).

Materializing Megaliths: Monumentality and Meaning

The Naga way of erecting stone monoliths, especially those related with the achievement of one's status, is done by duly organising 'feasts' by an aspirant donor in whose name the stone is to implant. The procedure and way of organizing such feasts of merit is almost similar in all the Naga communities with some trifling deviations. As every village in the District and beyond have different dialects though belonging to the same Naga group, obviously such social occasion of feasting are referred with different nomenclatures. For instance, different Poumai Naga villages use different terms — such as, *zhousou* in Saranamei, *zhoushowe* in Laii, *trazho* in Chingmaikhullen, *kosodotah* in Oinam. To Mao Naga, it is called *ozo-ooso* or *ozhokoso*, while it is *okhooni/tasumdani* in some Maram Naga villages. Any male aspirant can go with the giving of feast of merit, but has to fulfil usually the following conditions (ManiBabu, 2014), such as: (i) one should be a married person; (ii) widows or widowers were restricted from performing feast of merit and erecting a stone monument. If a widower desires to erect, he is to remarry; (iii) if the first wife of a person dies after his performance of a Feast of Merit — he should remarry another and perform the erection procedure, so as to the get his second wife the right of putting on the special shawl (Oinam Poumai people called it *pheiju*); and (iv) if a potential donor died during the process but before its final erection, the stone should not erect, and so on.

Performance of feasts of merit is rather expensive in terms of commodities spent like rice, meat (such as of buffaloes, pigs, mithuns, etc. and rice beer. A huge monolith is to be dragged from a distance by the males partaking the ceremony, and is to be erected at a convenient place. The stone pulling is an occasion for great festivity for the people, and the host aspirant is to arrange many gallons of rice beer and huge quantities of meat which are to be served to all the participants and fellow villagers. There are a series of feasts, each one costlier than the preceding one. Any male aspirant is free to carry out a feast of merit and should go through a number of formalities, such as; seeking formal approval of the village authority well ahead of the performance (at least one year before) by way of registration with a nominal fee, and also by giving meat and rice beer etc. Once he gets approval, mental and physical preparation begins. The buffalo and pigs to be killed for the ceremony would be well tended well ahead the occasion. Such animal should be physically fit in all respect without blemish and deformity marks, such as all the teeth of the animal should be intact without any missing, there should be no wear and tear on its horn, no flecks in the colour of its pelt, no swirls on the pelt nearby the neck or behind the ears. As the time for the feast is approaching, preparation of rice beer[3] begins. This is mainly done by the aspirant's wife, her close friends and relatives. The clan members and relatives of the aspirant would collect firewood from the nearby forest that would be required in making rice beer, meat and rice.

Once an aspirant or *rongpa* (an Oinam Poumai Naga term) get registered himself to the village authority for the performance of a feast of merit, he is not only restrained from having sexual relationship with his wife, but also is not to eat rice cooked, or drink rice beer prepared/served by others. The village priest and the aspirant are to look for the stone from within the clan/*khel* land. Selection of the suitable stone is made through omen in the aspirant's dreams. In case he had a bad dream then it is taken that the stone that they had chosen is not suitable, and shall try for another one.

When a suitable block of stone is found, the priest performs ritual formalities beginning with wine oblation to the chosen stone boulder. Pulling of stone is usually done during the dry/cold season. It was a tradition where, the village priest and the donor should always be together till the end of the ritual performed. Pulling of stone is done by the village youths. Among the Poumai of Oinam village, for example, just before the initial displacement of stone block from its resource outgrowth, one buffalo and one pig are to be sacrificed. The blood of the pig is to be stained over the stone. It is done on a general belief that stones also have life, and if they put bloodstains over it the stone is perceived to be dead, and no harm will occur to them. As and when the stone is pulled out of the quarry site (*talladobe*), any piece of item/object is to be kept at the place of removal as a replacement for it. The large stone is usually dragged after being placed on a long wooden sledge-like framework being lashed with special creepers. Females are refrained from such manual works; however, they could serve rice-beer and meat to the team. It may take several days or months in transporting the stone to the site where the monolith is to be erected. In reality, transportation of the large mass of stone is not an easy option to the people, but involve particular skills and large labour force. The very size of the blocks, weighing as much as 100 tonnes or more would have made them difficult to transport and erect. In some cases, particular blocks were brought from a considerable distance. This provokes the importance of the stones themselves, the quarry sites and the place where the monoliths are to be erected. The shipped stone blocks are supposed to be erected at any convenient spot as dictated by the traditional norms — such as, within a *khel* and/or clan land to which the donor belongs, or adjacent to the previously erected menhirs in a row, or to the conformation of village landscape etc. A smaller monolith is usually implanted just behind the larger ones representing that of the donor's wife. After the stone is erected — relatives, friends and youth who took part in dragging the stone, joined a grand feast offered by the donor. Such communal feasts obviously create a social cohesion and integration of the villagers, reinforcing reciprocal obligations between the donor and his fellow villagers, which makes the achievement of status legal. In fact, such materialization centre upon an individual's economic base, forming as an active element in the process of building and consolidating his status as a person who can afford such huge costs to sponsor ritual feasts. Obviously, such stone monuments are the material manifestations of wealth of a person who, by virtue of his expensive gratification, earn respect and reputation of being generous and resourceful. These successful performers are automatically entitled to adorn a distinct cotton-embroided shawl (Oinam Poumai people called it *zhosa/pheiyu*), to own a decorated spear, to decorate his house in a particular manner with a 'Y'-shaped wooden mark (called *chikai*) fixed on the gable wall, and to embellish the walls with horns of the animals killed during the entire episode etc.

In fact, menhirs implanted with such an occasion of feasts of merit have symbolic meaning. An individual's identification is not detached from the monuments, but is dependent on how that person interacts with material culture and with other fellow subjects. Naturally, there is reciprocity between actors (the donors) and the monuments in configuring the actors understand themselves in the society in terms of their identity and status. Status, as such, is the relative social position of an individual, and is contingent on the significance and meaning that are accumulated in social life. A status thus achieved by a Naga male through "the feasts of merit were separate from the status of being chief or a member of a noble clan" (West, 1985:30). And also this schema did not reflect the hallmark of a stratified society as stipulated by many in as much as in public architecture (such as, by Childe, 1950; Sanders & Price, 1968; Drucker, 1981).

Among the present category of megalithic monuments, the menhir displays one of the strongest index of wealth, where wealthy persons in order to achieve a status in the society, organised a feast lavishly for the people and erect a large stone monument as a symbol of his wealth and power. Here, wealth in its simplest term refers to the economic possessions of an individual that can be used in exchange and displays of worth. Wealth, as items used in "display, ritual, and exchange" (LeCount, 1999: 240) can and often does reflect status. However, wealth, status, and class are related terms but not interchangeable (Babic, 2005: 74). In fact, monumentality constitutes conspicuous consumption that objectifies the social power used to mobilise human labour. In the same vein, DeMarrais *et al.* (1996) argue that the material presence and physical character of stone objects and monuments are the concrete example of materialising ideology as an integral component of human interactions and the power strategies that configure socio-political systems. The symbolic meaning of megalithic monuments, in spirit, lies at the community level, as these manifest material signatures of an individual's status at the expense of the fellow members' cognizance. Hence, such monuments are the signified 'prestige items' to the community to gauge status of concerned individuals, and not simply chunks of rock, strands of material culture or contexts of a social landscape. By way of channelising through the material world, the Naga ways of megalithic materiality (such as, activities) and monumentality (that is, the identities) become part of peoples' placid social system characterised by the "repetition of the practices". With such common practices, the society shared a 'community identity' through a 'shared system'. It emphasizes how these monuments are built on a 'shared knowledge system' providing mutually intelligible ideas of status and difference. It is perceived that megalithism has become an articulated attribute of Naga identity conventionalised through peoples' collective legacy and ideas of inheritance.

An apposite issue here lies with — why people choose large

heavy stone rather than other raw materials as a medium of their monumentality? In fact, people are well gratified in interacting megaliths by building and crafting them, by seeing them, and walking around them. Most likely, peoples' orientation in this regard may perch with the following rejoinders:

(i) That stones have universal intrinsic qualities in terms of durability, solidity, and weight. And also, these have more permanence than wood and any other materials, which require less maintenance and less replacement.

(ii) That, large stone blocks owing to the above facts, are costlier than any other raw material available or known to the people. And their handlings towards monumentality demand strenuous task which has eventuality to complaisant feasts and drinks. These tolls to immense consumption of wealth in terms of meat and drinks, which is hardly beyond anyone's ability. No question for such logistics and expenditure will arise in case of a lighter raw material. Hence, stone is opted as the right medium to exhibit one's affordances to its monumentality, exposing his power and wealth.

Megaliths as External Symbolic Storage

The symbolic meaning of megalithic monument, in spirit, lies at the community level, as this manifest material signature of an individual's status at the expense of his fellow members' cognizance. It is a fact that material presence and physical character of stone objects and monuments are the concrete example of materialising ideology as an integral component of human interactions and the power strategies that configure socio-political systems (DeMarrais *et al.,* 1996). Here, the Naga menhirs are not simply chunks of rock, strands of material culture or contexts of a social landscape, but stand as the signified 'prestige items' to the community to gauge the socio-political status of concerned individuals. By way of channelising through the material world, the materiality (such as, activities) and monumentality (that is, the identities) schemata become part of peoples' placid social system characterised by the repetition of the practices. With such common practices, the society shared a 'community identity' through a 'shared system'. It emphasizes how these monuments are built on a "shared knowledge system" providing mutually intelligible ideas of status and difference. It is perceived that megalithism has become an articulated attribute of Naga identity conventionalised through peoples' collective legacy and ideas of inheritance. In such acts, *theoretical* rationality works more than *practical* one where erection of menhirs centred round the establishment embellishment of symbolic meaning of normative values. In spirit, theoretical rationality involves a conscious mastery of reality through the construction of increasingly precise abstract concepts surrounding monumentality. In reality, this issue of materiality obviously demands a *way of seeing* that "pinpoint and accentuate the importance of 'things' in human existence, self-understanding, self-definition and activity" (Lindstrom, 2015: 228). Through a deliberate and collective effort, large stone block/structure could enter into the domain of monumentality, embodying invisible but durable meaning in the form of what Aleida Assmann (1991) termed as *cultural memories*. This makes the understanding of a monumental mode of communication in the form of an *external symbolic storage* (Donald, 1991; Renfrew, 1998; Watkins, 2000). Of the three stages of increasing complexity of human mind in the hominine line from apes to modern humans — such as, the marked shift from 'episodic' primate mind into the 'theoretic' modern human mind through the 'mimetic' mind of early hominids (Donald, 1991) — eventually the final *theoretic* stage is characterised by the use of symbolism and of artifacts as external memory storage and retrieval devices. In the words of Donald (1998:184): "When I coined the term "external symbolic storage", I was simply singling out the most salient and indisputable property of material culture: it exists only in relation to interpretative codes stored inside the heads of the people who invented it, that is, inside their 'biological' memory systems. Written symbols, and even other less explicitly symbolic aspects of material culture, are external to biological memory, and serve as storage devices for the information needed to replicate entire cultures. This simple fact changes the nature of shared cognition. But it also makes the archaeologist's job very difficult, because the specific content of symbols can never exhaust their functions when in use. When in use, symbols engage biological memory, which is a creative, constructive, dynamic, force."

To Colin Renfrew (1998), the *external symbolic storage* concept applies to monuments (prehistoric megaliths) in the sense that monuments are often memorials built for remembrance, and "it is the role of a memorial to serve the memory, often the collective memory. ... Sometimes indeed they are the means by which memories are preserved which would otherwise be lost" (p. 5). As argued by DeMarrais *et al.* (1996) the material presence and physical character of stone objects and monuments are the concrete example of materialising ideology as "an integral component of human interactions and the power strategies that configure socio-political systems." As rightly commented by Furholt and Muller (2011) monuments are not only vehicles for the storage and communication of meaning, but they are also indispensable agents of the creation and maintenance of society, and are produced by the people as their physical world that make an indivisible bond of the human-material-technological relationship (Latour, 1991, 2002; Ingold, 2000).

In the present perspective, particularly with the erection of standing stones in commemorating one's status, rationality appears to be fundamental to the understanding of peoples' mind and behaviour. Symbolic interactionism, as a major framework of sociological theory, relies upon the symbolic meaning that people develop in the process of social interaction. People are motivated by a vintage goal for achieving status, and are supposed to do almost anything which is socially sanctioned, and monuments are the rewards that reinforce particular tendencies to this status-achieving behaviour. The rewards, that is, the status thus achieved include the intrinsic satisfactions to the actor and it is at the expense of the actor's wealth consumed. Obviously, there flares up a symbolic interaction between monument erected and the wealth expended. Here, menhirs display as one of the strongest index of wealth. The Naga example reveals that accumulation of enough wealth well before the performance of *feasts* is a precondition to the erection of monument. Wealth in its simplest term refers to the economic possessions of an individual that can be used in exchange and displays of worth. Wealth, as items used in "display, ritual, and exchange" (LeCount, 1999: 240) can and often does reflect status. However, wealth, status, and class are related terms but not interchangeable (Babic, 2005: 74). But it may be conceded that the Naga megalithic monuments discern as the external symbolic storage closely associated with the notion of meaning that the people assign to them in terms of the strategic activities on the dynamics of wealth, power and status.

Space and Megalithic Landscape

Significance of landscape, to post-processual archaeologists lies with its active role as a set of elements that acts as signs, symbols and messages interacting with society as a whole, in its parts and with the individual (Garcia, 2005). Through visibility, landscape can be perceived both "from a practical point of view (control of the territory and defence of settlements) or from a symbolic perspective (e.g. visibility of the anthropic elements and/or artistic, religious or funeral ones). And also, we can differentiate between quantitative methods for studying spatial aspects of a visual event (processual perspective) and the phenomenological analysis of the visible elements in the landscape (post-processual perspective)" (Oritiz, 2016: 85).

The presently scattered megaliths widely in the Naga-inhabited areas in the northern uphill of Manipur are a matter of great concern in terms of their distributional pattern amidst the habitation sites. These monuments do not exist in a void. They are seen scattered in clusters manifesting a relationship between village landscape/ boundary and their locational pattern. These built village-landscapes are part and parcel of human interaction with monuments that are performed, and hence forms part of the context in which other material objects are produced, used, and understood.[4] However, the Naga mode of megalithic erection is not done at random and cannot erect at any place, but at specific locations in accordance with their assigned functional attributes. It depends on the dictation of the peoples' long standing practices. These are installed accordingly by the side of terraced or *jhum* fields, by the sides of the inter- or intra-village roads, in the courtyard of the village chief, at the burial sites, at or near the important public places/gathering sites etc. Thus, distributional pattern of megaliths is categorically projected in the light of their action radius which obviously creates a megalithic landscape, revealing an existence of symbiotic relation between monuments and their physical surrounding. Their spatial distributional pattern gives rise to the characterization of a megalithic landscape that is operated at a variety of scales. This obviously makes a key to understand their salience and potential symbolic embodiment, their architectural and landscape attributes towards establishing an encoded grammar known to the builders and the users.

From the general distributional pattern of the monuments, a few basic operative modes can be discerned within the theoretical perspective of *space syntax analysis* (SSA). The dictum of this analytic thinking is that spaces can be broken down into components, analysed as networks of choices, and then represented as maps and graphs that describe the relative connectivity and integration of those spaces. This theoretical paradigm outlines for a cognitive approach to the environment (landscape) where megalithic monuments are located and aims to understand and explain certain aspects of human behaviour and their relation to the environment which the people have built and dwelled in (Dimitriadis, 2008). Through SSA paradigm, the following characters of megalithic distributional pattern could be observed (Manibabu, 2014):

1. There is a *spatial cognition* with the people to the erection and placement of monuments based on a correlative arrangement between landscape and human movement. The spatial distributions of monuments, irrespective of their typological categories, are related with the spaces where there is a maximum accessibility of human movement. It is a regular phenomenon that menhirs, alignments and stone seats are located either by the sides of the inter-village lanes or at the core areas (central places) of the village. Many of the stone seats are also seen by the side of the village road leading to the forest or terrace fields. Thus, a *spatial logic of human movement* can be identified according to the SSA theorems that more integrated spaces are associated with higher densities of movement. Such a relationship can be used to predict the flows and helps to formulate alternative scenarios to fit development sites into their surroundings (Peponis, 2001).
2. While selecting space for erecting monument, obviously one is to erect within the boundary of a *khel* where the donor belongs. However, this condition refers specially for those menhirs erected for one's attainment of status. The management of space by a donor is, thus attested with his belongingness to a spatial boundary by virtue of his *khel* affiliation. The mental space is thus related with human behaviour on management of space which manifests the concept the spatiality within a settlement area.

The very *megalithic space* thus created represents a sequence of contemporary megalithic tradition, reflecting how architecture, space structures and materiality entangled themselves to give meaning of the stone structure. As 'space' is both visual, like the physical environment created by architecture; and invisible, like a social space (Bourdieu, 1998), it embodies a sense of shared meaning and feelings of the people. Such a megalithic landscape as a component of larger social space bears meaning in terms of its spatiality within a specific area (such as, *khel*). The monuments are not implanted randomly and aimlessly, and devoid of territorial boundary of the people in question. The human actions in this regard, make the landscape an embodied multi-sensorial experience, a part of people's repetitive movements and activities. There also exists an intrinsic relationship between the sources of raw material and the space for erecting the megalith within the landscape. One is to exploit stone block from the corresponding village territory (*khel*) to which the person who initiates to erect the monument belongs. So, one's belongingness to a spatial boundary by virtue of his clan/ *khel* affiliation is an important factor. The spatial dimension of megalithic distribution, hence accentuates to the interpretation of social practices of Naga megalithism that corresponds to the community's socio-political dictum.

Concluding Remarks

The present discourse on Naga megaliths is an attempt to get along a compelling agenda towards theorising what materiality is in order to excel the threadbare duality of people (subjects) and monuments (objects), and comprehend how people simultaneously engage with their material existence. The discourse on megalithism, operated at multiple levels (economic, social, and ideological), reveals how the indigenous people manage themselves at materialising the naturally-occurred stones as monuments, and at outlining a theoretical treatment on monuments as symbolic forms which express a wide range of meanings within the given social matrix and milieu. In the present chapter, discussion has been bounded on the single erecting stone, the menhir, which form a fascinating breed among different megalithic classes in many Naga inhabited territories in Manipur, the erection of which is still a living tradition[5] though in lesser cases than earlier. One of the captivating items of menhir is that of implanting it by a male individual to commemorate his capability at its materialisation at the expense of his wealth, in order to achieve a status in the society. A person's achievement of social status, thus, is at the expense of erecting a menhir that entails conspicuous consumption of his wealth in the notion of exposing wealth to the fellow villagers as against their simple accumulation. J.P. Mills (1935) also noted that status was not conferred by wealth but by giving feasts. Here Naga way of conspicuous consumption stands as an important factor in transforming material wealth into status symbol in the process of status emulation, which has related standing locus with Vablen's (1899) archetypical example of conspicuous consumption concept to monumental architecture. In fact, raising the large mass of stone was not an easy option. The amount of energy expended during single episode of construction reflects the involvement of large numbers of manpower, the societal requisite for mobilising the labour force, the presence of craft specialists sufficiently trained and skilled to contribute to the transportation and construction process, and so on. Through materiality large stone blocks could make into *prestige artifacts* performing not a practical task, but to display wealth, success, and power (Hayden, 1998), which is logically and strategically different from accomplishing/creating practical artifacts. In reality, the main goal of prestige technologies is to employ as much surplus labour as possible to create objects that will appeal to others and attract people to the possessor of those objects due to admiration for his or her economic, aesthetic, technical, or other skills (*ibid.*). Dimensional features of a monument — small or large, short or tall — have nothing to do with a donor's achievement or conferment of status — the monumental configuration lies with the meaning that they convey to others. The material characteristics of the monument, such as visibility, durability and also uniqueness are seen as a means to achieve the aim of an intentional communication of distinct meanings and an indirect measure of wealth and power. Here, power refers to the ability of an individual or group to influence/control the decisions and behaviour of others, thereby making one's 'wealth' a platform to reciprocate the services of fellow villagers with feasting, which acts as a solid opportunity towards reinforcing social ties and community unity. Certainly monumentality can be examined with regard to original intentions and it is clear that the conscious act of memorialising is one part of monumentality; but that is not the end of the issue, however. And both materiality and monumentality of megaliths demonstrates the solidity of these concepts as building blocks for social knowledge system.

In fact, the indigenous means of planting menhirs displays engagement between means and goal, between humans and things. This dialectical struggle within "dependence and dependency" is one of the important components of the *entanglement* framework (Hodder 2011, 2012, 2014), which refers to "the sum of four types of relationship between humans and things: humans depend on things (*HT*), things depend on other things (*TT*), things depend on humans (*TH*), and humans depend on humans (HH)" (Hodder, 2014: 19-20). While these relationships are relationally produced, the organizational network of Naga megalithism demands a web of codependency of embodied cognition, social, technical, and financial upkeeps. This entanglement network implicates all the above four modes of dependencies which are thoroughly weaved into each other and hence, each has their own entities as components of the system. For instance, an enthusiastic person who endeavours for a megalithic monument for achieving status would depend on other humans, especially the primary and secondary kins (wife, family members, in-laws etc. and the members of the village council. This *HH* dependency and relationship entails their approval and support. Another example of *HH* dependency involves those human work-forces, who involve in the works of searching, transporting and erecting the monument. Likewise, in terms of *HT*, not only the large lump of stone chosen; other items like rice beer, meat, earthen and wooden casseroles, wooden sleigh for transportation of heavy rock etc., may be counted. Here, *HT* entanglement makes cause to the manipulation of wealth and power towards achieving goal as well as gaining dominance over others. There exist a good number of dependencies between thing and thing (*TT*) also. Besides, humans (labour) depend on wooden sleigh in accommodating the huge rock lump for its transportation; there exists entanglement between the timber bar, the slots and the creeper in mounting and fastening the large rock with the wooden frame of the sleigh. These 'things' in *TT* dependencies have their own distinct entities and also relative values. A good number of linkages and dependencies come up when we go deeper into the issue of 'entanglement' in which humans have socio-economical, physical and mental dependencies on *things*. In reality, as rightly commented "dependencies are not inherent in the things themselves, but in the interactions between humans and things" (Hodder, 2012:18).

The basic premise for this interpretative article arises from the belief that technological practices are an embodied way that people create their physical world and that the human-material-technological relationship is indivisible (Latour, 1991, 2002; Ingold, 2000). The discourse can make establishment of a dialectic relationship between the way the monuments are materially produced and the way the monuments itself are experienced and conceptualised. The Naga way of megalithism entails dialectic between the internal life of the individual (the donor) and the external realm of society in the process of synthesising one's social identity. Focusing on the social dimensions of a person will reveal a series of social relations and commitments that define who they are within the community. It is seen that donors as human agency insinuates power because it offers a social choice sanctioned with the peoples' normative value, which has relevancy to recall Tammy Stone's (2003: 61) observation that "which role an individual chooses to perform at any one time and the frequency of that performance is tied to the strategies for achieving personal goals within the social structure in which they live." This implies that "human goals are relevant to cultural outcomes" (Brumfiel, 1992: 559), and that individuals can pursue goals that might not completely agree with their social milieu, but must at least be intelligible to the rest of society to have salience. Thus, any Naga male aspirant could not exert exclusive ideology of status until he fulfilled the socially demanded formalities. The significance of a person's status thus lies with other systems of formalities to see how materialisation permits a person to consolidate and institutionalise status.

The present contention on the commemoration of a person's capability with erection of menhir can be backed up by the fact that the stones are in a sense to 'display'. And materialising stone blocks into monuments is none other than the transformation of ideas and values, and propagation of meaning of a system into a physical reality as a symbolic object — sharing and participating with the viewers. It thus reveals that the means and forms of materialisation are related with the investment of resources and transportation of wealth into prestige, power and status. Power, here, refers to the social power as a construct where its exercise may have material consequences far beyond the identity-based inequalities that many artifacts come to symbolise (Walker & Schiffer, 2006), and may be taken to mean that individuals having privileged of social identities that can exercise their will or exert 'power' over others (Giddens, 1993). The present example indicates that competition for prestige and power meshes with conspicuous consumption of wealth in the form of feasting, the *feast of merit*, which is a part of the social reciprocal system manifesting generosity, compassion and concern to the fellow community. Hence, the three components – *wealth, feasting* and *status* — are complementary and reciprocal themselves. A wealthy person's endeavour to achieve social status is at the expense of his accumulated wealth by way of organizing feasts lavishly to the fellow people and especially to those individuals involved reciprocating their labour. However, this is not the end of the issue and social dictums firmly mesh with the system. A male aspirant is yet to fulfil the normative conditions of the system though he possesses enough wealth to throw feast to the people. Yet, the present discourse on Naga living megalithism forcefully comes to such a proposition that prestige, power and status in the society can be achieved through wealth *via* communal feasting as a substantial social strategy. Here Naga ideology of monumentality is centred round the status symbol not only with the megaliths erected, but also with the ethnic insignia of special cloth, decorated spear, decorated house with a special mark, animal horns, and so on. The peoples' subjective meaning impose on megaliths thus has normative foundation of the system of what they believe and not just on what is objectively true.

NOTES

1. In archaeological literature definition of materiality is still unequivocal. To refer a few it is,
— "concern not only the study of the characteristics of objects, but also the as conscious agents and are themselves shaped by those experiences" (DeMarrais *et al.*, 2004: 2).
— "the ephemeral, the imaginary, the biological, and the theoretical; all that which would have been external to the simple definition of an artifact" (Miller, 2005: 4).
— "the fleshy, corporeal and physical, as opposed to spiritual, ideal and value-laden aspects of human existence" (Tilley *et al.*, 2006: 3).
— "materialities can involve a great variety of things, from artefacts, the landscape, layout and material of buildings and settlements, to trees and vegetation, animals, bodies and less evident material matters such as rain, ice and snow" (Fahlander & Oestigaard, 2008: 4) and so on.

2. Mehirs at Mao Naga inhabited villages of Makhel, Rabunamei and Makhan, and carved out standing stone at Willong come under this category. A general belief in case of Makhel is that if any male individual could climb the slanting stone (*napfuto kohrii tu*) without the support of his upper limbs or otherwise, he will be blessed with seven sons. A lean menhir (*bokho kane tsii*) at Rabunamei is a scale for measuring height of a boy — if he could touch the highest tip of the stone with his chin; he is entitled to join the group who watch the herd.
3. Different categories of rice-beer are prepared to serve to different groups of people during a feast of merit. Altogether nine categories of rice beers (*ju*) are known to the Poumai Naga tribe of the Oinam village which is to serve to different individuals who are engaged in different stages of the stone erection activities. These comprise *chameju* (rice beer used at the initial registration for the feast of merit), *thingreju* (meant for the firewood cutters), *thingfungju* (for fire-wood collectors), *taseju* (for the stone draggers and erectors), *duichang* (meant for all the participants), *duipoh* (second best rice beer for all the participants), *popohonju* (meant only for the village elders), *nampubaoloju* (special beer for the village priest), *loudaju* (rice-beer to serve at the time of erecting the monument) etc.
4. In fact, this issue entails the potential of a sensuous archaeology with landscape studies and embodiment perspective through the embracement of phenomenological approaches. Under landscape studies pertaining to monumental sites, space acts as a proxy for understanding the distribution of groups across the landscape and the degree to which their experience of the landscape was dictated by social concerns over other realms of physical needs.
5. One pertinent issue with megalithic monuments where their erection and use is still a 'living tradition' is with their status in terms of temporality within the context of human prehistory. Practically, these monuments are not being totally detached from their living systemic context, but still the integral part of socio-cultural entities participating behavioural domains of making and using with known symbolic meaning. Hence, these are still in their living/dynamic *systemic context* and do not enter into the dead/static *archaeological context.* In fact, the systemic context of a man-made artifact, along its *chaîne opératoire* (Leroi-Gourhan, 1964) domain refers to "the condition that an element is participating in a behavioural system" (Schiffer, 1972), which subsequently enter into *archaeological context* when it is discarded and abandoned. Knowing the behavioural matrix related with cultural intentionality of materiality and monumentality, we can say that the megaliths are within the realm of 'use' within its *chaîne opératoire* process.

REFERENCES

Assmann, A., 1991. "Kultur als Lebenswelt und Monument". In A. Assmann and D. Harth (eds.), *Kulturals Lebenswelt und Monument*. Frankfurt: Main, pp. 11-25.

Babic, S., 2005. "Status, Identity and Archaeology". In M. Diaz-Andreu, S. Lucy, S. Babic, and D. N. Edwards (eds.), *The Archaeology of Identity: Approaches to Gender, Age, Status, Ethnicity, and Religion*. New York: Routledge, Kegan & Paul Ltd., pp. 67-85.

Bawden, G., 1996. *The Moche*. London: Blackwell.

Binford, L., 1965. "Archaeological Systematics and the Study of Culture Process". *American Antiquity*, 31 (2): 203-109.

_____. 1983. *In Pursuit of the Past: Decoding the Archaeological Record*. London: Thames & Hudson.

Bintliff, J., 1991. "Postmodernism, Rhetoric and Scholasticism at TAG: The Current State of British Archaeology". *Antiquity*, 65: 274-78.

Boivin, N., 2008. *Material Cultures, Material Minds: The Impact of Things on Human Thought, Society and Evolution*. Cambridge: Cambridge University Press.

Bourdieu, P., 1998. *Practical Reason: On the Theory of Action*. Stanford: Stanford University Press.

Brumfiel, E., 1992. "Breaking and Entering the Ecosystem: Gender Class and Faction Steal the Show". *American Anthropologist*, 94(3):551-67.

Childe, V. G. 1950. "The Urban Revolution". *Town Planning Review*, 21 (1): 3-17.

_____. (1956). *A Short Introduction to Archaeology*. London: Muller.

Conkey, M. W., 1989. "The Place of Material Culture in Contemporary Anthropology". In A. L. Hedlund, (ed.), *Perspectives on Anthropological Collections from the American Southwest: Proceedings of a Symposium*. Anthropological Research Papers, No. 40. Tucson: Arizona State University Press, pp. 13-31.

Cunningham, J.J., 2003. "Transcending the "Obnoxious Spectator": A Case for Processual Pluralism in Ethnoarchaeology. *Journal of Anthropological Archaeology*, 22 (4): 389-410.

David, N. and C. Kramer. 2001. *Ethno-Archaeology in Action*. Cambridge: Cambridge University Press.

DeMarrais, E., L. J. Castillo and E. Timothy. 1996. "Ideology, Materialisation, and Power Strategies". *Current Anthropology*, 37 (1): 15-31.

DeMarrais, E., C. Gosden and C. Renfrew. 2004. *Rethinking Materiality: the Engagement of Mind with the Material World*. Oxford: McDonald Institute for Archaeological Research.

Dimitriadis, G., 2008. "Looking for Metals: Megalithic Monuments between

Reality and Mythology". In R.I. Kostov, B. Gaydarska, and M. Gurova (eds.), *Geoarchaeology and Archaeomineralogy – Proceedings of the International Conference*. Sofia, Bulgaria: St. Ivan Rilski, pp. 205-10.

Donald, M., 1991. *Origins of the Modern Mind: Three Stages in the Evolution of Culture and Cognition*. Cambridge: Harvard University Press.

_____. 1998. "Material Culture and Cognition: Concluding Thoughts". In C. Renfrew and C. Scarre (eds.), *Cognition and Material Culture: the Archaeology of Symbolic Storage*. Cambridge: McDonald Institute for Archaeological Research, pp. 181-87.

Drucker, P., 1981. "On the Nature of the Olmec Polity". In E. Bensen (ed.), *The Olmec and Their Neighbours.* Washington DC: Dumbarton Oaks, pp. 29-47.

Duke, P., 1995. "Working through theoretical tension in Contemporary Archaeology: A practical attempt from South-western Colorado". *Journal of Archaeological Method and Theory*, 2 (3):201-29.

Fahlander, F. and T. Oestigaard. 2004. "Introduction: Material Culture and Post-Disciplinary Sciences". In F. Fahlander and T. Oestigaard (eds.), *Material Culture and other Things— Post-disciplinary studies in the 21st Century.* Gotarc Series C, No. 61. Gothenburg, pp. 1-18.

_____. 2008. "The Materiality of Death Bodies, burials, beliefs". In F. Fahlander and T. Oestigaard (ed.), *The Materiality of Death Bodies, Burials, Beliefs.* BAR International Series 1768. Oxford: Archaeopress, pp. 1-16.

Friedman, J. and K. Rowlands. 1978. "Notes towards an epigenetic model of the evolution of "civilization". In J. Friedman and K. Rowlands (eds.), *The Evolution of Social Systems.* Pittsburg: University of Pittsburg Press, pp. 201-76.

Furholt, M. and J. Müller. 2011. "The Earliest Monuments in Europe – Architecture and Social Structures (5000-3000 BC)". In M. Furholt, F. Lüth and J. Müller (eds.), *Megaliths and Identities Early Monuments and Neolithic Societies from the Atlantic to the Baltic.* Bonn: Dr. Rudolf Habelt GmbH, pp. 15-32.

Garcia, L., 2005. *Introduccion al Reconocimiento y Analisis Arqueologico del Territorio*. Barcelona: Ariel.

Giddens, A., 1993. *New Rules of Sociological Method.* Stanford, CA: Stanford University Press.

Hayden, B., 1993. Archaeology: *The Science of Once and Future Living Things*. New York: W. H. Freeman.

_____. 1998. "Practical and Prestige Technologies: The Evolution of Material Systems". *Journal of Archaeological Method and Theory*, 5 (1): 1-55.

Hodder, I., 1982a. *Symbols in Action.* Cambridge: Cambridge University Press.

_____. 1982b. *Symbolic and Structural Archaeology.* Cambridge: Cambridge University Press.

_____. 1986. "From Ethnoarchaeology to Material Culture Studies". *Dialoghi Di Archeologia,* 3 (1):93-97.

_____. 1992. *Theory and Practice in Archaeology.* London: Routledge Kegan and Paul Ltd.

_____. 2011. "Human-Thing Entanglement: Towards an Integrated Archaeological Perspective". *Journal of the Royal Anthropological Institute (N.S.),* 17 (1): 154-177.

_____. 2012. *Entangled: An Archaeology of the Relationships between Humans and Things*. Malden, MA: Wiley-Blackwell.

_____. 2014. "The Entanglements of Humans and Things: A Long-Term View". *New Literary History,* 45(1):19-36.

Hodson, T.C. [1911] 1984. *The Naga Tribes of Manipur*. Delhi: Neeraj.

Horam, M., 1977. *Social and Cultural Life of Nagas (The Tangkhul Nagas).* Delhi: B.R. Publishing.

Hutton, J.H., 1965. *"The Mixed Culture of the Naga Tribes". The Journal of the Royal Anthropological Institute of Great Britain and Ireland,* 95(1): 16-43.

Ingold, T., 2000. *The Perception of the Environment: Essays in Livelihood, Dwelling and Skill*. London: Routledge Kegan and Paul Ltd.

_____. 2007. "Materials against Materiality". *Archaeological Dialogues,* 14(1): 1-16.

_____. 2012. "Toward an Ecology of Materials". *Annual Review of Anthropology,* 41: 427-442.

Jones, A., 2004. "Archaeometry and Materiality: Materials-based Analysis in Theory and Practice". *Archaeometry,* 46 (3): 327-38.

Knapp, A.B., 1996. "Archaeology without Gravity: Postmodernism and the Past". *Journal of Archaeological Method and Theory,* 3 (2):127-158.

Latour, B. 1991. "Technology is Society made durable". In J. Law (ed.), *A Sociology of Monsters: Essays on Power, Technology and Domination.* London: Routledge Kegan and Paul Ltd., pp. 103-31.

_____. 2002. "Morality and Technology: The Ends of the Means". Trans. C. Venn. *Theory, Culture and Society,* 19(5/6): 247-60.

LeCount, L.J., 1999. "Polychrome Pottery and Political Strategies in Late and Terminal Classic Lowland Maya Society". *Latin American Antiquity,* 10 (3): 239-58.

Leone, M.P., 1982. "Some opinions about recovering mind". *American Antiquity,* 47 (4): 742-60.

_____. 1986. "Symbolic, Structural, and Critical Archaeology". In D.J. Meltzer, D.D. Fowler and J.A. Sabloff (eds.), *American Archaeology: Past and Future.* Washington, D.C.: Smithsonian Institution Press, pp. 415-38.

Leroi-Gourhan, A., 1964. *Les religions de la préhistoire*. Paris: Albin Michel.

Lindstrom, T. C., 2015. "Agency "in Itself" — a Discussion of Inanimate, Animal and Human Agency". *Archaeological Dialogues*, 22 (2): 207-38.

Longchar, A.W., 2000. *The Tribal Religious Traditions in North East India.* Jorhat, Assam: Eastern Theological College.

Manibabu, M., 2014. "Making Sense of Stones: Wealth, Status and Indigenous Management Strategy". In K. Jose, and G.K. Bera (eds.), *Indigenous Resource Management in North East India.* New Delhi: Omsons Publications, pp. 192-17.

Meskell, L., 2005. "Objects in the Mirror appear closer than they are". In D. Miller (ed.), *Materiality*. London: Duke University Press, pp. 51-71.

Miller, D., 1985. Artefacts as Categories: A Study of Ceramic Variability in Central India. Cambridge: Cambridge University Press.

_____. 1987. *Material Culture and Mass Consumption*. Oxford: Basil Blackwell.

_____. 1994. "Artefacts and the Meaning of Things". In T. Ingold (ed.), *Companion Encyclopaedia of Anthropology*. London: Routledge Kegan and Paul Ltd., pp. 396-419.

_____. 2005. *Materiality*. Durham, N.C.: Duke University Press.

Miller, D. and C. Tilley. 1984. *Ideology, Power and Prehistory.* Cambridge: Cambridge University Press.

_____. 1996. 'Editorial'. *Journal of Material Culture*, 1(1): 5-14.

Mills, J.P., 1935. "The Effect of Ritual upon Industries and Arts in the Naga Hills". *Man*, 35: 132-35.

_____. 1937. *The Rengma Nagas*. London: MacMillan & Co.

Oestigaard, T., 2004. "Approaching Material Culture: A History of Changing Epistemologies". *Journal of Nordic Archaeological Science*, 14: 79-87.

Oritiz, N.S., 2016. "Towards a Definition of the Prehistoric Landscape in the Plateau of Sigarra: Visibility and Territoriality between the Middle Neolithic and Bronze Age". In V. Ard and L. Pillot (eds.), *Giants in the Landscape: Monumentality and Territorialities in the European Neolithic* [*Proceedings of the XVII UISPP World Congress* (1-7 September, Burgos, Spain)]. Oxford: Gordon House Archaeopress Publishing Ltd., pp. 85-94.

Oslen, B., 2003. "Material Culture after Text: Remembering Things". *Norwegian Archaeological Review*, 36(2): 87-104.

Peponis, J., 2001. "Interacting Questions and Descriptions". *Proceedings of 3rd International Space Syntax Symposium Atlanta 2001.* Atlanta, Georgia, pp. 13-26.

Pfaffenberger, B., 1992. "Social Anthropology of Technology". *Annual Review of Anthropology*, 21: 491-516.

Preucel, R., 1991. *Processual and Postprocessual Archaeologies: Multiple Ways of Knowing the Past.* Centre for Archaeological Investigations. Carbondale: Southern Illinois University.

Rathje, W.M. Shanks and C. Witmore. 2013. *Archaeology in the Making: Conversations through a Discipline*. London: Routledge Kegan and Paul Ltd.

Renfrew, C., 1998. "Mind and Matter: Cognitive Archaeology and External Symbolic Storage". In C. Renfrew and C. Scarre (eds.), *Cognition and Material Culture: The Archaeology of Symbolic Storage*. Cambridge: McDonald Institute for Archaeological Research, pp. 1-6.

Rosenau, P.M., 1992. *Post-Modernism and Social Sciences: Insights, Inroad and Intrusions*. Princeton: Princeton University Press.

Sabloff, J., 2005. "Processual Archaeology". In C. Renfrew and P. Bahn (eds.), *Archaeology: The Key Concepts.* London/New York: Routledge Kegan and Paul Ltd., pp. 159-64.

Sackett, J.R., 1982. "Approaches to Style in Lithic Archaeology". *Journal of Anthropological Archaeology*, 1(1): 59-112.

Sanders, W. and B. Price. 1968. *Mesoamerica: The Evolution of a Civilization.* New York: Random House.

Semaw, S., 2000. "The World's Oldest Stone Artifacts from Gona, Ethiopia: Their Implications for Understanding Stone Technology and Patterns of Human Evolution between 2.6 and 1.5 Million Years Ago". *Journal of Archaeological Science*, 27 (12): 1197-214.

Shanks, M. and C. Tilley. 1987a. *Social Theory and Archaeology*. Oxford: Polity Press.

_____. 1987b. *Reconstructing Archaeology*. Cambridge: Cambridge University Press.

Schiffer, M.B., 1972. "Archaeological Context and Systemic Context". *American Antiquity*, 37(2): 156-65.

Shimray, R.R., 1985. *Origin and Culture of Nagas.* New Delhi: Pamleiphi Shimray.

Stone, T., 2003. "Social Identity and Ethnic Interaction in the Western Pueblos of the American South-west". *Journal of Archaeological Method and Theory*, 10(1): 31-67.

Thomas, E., 2007. *Monumentality and Roman Empire: Architecture in the Antonine Age*. Oxford: Oxford University Press.

Thomas, J., 1996. *Time, Culture and Identity.* New York: Routledge Kegan and Paul Ltd.

Tilley, C., 2004. *The Materiality of Stone: Explorations in Landscape Archaeology*. Oxford: Berg.

_____. 2006. 'Introduction'. In C. Tilley, W. Keane, S. Kuchler, M.J. Rowlands and P. Spyer (eds.), *Handbook of Material Culture Studies*. London: Sage Publications, pp. 1-6.

_____. 2007. "Materiality in Materials". *Archaeol. Dialogues*, 14 (1): 16-20.

Tilley, C., W. Keane, S. Küchler, M. Rowland and P. Spyer. 2006. *Handbook of Material Culture*. London: Sage Publications.

Vablen, T., 1899. *The Theory of the Leisure Class*. New York: MacMillan & Co.

VanPool, C.S. and T.L. VanPool. 1999. "The Scientific Nature of Postprocessualism". *American Antiquity*, 64(1): 33-53.

Venuh, V., 2004. *Naga Society: Continuity and Change*. Delhi: Shipra Publication.

Walker, W.H. and M.B. Schiffer. 2006. "The Materiality of Social Power: The Artifact-Acquisition Perspective". *Journal of Archaeological Method and Theory*, 13(2): 67-88.

Watkins, T., 2000. "Memes, Memeplexes and the Emergence of Religion in the Neolithic". Paper presented at the Second International Congress on the Archaeology of the Ancient Near East, Copenhagen.

Watson, R., 1990. "Ozymandias, King of Kings: Postprocessual Radical Archaeology as Critique". *American Antiquity*, 55 (4): 673-89.

Watt, G., 1887. "Aboriginal Tribes of Manipur". *The Journal of the Anthropological Institute of Great Britain and Ireland*, 16: 346-70.

West, A.C., 1985. "Nineteenth Century Naga Material Culture". *Newsletter (Museum Ethnographers Group)*, 18: 21-34.

Yoffee, N. and A. Sherratt. 1993. *Archaeological Theory: Who Sets the Agenda?* Cambridge: Cambridge University Press.

8
Monumentality, Social Memories and the Idea of Landscape in Naga Megalithic Tradition

Tiatoshi Jamir

Introduction

The main title to this chapter partly stems from Lefebvre's *The Production of Space* (1991) and Holtorf (1996) that brings to discussion how natural metaphors of the raw material (i.e. stones) such as size, durability and permanence helps megaliths achieve its monumental beauty. Natural landscapes have often been perceived as one of the prominent spaces from which people of different historical and cultural milieu inscribes the human experience. It is, therefore, the bodily movement of human beings through space which is directly implicated in both their interpretation of the world and the formation of their subjectivity (*see* Thomas, 1993). An immediate corollary to this notion is the megalithic monuments dotting the landscape built throughout the various stages of human history. It is here that an attempt is made to explore how ideas of landscapes and social memory may be derived from the Naga stone monuments, an idea previously discussed by Jamir (2005) and Blackburn (2008) and later more elaborately explored by Khongreiwo (2014) and Wangjin (2014). Recently, Wouters' (2015) work in a Chakhesang village also brings to mind the social role of these monuments and the potential it holds for understanding a village ethnohistory.

In many respects, the study of megaliths in North East India occupies a prominent position due to several reasons. Firstly, colonial ethnographers posted in the region for various administrative assignments were intrigued not only by their sheer massive size and variety of forms, but also because of their striking similarities with those found in South East Asia (*see* Hutton, 1926a, 1928a; Fürer-Haimendorf 1939, 1943, 1945, 1971) and Europe (*see* Walters, 1832; Fergusson, 1872) while approaching the subject of their supposed origin based on broad general comparisons. Such observations have also offered a basis for geographer and anthropologists such as W.J. Perry (1918) and Katz (1928), and prehistorians alike (*see* Heine-Geldern 1935; Schnitger, 1939) to serve their diffusion and migration theories as testing models. Secondly, in spite of the few dates emerging from both old and new excavations (*see* Rao, 1977; Nienu, 1983; Hurst & Lawn, 1984; Jamir, 2014, Jamir *et al.*, 2014a & 2014b; Mitri *et al.*, 2015), the obscure antiquity to this living tradition in North East India continues to linger on (on a similarly concerned view, *see* Sarma & Hazarika, 2014). Thirdly, realizing their archaeological potentials, the post-Independence in North East India witnessed at least several research dissertations and few published volumes dedicated to megalithic research of North East India (Bareh, 1981; Syiemlieh, 1981; Devi, 1993, 2011; Mawlong, 1996; Jamir, 1997; Mitri, 1998, 2016; Venuh 2000, 2005; Bezbaruah, 2003; Choudhury, 2004; Jamir, 2005; Sarma 2011, 2014a, 2014b; Malsawmliana, 2011, 2016). These works present us with exhaustive accounts on their typo-morphological variations and the complex multifarious functions associated with stone monuments of North East India.

Parallel to such developments are the epistemological shifts that took to autochthonous origins seeking alternative explanation away from diffusionism. Inspired by new theoretical and methodological concepts current in archaeology, few archaeologists brought about fresh perspectives to the study of stone monuments of the region. Such paradigmatic shifts are evident in the works of Mawlong (2004), Mitri (2009, 2016), Jamir (2005, 2006, 2015), Khongreiwo (2014, 2015), Wangjin (2014), Burke (2014), Marak (2014), Wouters (2015) and Wunderlich (in press) who not only utilised historical accounts, oral tradition, family histories, ecological, landscape concepts and other spatial analyses to stone monuments, but also examined the beginning of megalithic culture alongside social formations, territoriality, resource utilisation and neolithic-megalithic transition, social memories, notion of ideology, identity and cosmology.

Types of Naga Monuments, Their Relative Function and Location Pattern

Based on a detailed list of types and their distinctive features and functions reported by Hutton (1927), W. Jamir (1997, 1998), Venuh (2000, 2005, 2008), T. Jamir (2005), Mushrif *et al.* (2008) and Wangjin (2014), we can now view the function of these megaliths based on their following broad types:

Commemorative or Memorial Stones

It consist mainly of standing stones whether large or small associated with feasting, with local legend and folklore, warrior stones, oath stone, to mark the establishment of a village, to mark a man's romantic favours with women, stones erected by childless widow, to perpetuate memory of a childless man, commemorating peace treaties and victory in war and memorials for the dead. Stone pillars are also erected to mark the territory of plots between two or more individuals to define the extent of land a person owns.

Location pattern: They are both found within the settlement area and outside the village periphery. Generally, stones in commemoration of a peace treaty or victory are set up in the heart of the village. Stones associated with feasting, territorial markers, warrior stones representing carved enemy heads and stones recording a man's romantic ties with women (in the Chakhesang case) seem to occur away from the settlement area in conspicuous locations.

Stone Platforms

They are raised platforms surmounted by massive stone blocks which are either quarried or naturally rolled river boulders. It is found in various forms and sizes (roughly 2-10 feet in height) — square, rectangular, circular, semi-circular or oblong. While such structures are often linked with the highest stages of the feast of merit and used for holding clan meetings, there exist other similar structures that are simply built by members of the clan that bears no meritorious significance. But when found outside the village on wayside to agricultural fields, they serve as resting places constructed in memory of surviving members to perpetuate their own memory or even for the dead. They also serve as a memorial for the dead (a lost son, a warrior, a seer or even an influential person), a grave marker, or as a mark of prestige commemorating the completion of the whole feasting process.

Location pattern: They are distributed around the village *khels*, in front of a house compound, by the side of the village streets and by the footpaths to the fields.

Table Stones

Large flat slabs supported by three or more vertical stones with multiple functions – serves as a pronouncement platform for the village priest, an altar for the ritual ceremony, set up in the name of a woman, particularly the spouse of a feast-giver. Such stones may at times be marked with local legends and beliefs.

Location pattern: Such structures are mainly found within the settlement area—by the corner of a house at the front and beside the village streets. For the priest pronouncement place, they are generally set up in an elevated area facing the *khels* in the village.

Burial Chambers

They are simple cist burial, rectangular or oblong cut earth-cut pits lined with small upright stones around the pit wall meant for primary burial. Several capstones are topped over this stone-lined grave giving the appearance of a hollow chamber. Occasionally, a rough transept is laid between two graves and covered with capstones above each individual pit. Among the Semas, the niche burial with the capstones in an inclined position is common.

Location pattern: Burials are seen to occur within the village premises around the house compounds marked with rough, undressed stones. However, burial of a person from unnatural death are found outside of the settlement area, beyond the village gate.

Skull Cist

They are stone cist carved out of a solid stone block in either square or conical shape measuring about 2-3 feet in height and about 2-4 feet maximum girth with various incised geometric patterns. The cist contains a deep cavity on one side of the face meant for interring the detached skull of the deceased after corpse exposure, a practice known among the Konyaks, particularly in Wakching and Kongan.

Location pattern: Such stone cists are found outside the village grouped in huge clusters, each cluster representing a *morung* of the village.

There is further scope to consider more systematic typologies for these megaliths. Besides a description of their primary attribute like height and size, other qualities of the stones such as shape, texture, colour, rock type, presence or absence of weathering lines, cracks, depressions, the aural experiences from the acoustics of the rocks, the relationship of such types with the local settings and wider landscape contexts have not been considered systematically, which instead are equally important for creation of difference, meaning and identity (on detailed discussions, *see* Tilley, 2004a: 35-38).

Quarrying and Transporting

As described by Hutton (1922a, 1922b, 1928b, 1929) and Fürer-Haimendorf (1976), the stones to be pulled and erected are the locally available sandstone, which is either quarried from a massive strata or are simply natural slab or boulders lying close to a stream or from a nearby rock outcrops around the peripheral area of the village. Most stones appear to have been found within the vicinity of the village not far from where they were erected. The sledge is generally made from the forked branch of a massive tree and is shaped to a 'V'.

In other cases, they are made from two parallel branches or tree trunks that serve as runners (Fig. 8.1). Once on the sledge, the stone is lashed with ropes of creepers and dragged to the desired site and erected. In another case, for transporting smaller monoliths, a huge rectangular frame of poles crossing at right angles is made as rigid as possible while the stone is lashed to the centre of the frame. About 60 men lift the wooden framework and carry the stone to the site. The pulling of a stone and the organisations of feasts thus involves a good deal of labour mobilization, cooperation and economic resources that bear potential social implications along socio-economic lines.

Fig. 8.1: A parallel wooden sledge used by Chakhesangs, Phek village (*Photo* courtesy: Venuh, 2002)

Monuments, Memories and Landscape: A Naga Context

The concern with monuments, memories and ideas of landscapes in the context of Naga pre-Christian belief systems and worldview has been a subject of emerging interest in recent works. I explore and highlight three works mainly in this direction to present an overview, thereafter followed by a discussion of my own work in my earlier doctoral research (Jamir, 2005) combined with relatively recent research undertaken on megalithic monuments as part of a larger research initiative on Naga ancestral sites (*see* Jamir *et al.*, 2014a, 2014b).

Blackburn (2008) in writing about oral tradition and the stories that Naga stones tell draws the importance of stones in the oral narratives of migration histories and origin myths. In his observation, he notes, "Naga stones tell, or told, many types of stories. Some stones mark the origin and dispersal of tribes and sub-groups, whilst some are characters in legends of war and still, others are associated with less dramatic historical events; then there are the magic stones that generate tales about those who use or abuse them. Social memory is also inscribed in the large memorial stones dragged and set up to mark the performance of a feast of merit…" (Blackburn, 2008: 265). He further argues that it is the permanence and the durability that stones, megaliths, and monuments are perhaps the most common objects for transmitting social memory. The other work is that of Khongreiwo (2014, 2015) who explores the significance of landscape in the pre-Christian belief systems of the Nagas of Nagaland and Manipur. His notion of landscapes, monuments, and collective memories draws the ancestral landscapes imbued with legends and their pivotal role in Naga belief systems. Memories of the past can be reconstructed by reading the landscape through certain topographic features that mark the abode of spirits, land of the Dead, associated monuments instilled with a sense of supernatural powers while others are associated with popular tales. The concept of the soul and the idea of perpetual existence and immortality of the soul, life after death and need to settle the dead in the land of the dead, were instrumental in the construction of memorials to the dead (Khongreiwo, 2014: 314).

Another interesting piece of work is by Wangjin (2014). While making a comparative study of the Konyak and Angami monuments, he draws the relevance of ideology, identity, landscape and social memories to the Naga monuments. Visualising the landscape as both the physical and memory aspect, he suggests that the transformation of the landscape through monumental space is the very act of transforming the perception of that landscape. Such constructed landscape, therefore, becomes a powerful tool for invocation of the past through rituals and through memories, the identifier of their ancestors. His example to such constructed landscapes lies in the carefully chosen areas for erecting monuments and burials among Angamis and Konyaks. In linking social memories to megaliths, he maintains, "Stones, therefore, was a medium through which knowledge was represented and interpreted consciously, and also a receptacle through which feelings, emotions, events was manifested and consciously passed down" (Wangjin, 2014: 330).

Landscape Dimensions of Naga Megaliths

The Nagas perceived themselves as part of nature. In a balanced, harmonious, and steady state of nature, they maintained balance and harmony — a state of ideal equilibrium. Mountains, hills, forests, and rivers were held sacred and respected, for they were the source of all good things and had the power to affect crops and fertility — all believed to be controlled by supernatural forces (*see* Neinu, 2015:

33-50). Similar to what is described by Turnbull (1961, 1965, 1983) for the Mbuti hunter-fisher-gatherers of the Ituri rain forest, the generalised significance of the forest as "the provider, spiritual entity and mystical force" (cited in Tilley, 1994: 36) also applies the same in the Naga case. The landscape among the Nagas is one which is replete with elaborate social meanings linking together place and people through social memories derived from the landscape. This notion of nature perceived as cultural landscape fashioned by a cultural group (Evans, 1985) is aptly described by Nienu (2015:14): "Particular places in the mountains, especially peaks, springs, knobs, caves and caverns, and streams and rivers became associated with important oral traditions that explained the Naga beliefs and/or the source of their origin or such other important historical or mythological events" (p. 41).

Approaching the landscape dimensions to the megaliths found particularly in the Angami (Kohima District) and Chakhesang (Phek District) area, based on my preliminary field observation, I propose few fundamentally distinguishable variables in respect of their locational points chosen by the community for retention and transmission of social memories. These examples are specific to the menhirs and the raised stone platforms commonly constructed in the villages of these districts. Menhirs from the region are either found singly or in a single pair, cluster or form rows of alignments, while the stone platforms are constructed in various forms — square, rectangle, oblong, circle or semi-circle. All the stones are of the Barail formation, a local sandstone, medium coarse-grained and hard sandstone with a bright greyish texture when freshly quarried, found widely distributed within these districts. Prominent physiographic features such as hills, mountains, spurs, nearby rock outcrops, rivers and other small watercourses, proximity to natural ponds and a valley surrounded by wet-rice terrace fields are some of the most common topographic features taken into consideration. If this is so, the distribution of such monuments should draw their significance to several distinct landscape referents. However, when built inside the village, such structures takes their places in prominent locations such as the central portion of a *khel* (a division within a village based on clan) or over a prominent ridge around the margin of a *khel*. As a result, the precise location of the monuments forms an essential feature of its architecture and is never a matter of chance. It was the result of a deliberate choice, based on identifiable criteria (Criado-Boada *et al.*, 1994: 39).

Preferably, the first locational points that come to mind are wide open clearings, situated on high elevations offering good visibility points of the surrounding landscape. The menhirs here occur as single standing stone, in pairs or at times found in a cluster adjacent to a footpath or away from it and are inter-visible to each other (Fig. 8.2). When occurring in alignments, they are often found by narrow paths within close proximity of settlements (Fig. 8.3). Their dense

Fig. 8.2: A menhir at Zhavame village (Chakhesang) inter-visible to another menhir standing downhill

Fig. 8.3: Parallel rows of monuments erected alongside the village path at Zhavame village (Chakhesang)

concentration close to settlement proximities and their sparse distribution further away from settlement areas is well illustrated from the distribution pattern of the monuments from Khezhakeno and adjoining sites, Khusomi, Phek village and Chiethu (Figs. 8.4-8.7).

Fig. 8.4: A 2-dimensional GIS generated model (with hillshade illumination) of Khezhakeno village (Chakhesang) and adjoining sites showing the locational pattern of monuments

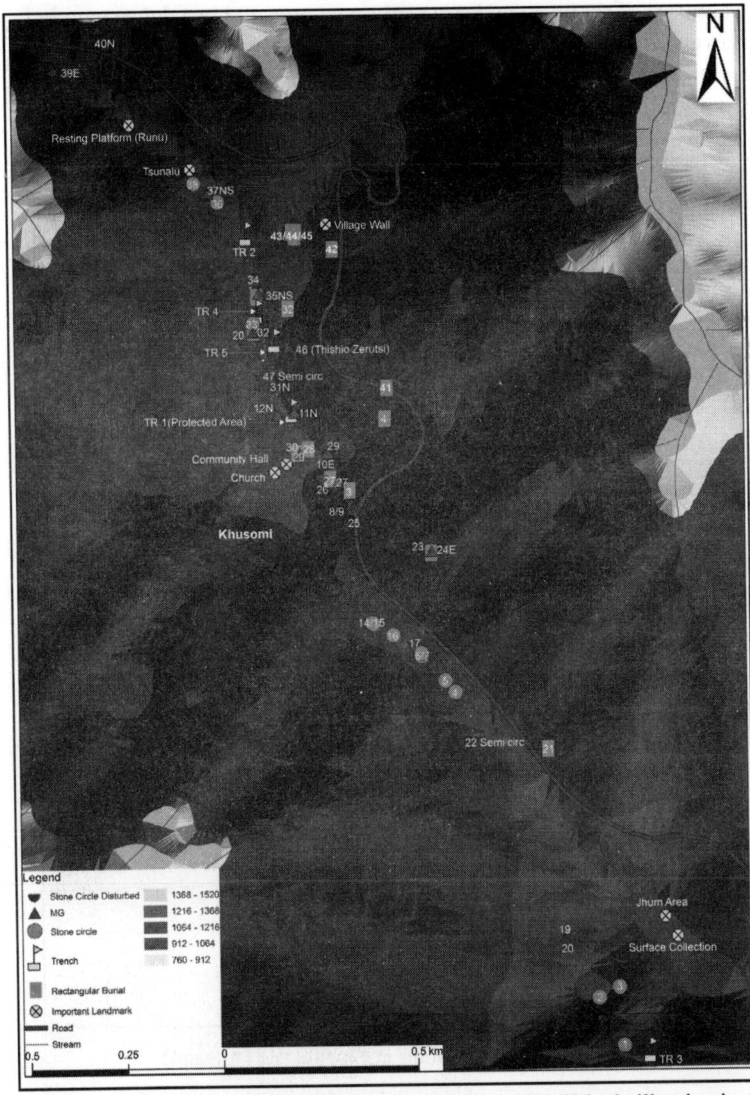

Fig. 8.5: A 2-dimensional GIS generated model (with hillshade illumination) of Khusomi village (Chakhesang) showing the locational pattern of monuments

By contrast, if set up away from settlement area and in a dense wooded environment, whilst they obstruct the visibility of the stones, the favoured locations are nevertheless the footpaths leading to agricultural fields.

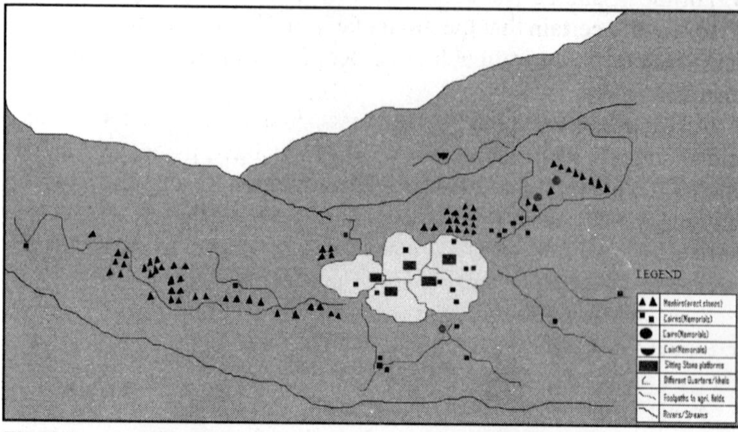

Fig. 8.6: Locational pattern of megaliths in Phek village (Chakhesang) (After Zokho Venuh 2005)

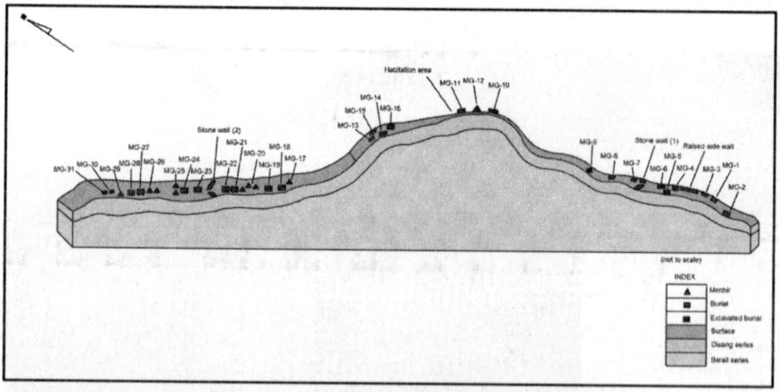

Fig. 8.7: Locational pattern of megaliths at Chiethu site (Angami)

Here "the menhirs stand prominent in an otherwise fairly featureless landscape" (Tilley, 2004a: 82). In such cases, it is the visual prominence of the monuments that enhances and impacts on the surrounding landscape.

Other visibility locations are mostly prominent flatlands with gentle undulating slopes, with the terrace fields in the background.

Landscapes dotted with terrace rice fields provide one of the most spectacular panoramic sights in the region. If such magnificent sights and surrounding mountains had the effect of inspiring early travellers referring the region as "towering heads of majesty" (King, 1879: 145) or the "Land of Wonders" (Houston & Houston, 1953), we can be reasonably certain that the mountains, similarly, must have been a great source of inspiration for the people living in the region for generations.

A significant number of monuments are also found in the terrace fields itself. Rows of menhirs or at times isolated pairs are noticed standing on the rice field bunds (large baulks about 4 ft generally left untilled in between plots of fields) (Figs. 8.8, 8.9). While it is the panoramic visuals and the monumental features intrinsic of the terrace fields that enhances the surrounding landscape where the megaliths are seen standing, such a landscape with relatively few or barely any trees transform the significance of the place by "its relationship with other 'natural' and 'cultural' places" (Tilley, 2004a: 221).

What constitutes as 'bad' and 'good' stones are also judged from the intrinsic qualities of the menhirs found in these landscapes. Features such as deep grooves or depressions on the face of the stone are believed to bring misfortune or poverty to the one who drags

Fig. 8.8: A row of menhirs erected on the bunds of terrace fields, Mesulumi village (Chakhesang)

Fig. 8.9: Single inter-visible menhirs in a terrace field, Khezhakeno village (Chakhesang)

them, while scally features on the rock face speak of ill omen, bringing misfortune in the form of sudden death to the one in whose memory they are set up. In contrast, a straight feature and an even surface bring fame to the owner of the stone. Other characteristic feature such as a smooth surface and stoutness speaks of the strength of the stone and brings wealth and wisdom to its owner (*see* Venuh, 2005).

Given the purpose of these monuments, the orientation of the menhirs is directed in such a manner that the face of the megaliths is immediately visible to any passer-by. However, due to space constraints within the confines of the area, the face of the menhir is arranged parallel to the footpath. Such differences in orientation as we were informed are a matter of availability of space or the direction of ridge patterns and bear no astronomical significance. The directional orientation, therefore, differs greatly following an E-W, N-S or NE-SE pattern. Thus, commemorative and memorial stones meant to perpetuate the memory of the living members or the dead occupied a permanent place in the landscape and offered new meanings to places by establishing a link with the people who raised them. It is also the durability of the material that enhanced the monumental nature of the structures for social memories to be encoded not only for the present generation, but also as vehicles through which memories can be transmitted to the future.

Another notable monument is the small raised rectangular or semi-circular stone platform arranged with stone seats known as *badze*. They generally occur outside the village walls and are built in one's memory or a memorial for the dead. At Khusomi village (Chakhesang), such structures are circular or oblong in shape and take their place over the burial of influential people. They are set up following the linear ridge pattern outside the settlement. Here, the prefix "*ba*" refers to "a place or a seat", and "*dze*" meaning, "to build or arrange" (Venuh 2000: 19). Consequently, the purpose of the memorial relates to something which is associated with either "sitting or resting place". They lie close to spots where menhirs are set up or preferably built following the ridge, right around the edge where they offer a good view of the surrounding valley. Given the mountainous topographic feature, the locational pattern of such memorials are ideal resting points after an arduous steep climb from the terrace fields or also affords the same for those trailing down the fields (Fig. 8.10).

Fig. 8.10: A raised stone platform with a picturesque view of the valley below, Kalozie (Chakhesang)

For the monuments that are found in the village, they are chiefly the *kwehou* and the *theuba* that are most conspicuous. In some Angami villages of the western region, these circular *kwehous* are associated with the highest feasts, which are either built in his name or his deceased members. It literally means, "a place for discussion"

(Venuh, 2000: 19) and serves as meeting places of the village and *khel* members. By choice, they are built in flat lands, but take a commanding presence when viewed from the *khel*. They are built around the front of the house compound, but around the centre, if space is generally available. Nonetheless, the preference is towards the edge or along the ridge of the settlement (Fig. 8.11).

Similarly is the case with the *theubas*. These massive structures made from blocks of stones are raised rectangular platforms built by the clansmen and are mainly located in strategic locations around the village offering good vantage points.

Fig. 8.11: A stone circle or *kwehou* built around the ridge of the settlement area, Khonoma village (Angami)

Discussion

Landscapes represent "a way in which... people have signified themselves and their world through their... relationship with nature, and through which they have underlined and communicated their own social role and that of others with respect to external nature" (Cosgrove, 1985: 15). Quite parallel to this, even to the Nagas, the landscape is more than simply a complex network of mountains and rivers. Such physical features are a reservoir of detailed ecological knowledge and a repository for the memory of past events (Nienu, 2015: 43). The stone monuments of the Naga Hills have been a subject of much interest ever since its first report in 1872 (Godwin-Austen, 1872-73). While the interest in such monuments was initially confined to the colonial ethnographic tradition of description, followed by later ethnoarchaeological research in post-Independence times (Jamir, 1997; Venuh, 2000, 2005; Jamir 2005), their relation to landscapes and metaphors of social memories is a subject of very recent concern. Menhirs distributed within a given landscape denotes much beyond notions of fertility and embodiment of the phallic principle, an idea previously understood as a central and underlying feature of these stones (*see* Hutton, 1922a,1926a, 1926b, 1928c,1929; Jamir 2004). We do not deny the embodiment of such innate virtues of stones in the Naga traditional belief systems as jotted by Hutton manifold times, yet when local people are asked why standing stones are set up outside their village, the reaction is prompt and immediate: "The stones must be set up in a place where all can see" thus acting as personal biographies of their lifetime achievements. So far as their social significance is concerned, this straight forward and prompt response brings to mind several implications for drawing the ideas of landscapes, the monumentality of stone monuments and the social memories they embody.

According to Aleida Assmann (1991), "monuments are that part of culture, which stage-manage it: they want to be seen, preserved and remembered by contemporary and later generations. The monument is an erected sign, which encodes a message in a permanent way for communicating with people that are (possibly) millennia away: a monument is designed to survive the present and to enable cultural communication with the distant future" (Assmann, 1991: 13; cited in Holtorf, 1997: 47). The monuments, therefore, were built as "cultural mnemonics" and their builders hoped that they carried out a particular message into the future (*ibid.*: 60). While such notion of memories is clues to understanding the monumentality of megaliths, their permanence, size and visibility is also another that particularly influenced its location within a given landscape. Given its location in the backyard of a house, a menhir or stone platform would appear to lose its profound visual significance unless located elsewhere at a place where "meaning is created with the dialectics of place and surroundings" (Tilley, 2004a: 221). An example is a monument *Terhuo Tsiese* at Khonoma village where the significance of the place (a folklore popularly recounted by the people) was what might have equally inspired them to set up megaliths within the immediate vicinity of this stone erected by spirits (Fig. 9.12). According to Khongreiwo (2014: 305), "Some people of the village believe that humans learnt the tradition of erecting menhirs from this episode". Because of the mountainous area, day-to-day mobility routes of a village are taken following an energetically optimal path from the village to the fields and other known paths leading to a neighbouring village. As in the Angami and Chakhesang case, rather than by chance, because most megaliths appear to occur by the waysides, a spatial relationship between such mobility pattern and the megaliths seems apparent. Megaliths appear to densely occur by the side of daily routes either singly, in pairs, or in clusters within close radius of the settlement, beyond which their numbers appear to decrease gradually (on a detailed study using GIS in monument landscape studies, *see* Wheatley *et al.*, 2010).

Fig. 8.12: Cluster of monuments seen standing around the *Terhuo Tsiese* monument, Khonoma village (Angami)

Monuments within the landscape also inform of a collective past and the potential to transmit 'prospective memories' (Holtorf, 1996) to the future. It is the permanency of the megaliths that not only aid in inscribing people's personal memories of their lifetime achievements, but also carry forward a community's shared memories of the past to the future. In most Chakhesang villages, such social memories in stones continue to inspire the community when the past deeds and personality of their ancestors are actively imagined and remembered. Given their durable character, their wide visibility in the landscape and permanence, the monuments guarantee a potential medium for carrying memories to the future. If this is so, when did such megaliths come to occupy the landscape in the Angami and Chakhesang region? What were the social circumstances that led societies to mark memories with stones? What were the changing economic and socio-cultural dynamics at the time when megalithism and idea of monumentality emerged? From where were the main ideological sources of monumental behaviour drawn from? Were they rooted alongside the beginning of farming in the region? These are far-reaching queries where we need to seek corresponding answers at the economic, social and ideological levels, a considerable body of archaeological evidence and further reinforced by a strong chronology of these megaliths. New excavations at Chungliyimti, Khezhakeno, Movolomi and Khusomi provide radiocarbon dates for such monument building activity not earlier than 10th to 14th centuries AD (*see* Jamir *et al.*, 2014a, 2014b). However, an indirect lead to the beginning of early monumentality may perhaps lie within a popular Angami folktale of Sopfunuo:

> "If I become a piece of wood,
> I will become rotten and mingle with the earth;
> So I must become a stone".
>
> (*Folktales from Nagaland*, Parts I and II, 1971)

The above narrative from this Naga folktale and the Angami practice of erecting 'Y' shaped wooden post prior to the commencement of the stone pulling ceremony previously documented by Hutton in 1921 (Hutton, 1922a, b; also *see* Venuh, 2005) may provide vital clues to the rise of monumental behaviour in the region. There could, of course, be a myriad of linkages between megalithic construction, organisation of feast, labour and resources. But the context within which such shifts may occur might appear to be linked to the emergence of a 'big-man' like social institution where competition for social status fell entirely along the principal lines of feasting, valour in war, skill in oratory etc. Perhaps it was during this time that megalithism developed whereby its permanence in stones spoke of an individual's lifetime achievements as well as those of his dead ancestors (on a proposed model, *see* Jamir, 2005). Consequently, such a process may have led to circumstances, not only to receive ideas but also to create new ideas and symbols to express them. Thus in replacing with a new material agency and added significance, "the megalith-builders must have had every intention to transform a particular message into permanent memory" (Holtorf, 1996: 123).

Concluding Remarks

Just as social memories, commemorative ceremonies, and bodily practices go beyond the bounds of the individual and the personal for conveying and sustaining the memory of social groups (on a detailed discussion, *see* Connerton, 1989), megaliths and landscapes are but one medium through which memories of a particular community are inscribed and transmitted. My preliminary field observation in noway attempts to provide a thick description of space or place through a bodily experience of a contemporary body, a theory of phenomenology and its methodology exhaustively espoused by Tilley (1994, 2004a, 2004b, 2004c), but instead outlines future scope in the region for an alternative understanding of monuments in relation to landscape features and their insightful meanings that can hitherto be derived. This is conceivable not only by drawing the significance of monuments themselves, but also it is wider added significance if the field of inquiry is expanded towards metaphors of the landscape. For that reason, it is important to understand landscapes as a territory which can be apprehended visually, and as a set of relationships between people and places which provide the context for everyday conduct (Thomas, 2001: 181). Megaliths, like other forms of material culture, are also continually being reinterpreted in new historical contexts, an idea previously explored by Hodder (1992, 1994) and also Barrett (1994). Thus, what these monuments serves to the present is crucial to the understanding of their changing social meanings (*see* Holtorf, 1996; on the ancestral 'six stones' or *Longterok* in the Ao Naga context, also *see* Aier & Jamir, 2009). The perception and meanings of these monuments by the present generation are one of mixed reactions and hence encompasses a wide range of collective memories attached. While a few still considers these stones as relevant in people's lives, providing a valuable link to their past and evoke a sense of cultural identity from the narratives embodying the monuments, and also perceived as sites of tourist attractions etc.; others considers these monuments as a thing of the distant past, neglected, lost and forgotten. This neglect, as observed by Wouters (2015: 25), "appears in parts related to the notion, propagated in certain circles, that stone rituals and beliefs are part and parcel of a non-Christian past, a period some seek to denounce, perhaps unfortunately so, as 'heathen worship' that is best forgotten". Whatever monuments are considered obstructions during developmental programmes in the region are obliterated from the landscape — expansion of roads connecting to fields and neighbouring villages, the establishment of a new settlement in the area, or either used as foundation walls, for road constructions or reused to meet other needs. Nonetheless, the ones that survived, once again, play out new prospective memories to be engaged, recreated and imagined intertwined within a sense of place alongside new monuments erected to celebrate jubilees commemorating such milestones either of a village or town, thus, recasting old cultural expressions in contemporary times.

Acknowledgements

Part of the GPS survey data on the monument distribution is derived from the field season of 2009. I wish to thank my team particularly Dr. David Tetso, Dr. Zokho Ṿenuh, Mepusangba and Yapangri Changkiri for all assistance rendered in the field. A special note of gratitude is also extended to the Department of Art and Culture, Government of Nagaland for all financial support towards the research programme.

REFERENCES

Aier, A. and T. Jamir. 2009. "Re-interpreting the Myth of Longterok". *Indian Folklife*, (33): 5-9.

Bareh, A., 1981. Megalithic Culture among the Khasis with Special Reference to Mawiong village. M.Phil. Dissertation, North Eastern Hill University.

Barrett, J., 1994. *Fragments from Antiquity: An Archaeology of Social Life in Britain, 2900-1200 BC*. Oxford: Blackwell.

Bezbaruah, D., 2003. *Megalithic Ruins in Karbi Anglong District of Assam: A Study in the Context of Karbi Culture*. Ph.D. Thesis, Gauhati University, Guwahati, Assam.

Blackburn, S., 2008. "The Stories Stones Tell: Naga Oral Stories and Culture". In M. Oppitz, T. Kaiser, A. von Stockhausen, and M. Wettstein (eds.), *Naga Identities: Changing Local Cultures in the North East of India*. Ethnographic Museum of Zürich University: Snoeck Publishers, pp. 259-69.

Burke, D., 2014. "*Jingkynmaw*: Memories written in stone". In T. Jamir and M. Hazarika (eds.), *50 Years After Daojali-Hading: Emerging Perspectives in the Archaeology of North East India* (Essays in Honour of T.C. Sharma). New Delhi: Research India Press, pp. 360-75.

Choudhury, K., 2004. *The Megaliths and their Associated Remains in Dimoria Area of Kamrup District, Assam*. Ph.D. Thesis, Gauhati University, Guwahati, Assam.

Connerton, P., 1989. *How Societies Remember*. Cambridge: Cambridge University Press.

Cosgrove, D.E., 1985. "Prospect, Perspective and the Evolution of the Landscape Idea". *Transactions of the Institute of British Geographers*, 10: 45-62.

Criado, Boado F., R. Fabregas Valcarce and J. Vaquero Lastres. 1994. "Regional Patterning among the Megaliths of Galicia, North-West Spain". *Oxford Journal of Archaeology*, 13(1): 33-47.

Devi, P. B., 1993. *Studies on the Megalithic Remains of Manipur*. Ph.D. Thesis, Gauhati University, Guwahati, Assam.

_____. 2011. *The Megalithic Cultures of Manipur*. Delhi: Agam Kala Prakashan.

Evans, C., 1985. "Tradition and the Cultural Landscape: An Archaeology of Place". *Archaeological Review from Cambridge*, 4 (1): 80-94.

Fergusson, J., 1872. *Rude Stone Monuments in all Countries: Their Age and Uses*. London: John Murray.

Folktales from Nagaland, Parts I and II. 1971. Kohima: Directorate of Art and Culture.

Fürer-Haimendorf, C. von., 1939. "The Megalithic Culture of Assam". In F. M. Schnitger (ed.), *Forgotten Kingdoms of Sumatra*. Leiden: E.J. Brill, pp. 215-22.

_____. 1943. "Megalithic rituals among the Gadabas and Bondos of Orissa". *Journal of Royal Asiatic Society of Bengal*, IX (1): 149-78.

_____. 1945. "The Problem of Megalithic Cultures of Middle India". *Man in India*, XXV (2): 73-90.

_____. 1971. "Comparisons between the Mountain peoples of the Philippines and some tribes of North East India". *The Geographical Journal*, 137 (3): 339-48.

_____. 1976. *Return to the Naked Nagas*. London: John Murray.

Godwin-Austen, H. H., 1872-73. "Report on the Survey Operations in the Naga Hills and Manipur during the Field Season 1872-73". *General Report on the Topographical Surveys of India for the Season* 1872-73, Appendix: pp. 74-87.

Heine-Geldern, R. von., 1935. *Sumatra: The Archaeology and Art of Sumatra*. Verlog Des Institute Fur Folkenkunde Des Universital Wein.

Hodder, I., 1992. *Theory and Practice in Archaeology*. London: Routledge Kegan and Paul Ltd.

_____. 1994. "The Interpretation of Documents and Material Culture". In N. K. Denzin and Y. S. Lincoln (eds.), *Handbook of Qualitative Research*. London: Sage Publications, pp. 393-402.

Holtorf, C., 1996. "Towards a Chronology of Megaliths: Understanding Monumental Time and Cultural Memory". *Journal of European Archaeology*, 4: 119-52.

_____. 1997. "Megaliths, Monumentality and Memory". *Archaeological Review from Cambridge*, 14(2): 45-66.

Houston, H. and H. Houston. [1953] 1987. *Nagaland Adventure: 1947-53*. Kohima: Kohima Lotha Baptist Church.

Hurst, B.J. and B. Lawn. 1984. "University of Pennsylvania Radiocarbon Dates XXII". *Radiocarbon*, 26 (2): 212-40.

Hutton, J. H., 1922a. "The Meaning and Method of Erection of Monoliths by the Naga Tribes". *The Journal of Royal Anthropological Institute*, 52: 242-49.

_____. 1922b. "Carved Monoliths at Dimapur and an Angami Naga Ceremony". *The Journal of Royal Anthropological Institute*, 52: 55-70.

_____. 1926a. "The Use of Stone in the Naga Hills". *The Journal of the Royal Anthropological Institute*, 56: 71-83.

_____. 1926b. "A Carved Stone at Kigwema in the Naga Hills". *Man*, 26: 74.

_____. 1927. "The Disposal of the Dead at Wakching". *Man*, 27: 61-64.

_____. 1928a. "The Ao Nagas". *Folklore*, 39 (1): 93-95.

_____. 1928b. "Prehistory of Assam". *Man in India*, VIII (4): 228-32.

_____. 1928c. "The Significance of Head-Hunting in Assam". *Journal of the Royal Anthropological Institute of Great Britain and Ireland*, 58: 399-408.

_____. 1929. "Assam Megaliths". *Antiquity*, III (2): 399-408.

Jamir, T., 2004. "Megaliths of Nagaland: Reflections of Material Milieu and Social Values". In M. Momin and C. Mawlong (eds.), *Society and Economy in North East India* (Vol. 1). New Delhi: Regency Publication, pp. 105-17.

_____. 2005. *Megalithic Burial Tradition of the Nagas (with special reference to the Angami and Chakhesang Nagas): An Ethnoarchaeological Perspective*. Ph.D. Dissertation, Deccan College PG and Research Institute.

_____. 2006. "A Burial site at Jotsoma and the Mortuary Customs of the Angami Nagas: An Ethnoarchaeological Approach". In G. Sengupta, S. Roychoudhury and S. Som (eds.), *Past and Present: Ethnoarchaeology in India*. New Delhi: Pragati Publications, pp. 449-63.

_____. 2014. "Rethinking the Chronology of Chungliyimti, an early Naga

Ancestral Site: views from recent AMS dates". *Nagaland University Research Journal*, 7: 264-73.

_____. 2015. "Death, Memory and Society: An Ethnoarchaeological study of Angami Mortuary Practices". In K.K. Basa, R.K. Mohanty and S.B. Ota (eds.), *Megalithic Traditions in India: Archaeology and Ethnography*. New Delhi: Aryan Book International, pp. 609-40.

Jamir, T., D. Vasa and D. Tetso. 2014a. *Archaeology of Naga Ancestral Sites: Recent Archaeological Investigations at Chungliyimti and Adjoining sites* (Vol. 1). Department of Art and Culture, Government of Nagaland. Dimapur: Heritage Publishing House.

Jamir, T., D. Tetso, Z. Venuh, V. Mushrif-Tripathy and A. K. Pokharia. 2014b. *Archaeology of Naga Ancestral Sites: Recent Archaeological Investigations in Phek and Kiphire Districts of Nagaland* (Vol. 2). Department of Art and Culture, Government of Nagaland. Dimapur: Heritage Publishing House.

Jamir, W., 1997. *Megalithic Traditions in Nagaland: An Ethnoarchaeological Study*. Ph.D. Thesis, Gauhati University, Guwahati, Assam.

_____. 1998. "Megaliths in Nagaland". *Puratattva*, 28: 104-10.

Katz, M., 1928. "Genna in South-Eastern Asia". *American Anthropologist* (NS), 30(4): 580-601.

Khongreiwo, R., 2014. "Landscapes, Monuments, Collective Memories: Understanding pre-Christian belief systems and socio-religious practices of the Nagas". In T. Jamir and M. Hazarika (eds.), *50 Years After Daojali-Hading: Emerging Perspectives in the Archaeology of North East India*. New Delhi: Research India Press, pp. 292-317.

_____. 2015. *Archaeologies of Landscapes: A Social and Religious History of the Nagas of Nagaland and Manipur*. Ph.D. Thesis, University of Delhi, Delhi.

King, C.D., 1879. "Among the Naga Hills". *The Baptist Missionary Magazine*, LIX: 144-46.

Lefebvre, H., 1991. *The Production of Space*. Oxford: Blackwell.

Malsawmliana. 2011. *Megalithic Monuments of Mizoram: A Descriptive Study*. Ph.D. Thesis, North Eastern Hill University, Shillong.

_____. 2016. *Megalithic Culture of Mizoram*. New Delhi: Research India Press.

Marak, Q., 2014. "Megaliths and Living Cultural Traditions". In S. Sengupta (ed.), *Explorations in Anthropology of North East India*. New Delhi: Gyan Books, pp. 31-51.

Mawlong, C., 1996. *Megalithic Monuments of Khasi-Jaintia Hills: An Ethnoarchaeology Study*. Ph.D. Thesis, North Eastern Hill University, Shillong.

_____. 2004. "Megaliths and Social Formation in Khasi-Jaintia Hills". In

M. Momin and C.A. Mawlong (eds.), *Society and Economy of North East India* (Vol. 1). New Delhi: Regency Publications, pp. 35-56.

Mitri, M.B., 1998. *Living Megalithism of the Khasis (with special reference to the Umniuh-Tmar village of the War Region)*. M.A. Dissertation, Deccan College PG and Research Institute.

_____. 2009. *An Outline of the Neolithic Culture of Khasi-Jaintia Hills, Meghalaya, India*. BAR International Series 2013, South Asian Archaeology Series (No.11).

_____. 2016. *The Living Megalithic Culture of Khasi-Jaintia Hills, Meghalaya*. Shillong: Don Bosco Centre for Indigenous Cultures.

Mitri, M. B., D. Kharmawphlang and H. Syiemlieh. 2015. A Preliminary Report on the Excavation at the Neolithic Site of Lawnongthroh (Sohpetbneng Hill), Khasi Hills Meghalaya. *Man and Environment*, XL (1): 33-42.

Mushrif, V., T. Jamir, D. Vasa and S.R. Walimbe. 2008. *Human Skeletal Remains from Jotsoma, Nagaland: Osteobiographic Studies*. Kolkata: Centre for Archaeological Studies and Training.

Nienu, V., 1983. *The Prehistoric Archaeology and Human Ecology of Nagaland*. Ph.D. Thesis, University of California.

_____. 2015. *Naga Cultural Milieu: An Adaptation to Mountain Ecosystem*. San Francisco, CA: Dorylus Publishing Group.

Perry, W. J., 1918. *Megalithic Culture of Indonesia*. Manchester: University of Manchester.

Rao, S.N., 1977. "Continuity and Survival of Neolithic Traditions in North Eastern India". *Asian Perspectives*, XX (2): 191-205.

Sarma, D., 2011. *Megalithic Traditions of the Karbis in the Hills and the Plains of Assam*. Ph.D. Thesis, Gauhati University, Guwahati, Assam.

_____. 2014a. *Khasi and Jaintia Megaliths and Culture*. Guwahati: Spectrum Publication.

_____. 2014b. *Karbi Culture and Megaliths*. Guwahati: Spectrum Publication.

Sarma, P.J. and M. Hazarika. 2014. "Situating North East Indian Archaeology in Chronological Perspective: Fresh Observations". In T. Jamir and M. Hazarika (eds.), *50 Years After Daojali-Hading: Emerging Perspectives in the Archaeology of North East India*. New Delhi: Research India Press, pp. 37-59.

Schnitger, F.M., 1939. *Forgotten Kingdoms in Sumatra*. Leiden: E.J. Brill.

Syiemlieh, J., 1981. *The Funeral Rites and Practices in the Khasi Mainland: An Anthropological study*. Ph.D. Thesis, North Eastern Hill University, Shillong.

Thomas, J., 1993. "The Hermeneutics of Megalithic Space". In C. Tilley (ed.), *Interpretative Archaeology*. Oxford: Berg, pp. 73-97.

_____. 2001. "Archaeologies of Place and Landscape". In I. Hodder (ed.), *Archaeological Theory Today*. Cambridge: Polity Press, pp. 165-86.

Tilley, C., 1994. *A Phenomenology of Landscape: Places, Paths and Monuments*. Oxford: Berg.

_____. 2004a. *The Materiality of Stone: Explorations in Landscape Phenomenology*. Oxford: Berg.

_____. 2004b. "Mind and Body in Landscape Research". *Cambridge Archaeological Journal*, 14(1): 77-80. DOI: 10.1017/S0959774304240057.

_____. 2004c. "Round Barrows and Dykes as Landscape Metaphors". *Cambridge Archaeological Journal*, 14(2): 185-203. DOI: 10.1017/S0959774304000125.

Venuh, Z., 2000. *Megalithic Traditions of the Chakhesang Nagas*. M.Phil. Dissertation, Dibrugarh University, Assam.

_____. 2005. *Megaliths and Megalithic Traditions of the Chakhesang Nagas: Myths, Facts and Interpretations*. Ph.D. Thesis, Dibrugarh University.

_____. 2008. "Megalithic Remains in Nagaland: A General Survey". *Nagaland University Research Journal*, 5: 228-41.

Walters, H., 1832. "A Journey across the Pandua Hills, Near Sylhet in Bengal". *Asiatic Researches*, 17: 472-99.

Wangjin, W., 2014. "Ideologies, Identities and Memories: Interpreting stone structures of the Konyak and Angami Nagas". In T. Jamir and M. Hazarika (eds.), *50 Years After Daojali-Hading: Emerging Perspectives in the Archaeology of North East India* (Essays in Honour of T.C. Sharma). New Delhi: Research India Press, pp. 318-32.

Wheatley, W.D., L.G. Sanjuán, P.A. Murrieta Flores and J. Márquez Pérez. 2010. "Approaching the Landscape Dimension of the Megalithic Phenomenon in Southern Spain". *Oxford Journal of Archaeology*, 29(4): 387-405.

Wouters, J.J.P., 2015. "The Social Lives of Stones: Studying the Past in the Chakhesang Naga Village of Phugwumi". *Anthropology Today: North East Institute for Research in Anthropology*, 1(1): 21-41.

Wunderlich, M., (In press.) "Social Implications of Megalithic Construction —A case study from Nagaland and Northern Germany". Paper read at the International Conference "*Megaliths, Societies, Landscapes: Early Monumentality and Social Differentiation in Neolithic Europe in the Session*" Monuments and their Builders, CAU, Kiel, Germany, 16-20th June, 2015.

9
Mortuary Behaviour of the Jaintias of Meghalaya

Akoijam Milan Meitei

Introduction

Mortuary behaviour is an accepted cultural norm and a part of the religious custom of a society, and thus a treatment to/for the deceased. It involves rites, rituals, emotions, mournings and disposition of the dead. These are well defined and meaningful expressive actions and not random occurrences (Gardener, 1988). On similar lines, Iguaz (1993) opined that disposal of the dead is a carefully thought out process and not a random one. It is transmitted to the present generation through various generations over a period of time. Mortuary behaviour of a society is also part of the so called "primitive religion" (Tylor, 1871). But according to Frazer (1886), stones like cairns and tombstones, are piled on the graves of the deceased to keep the deceased's soul underneath the stones. Thus, humans started mortuary rituals due to the fear of the deceased's soul turning into a ghost. The deceased souls are then turned into ancestors through mortuary rituals and practices (Porter, 2002). This ancestor's soul gives wealth to the descendents and protection from evil things. Thus, performing mortuary practices are seen as the 'duty' of the deceased's descendents (Meitei & Marak, 2015).

There are different stages to a mortuary ritual. It comprises, a series of burials or cremation processes (Ingham, 2001), and are seen in ethnographic writings too (Meitei & Marak, 2013, 2015). The identification of the degree of richness and poorness of the deceased from funerary remains can also be made (Ucko, 1969). Childe (1958) discusses the richness and poorness of the deceased through interpretation of the megalithic structures. In India too, it has been reported that mortuary practices of various communities are associated with megalithic structures — both directly and indirectly. Nagas of Manipur (Singh, 1985; Devi, 2011) and Nagaland (Jamir, 1998; Jamir, 2004), Karbis of Assam (Bezbaruah, 2003; Choudhury, 2004), Khasi-Jaintias (Roy, 1963; Bareh, 1967; Mawlong, 1996; Meitei & Marak, 2015) and Garos (Playfair, 1909; Marak, 2012) of Meghalaya and few tribes from central India (Fürer-Haimendorf, 1945).

Mortuary practices have been studied by scholars from various fields — anthropologists, archaeologists, historians and others. The burial position reflects the social context of the prehistoric or past people (Peterson, 1972). Bickler and Ivuyo (2002) found that megaliths were used as primary burial locations at first, and then later as secondary burial repositories. The occurrence of multiple burial rather than single burial has been witnessed in many places (Peterson, 1972), and such practices has transformed through time and space, from inhumation to cremation (Mizoguchi, 1993). According to Binford (1971), mortuary behaviours determine the social organisation and social identity. These transformations are additionally associated with political and socio-economic shifts (Curet & Oliver, 1998).

In the study area discussed in this chapter, some transformations in the traditional mortuary behaviours in connection to megaliths have taken place over time. The study space and population discussed in this chapter is the area presently occupied by the Jaintias of Meghalaya, a North Eastern state of the Indian Union. Jaintias locally prefer to call themselves *Pnar* or *Synteng* and inhabit predominantly the Jaintia Hills District of Meghalaya. They also reside in some adjoining areas of the region. Jaintia Hills is surrounded by Bangladesh in the south, Assam in the east and north, and Khasi Hills in the west. The Jaintia kingdom once flourished before the intervention of British in the region. Jaintias are a matrilineal society and belong to Mon-Khmer group of people. They are Mon-Khmer speakers of the Austro-Asiatic language family. Their unique features are the megalithic culture which still continues till today and their matrilineal descent. The traditional religion of the Jaintias is called *Niamtre* which is a belief in ancestor's soul, spirit/nature worship, and a belief in a number of local deities without any particular figures and figurines.

The archaeological and ethnographic interpretation of mortuary behaviours in the study area is negligible. This is due to the religious aspect connected to burial rituals, and due to changes that have come in with Christianity and modernization. Though the exact date of this tradition and erection of megaliths cannot be said, it is suggested that megaliths of Nartiang in Jaintia Hills were erected between 1250-1500 AD (Bareh, 1967) and possibly 1300 AD in Khasi Hills (Mawlong, 2004). But the lone C^{14} dating from a post-Neolithic site at Marakdola in Khasi Hills gives a date of 1296±100 years AD (Rao, 1991). However, at present there is no convincing record regarding the chronology of the origin of megaliths in this place.

Burial Stones — Types and Variations

Among the Jaintias, there are variations in burial stones — both structurally and functionally. Though the structures are different from each other, the function and internal meaning of burial stones remain more or less the same (Meitei & Marak, 2015). Moreover, the stones having the same structure sometimes are given different names due to different purpose and *vice versa*, and they also differ from village to village. This is the reason why the naming of a common specific burial stone for Jaintias is difficult. Essentially, there are primary or temporary burial stone and secondary or permanent burial stone. Here, the burial stones are classified based on their morphology.

Cairns

It is a heaped up man-made pile of stones placed one above the other. These stone structures are at present used as primary clan burial stones in many villages in Jaintia Hills like Shangpung, Raliang, Niawkmai, Mukroh etc. They are, however, not found among War Jaintias of southern Jaintia Hills or War Jaintia area.

Fig. 9.1: Cairns used as primary burial stone in Shangpung

This structure is conical in shape. It has three parts — (a) one flat stone on top (as opening); (b) a flat stone on the ground (as foundation); and (c) heaps/piles of stone rubble (as wall). Sometimes there is no flat stone on the ground, so only two parts are present. It is made into a shape that leaves a small hollowed portion in the middle of the main stone with an opening lid on top. The deceased's bones are deposited into the hollow space of this middle portion.

Dolmens

This is a box-like burial stone. It comprises a capstone on top of three or more vertical supporting pillar stones, i.e. orthostats. They are used as primary/temporary and secondary/permanent clan burial stone. There are two similar burial stones for each clan in Nangbah village. One is used at present and the other one is kept as extra reservoir, in case the first one becomes full. In other villages like Shangpung, Raliang, Niawkmai etc., they are used as secondary burial stone. However, dolmens are used as individual primary and secondary burial stone by War Jaintias of southern Jaintia Hills. But very uniquely here, it is meant only for deceased women.

Though the bottom of the capstone (i.e. cover of the dolmen) is flat, the top has various shapes — flattish circular to flattish convexo/

polygonal. However, the arrangement of vertical supporting pillars is either in a circular or polygonal shape and covers the ossuary from all sides. It is arranged according to the structure of the capstone itself. There is one other commonality of these stones, i.e. one small movable stone acting as the entrance to the dolmen. This is the only entrance for the deceased's bones.

Fig. 9.2: Dolmen in Shangpung

Fig. 9.3: Dolmen having flattish-convexo capstone in Raliang

Thus, the dolmens can be further classified on the basis of the capstone's morphology. They include:

(i) *Dolmen with flat capstone* – The capstone has a flat orientation on both the surfaces (top and bottom). However, the shape of the stone itself is circular, squarish, rectangular or polygonal.

(ii) *Dolmen with convex capstone* – The capstone is flat underneath, but the upper surface is dome-shaped. This capstone is found either in polygonal or round shape and sometimes, elongated, thinner and smaller at the back and larger at the front.

(iii) *Dolmen with flattish-polygonal capstone* – Here, the capstone is flat on its undersurface but variant shapes are seen on the upper surface. They are pyramidal (pointed and blunted showing four sides on upper surface) and trapezoidal (five sides on upper surface).

Dolmenoid Cists

This stone is a dolmen in appearance but the chamber is built underneath the ground. Other than the depression (i.e. partly above and partly below the ground) the purpose, shape, feature etc. are similar to the dolmen. Inner portion of most of these stones are not visible clearly, so it is difficult to identify the dimensions of the stone correctly. In addition, the sacred nature of the stone in connection to the religious belief of the people does not permit to conduct an extensive observation. But, it is clear from simple observation that these stones have a negative depression into the ground. These dolmenoid cists are found in Shangpung and Raliang.

Dolmen with Menhir

In this type, there is one dolmen and one standing stone. While the dolmen represents a female burial stone, dolmens with menhirs represent male burial stones. The structures of dolmens in Jaintia Hills are more or less similar but the addition of one menhir among the War Jaintias of southern Jaintia Hills makes it unique from the rest of Jaintia Hills. Moreover, the size of this menhir depends on the achievement and contribution during the deceased's lifetime.

Fig. 9.4: Dolmens with menhirs belonging to a clan in Nongtalang

The burial stone is, however, an individual's primary burial stone but in some villages like Lamin, it is also a secondary individual/family burial stone.

Dolmen with Enclosure

In this stone type, one or more dolmen is present inside a circular or geometric stone enclosure. An enclosure here is a group of small miniature megaliths that are arranged in a pattern — circular or square/rectangle/polygonal. This type is widely found in Nartiang, Raliang etc. but in scattered and broken condition, though the place where the stone lies is still considered a sacred place.

Various types of enclosures are found with a variation in the number of dolmens too. They are classified as follows:

(i) *An enclosure with a dolmen and a passage entrance* – The stone enclosure is arranged in a square within which a dolmen is present. A stone passage chamber is present and leads to the enclosure as an entrance;

(ii) *An enclosure with a dolmen inside* – Here, an enclosure is present within which a dolmen is placed; and

Fig. 9.5: An enclosure with a dolmen and a passage entrance

Fig. 9.6: An enclosure with a group of dolmens inside

(iii) *An enclosure with a group of dolmens inside* – Here, a circular or geometric shaped enclosure is present within which is a group of dolmens.

Cenotaph

It is the stone which is erected in remembrance of the deceased. In Nongtalang, this old structure comprises one or three menhirs and a flat stone (capstone) in front. However, it is now replaced by modern cemented structure with many designs.

Traditional burial structures are at present being replaced by modern cemented structures in many Jaintia villages. This is a slow process that happens in one's society knowingly and unknowingly. But, the cultural values among *Niamtre* Jaintias remain the same throughout generations.

Ethnographic Situation

Traditionally, Jaintias cremate the dead. This tradition is still followed by *Niamtre* Jaintias and not by the Christian Jaintias. Among them, small pieces of bones are collected after cremation. These are deposited in a bone repository (clan stone). The deposited bones are then taken out and deposited in a permanent clan stone. Thus, the belief goes that all the deceased souls of a particular clan are living together under a single roof of a particular clan's stones even after death.

In the following, the process of how the deceased's bones reach the different burial stones is discussed.

Cremation Ground

The clan is one of the most important social units among the Jaintias. Therefore, the importance of clansmen/women in the mortuary practices is clearly seen. As soon as one dies, all clansmen/women are informed as per tradition. The mortuary rite begins by giving bath to the deceased with warm water. Depending on the sex of the deceased, women/men take care of her/his bathing. During this time, all the family members of the deceased place a small amount of *nup* (a soap-like powdered substance made from the *nup* tree) on the head of the deceased. The deceased's body is clothed with the best

Fig. 9.7: Cenotaph in Nartiang

dress, preferably white in colour, and is kept on a new mat covered with a white linen cloth. Relatives and clansmen of the deceased's family bring eatable items like fruits, cakes, areca nuts, betel leaves etc. The gifting of these items indicates respect and love towards the deceased. Some of these items are offered to the deceased's soul and some are meant for guests and visitors who come to console the deceased's family and to attend the mortuary rituals. These items are kept separately and near the deceased's head in a small basket. Small amount of money are also placed in the hands of the deceased.

The cremation of the deceased is usually held within three days inclusive of the day the individual passed away. Though it is performed on the same day now-a-days, it is decided by the deceased's family. Gurdon (1907) observed that the deceased's body is placed for three days and three nights following some rites including the offering of betel leaves, areca nuts, rice and sacrifice of a fowl. On the cremation day, women are mostly engaged in household chores like cooking, serving food etc. The eldest woman of the house symbolically feed the deceased by putting little amount of food into his/her mouth. She then offers betel leaves and areca nuts to the dead person at the place of cremation, before the pyre is lit. Men undertake activities like

Fig. 9.8: Cenotaph in Nongtalang

carrying the dead body, making pyre, cremation etc. They also throw some coins in the cremation ground before the start of the cremation. The cremation is attended by relatives and neighours, but there are some nominated men who are assigned to conduct it. In every Jaintia village, they are known by different names.

On the way to the cremation ground, rice grains are scattered, music is played, and even gunshots are fired (if the deceased is respectable). This is believed to chase away the evil spirits who try to take the deceased's soul. They take out most of the deceased's belongings to the crematorium. Here, they place items like clothes, plates, knives, and even mobile phones in a large basket. A smaller basket with eatable items is also brought by the women of the family. Besides this, relatives offer money, eatable items etc., to the burning pyre. These items are burnt partly or fully together with the deceased's body. However, some of the valuable items like gold are just placed in the smoke of the burning pyre. These items are then taken out and reused.

It is also said that there are no immediate cremation of the deceased among the Khasis, if she/he died from some unnatural cause. They bury the dead for few months and then perform the cremation following the making of cist burial (Mitri, 2016). From this residue, they look for small pieces of bones which are not completely burnt. Four or five persons collect all these pieces of bones. The collected bones are put together in betel leaves only. Sometimes, they wash it. Women from the deceased's family sit nearby the crematorium. They prepare a clean white cloth to collect all the bones. The bones are collected and wrapped inside this white cloth.

Primary Burial Stone

Due to matrilineal descent, the collected bones of the deceased are carried by the youngest daughter or niece, in case of a male, from the cremation ground. The bones are then handed over to the eldest maternal uncle when she reaches the burial stone. The role of the maternal uncle in the life of the Jaintias is enormous — since birth to death and even in after-life. He is the only person who is to collect the bones from his niece and deposit it in the burial stone. He is accompanied by one religious specialist or elder who guides the recitation of saying goodbye to the deceased's soul from this world of living to the new world of ancestor's spirits/souls. He deposits the deceased's bones into the burial stone. Following the deposition, family members, relatives, and friends offer flowers, money, some eatable items to the burial stone where the deceased's bone is placed. Only men take part in the ritual. Women are also allowed to offer these items during the internment. These items are specially given to the deceased's soul with the concept of using them in her/his afterlife journey to the new world. This ritual, the Jaintias believe, will allow the deceased's soul to go happily and in peace.

The primary burial stone differs from village to village. It is represented by cairns (in Shangpung, Raliang, Niawkamai and Mukroh), and by dolmen or dolmenoid cist (in Nangbah). But in Nongtalang of southern Jaintia Hills, primary burial stone is an individual dolmen and if the deceased is male then it is accompanied by one standing stone behind the dolmen. This burial stone is made by relatives/villagers during the cremation. While the cremation is going on, some elders/youths of the clans clean the primary burial stone and the area near it.

Most of these places where burial stones lie are located inside an assigned place of the village. Every clan in Jaintia villages have separate cremation grounds near the clan burial stones (e.g. Nongtalang, Nangbah) and they are located inside an assigned clan area. In some villages, they are located at some distance away from the burial stones (e.g. Nartiang, Shangpung). A common crematorium made by modern cemented bricks is also seen in Nartiang, Nangbah and Shangpung. These places are considered sacred except in Nongtalang village. It is believed, that all the dead souls or ancestors of the village will meet and stay in their respective burial places. Thus, each of the matrilineal clans have their own plot for placement of a burial stone and a crematorium. However, inter-village differences are also seen in the study areas.

Secondary Burial Stone

The bones are taken out from primary burial stones and transferred into a secondary burial stone, after a period of one to three years. This is the last and final rite of the deceased's soul in order to reach the permanent burial stone of the clan. The collection and deposition of clansmen/women's bones is under the leadership of the clan elders, but in Nongtalang village it is held together on the same day, by all clans under the guidance of the *lyngdoh* (high priest) of the village. The transference of bones into the final resting burial stone is accompanied by feasts and offerings. In case of many individuals (bones) to be transferred, a big feast is prepared. It requires a large number of pigs, and a large amount of local rice beer, betel leaves, areca nuts, rice cakes, tea etc. The cooked food is first offered to the clan's ancestors and souls of the deceased. The food is then consumed by the living kin of the clan. This feast follows a prayer to the ancestors for their good journey to the after-life. At the same time, this is a ritual of joy and happiness. The deceased's family invites relatives to witness, to console the departed soul, and to share the happiness of the ancestors' reunion. The ritual is undertaken by lineal descendents and a sign to the deceased souls to stay together with their ancestors. Thus, it brings the unification and solidarity of all the clan's souls/ spirits in the secondary burial stone.

This secondary burial stone of the clan is the final destination of all the deceased souls belonging to one clan. The demarcation of burial stones according to clan is clearly seen in some villages, especially in Nartiang and Raliang. The strong bond of clan members symbolises the clan's identity and unity of lineal kinship even after death. Though the secondary clan's burial stones are found in plenty, they are in dilapidated condition. Most of these structures are broken and some abandoned. Non-practice of this ritual over a long period of time relegates the tradition to the background. The present generation does not know the processes and hymns involved in this ritual. The structure of this clan burial stone or bone repository is either a dolmen or a dolmenoid cist. But the structures are slightly different from one village to another. Thus, post-cremation/funerary ritual is related to megaliths and so it forms an important part of their religious and socio-cultural beliefs of mortuary behaviour.

Discussion

Traditionally, there are no known figures or figurines of worship among the Jaintias. According to Tylor (1871), animism might have originated from the context of dreams and the belief in the deceased's soul. Likewise, not gods or goddesses but the souls of the deceased become part of Jaintia life. Probably, they started conducting rituals connected to the dead and their souls. Ancestors or dead souls are also the centre of origin of animism and thus knowingly and unknowingly become a part of Jaintia religion known as *Niamtre*. The mortuary practices are associated with belief systems limited to the religious concept and ideology (Binford, 1971), and thus this practice is a part of the cultural whole.

Death and its rituals are directly connected to the social life (Abramovitch, 2001). Even though the ancestors or souls leave the world, they supposedly take care of their descendents. Offerings to the souls and accompanying rituals are important traditions followed by the living descendents. This is to make the deceased happy. This happy soul turns into a good spirit and brings fortune to the living; however, the evil spirit roams around and brings misfortune. An unseen bond thus exists between the living and the dead continuously throughout generations. Thus, they are active agents in the life of the living.

Among Jaintias, the mortuary practices and burial stones are two sides of a coin. Each clan has their respective burial stone. The primary burial stone is used for temporary period whereas the secondary clan burial stone is the final resting and bone depositing stone. The primary burial stones are represented by cairns, dolmen/ dolmenoid cists, individual burial stones, and even a tree (as seen in Nartiang). However, secondary burial stones are represented by flat stones, and dolmen/dolmenoid cists. These bones are transferred permanently to the secondary clan burial stones after a period of time. The time period of this transference of bones depends on the clan and sometimes on the village, if they want to have the ritual together as a whole. This clan burial stone is the only place/house where all the deceased souls of a clan stay in the after-life. It is believed that they cannot go and stay in another clan stone. Thus, the clan plays an important role in mortuary practices. The unity/ solidarity, and clan's identity among the clansmen/women even after life, is clearly symbolized in the clan burial stone. It is widely believed that the reunion of all deceased's souls of a clan take place here and they become the ancestors of this clan and their respective families. The deposition of bone in the clan stone is the sign of matrilineal kinship solidarity (Mawlong, 2004; Meitei & Marak, 2015) and a sign of respect (Mawlong, 2004).

Among Jaintias, religion plays the main role in traditional mortuary practices. It was the colonisation of British in the region which simultaneously brought Christianity through the missionaries. The last Jaintia kingdom was annexed by the British in 1835 AD (Lamare, 2005). Since then, a large number have started converting to Christianity. Though conversion takes place continuously, there are many who still believe deeply in their traditional practices and beliefs. This new faith/belief brings indirect impact to the traditional mortuary practice. Apart from this, there are other factors which affect this tradition — such as urbanisation, modernisation, education, modern economy etc.

Concluding Remarks

Death is followed by a series of rites, rituals, emotions, mourning, and all these become a part of mortuary behaviour everywhere. This behaviour of the society is directly associated with religion and belief. Traditional rituals and practices surround the phenomena of death in societies across the world, including the Jaintias of Jaintia Hills. According to lore, the deceased soul turns into a good spirit and eventually an ancestor, through this ritual process only. The ancestor is the agent of guiding the living. They are believed to be responsible for bringing fortune or misfortune to the descendents, and therefore, an unseen bond between the dead and the living is witnessed.

The deposition of the deceased's bones in clan/individual burial stone and transference to a secondary burial stone permanently makes the mortuary behaviours of Jaintias an interesting process. It clearly shows the unity and solidarity of clansmen even in the world of the dead souls. It is likely that the origin of Jaintia religion, *Niamtre*, might have sprung from this mortuary behaviour.

The traditional mortuary behaviours have been affected by a number of agents that entered in the life of the Jaintias since the recent past. Additionally, there are inter-village differences due to geographical space (Meitei & Marak, 2015), but as a whole, the internal ideology, concept, and belief system remain the same.

REFERENCES

Abramovitch, H., 2001. "Sociology of Death and Dying". In N.J. Smelser and P.B. Baltes (eds.), *International Encyclopaedia of the Social and Behavioural Sciences*. Berlin: Palo Alto, pp. 3266-70.

Bareh, H., 1967. *History and Culture of the Khasi People*. Calcutta: Naba Murdan Private Ltd.

Bezbaruah, D., 2003. *Megalithic Ruins in Karbi Anglong District, Assam: A Study in the Context of Karbi Culture*. Ph.D. thesis, Gauhati University, Guwahati Assam.

Bickler, S.H. and B. Ivuyo. 2002. "Megaliths of Muyuw (Woodlark Island), Milne Bay Province PNG". *Archaeology in Oceania*, 37 (1): 22-36.

Binford, L.R., 1971. "Mortuary Practices: Their Study and Their Potential". In James A. Brown (ed.), *Approaches to the Social Dimensions of Mortuary Practices.* Memoirs of the Society for American Archaeology 1. Washington, DC: Society for American Archaeology, pp. 6-29.

Childe, V. G., 1958. *The Prehistory of European Society*. Harmondsworth: Penguin Books.

Choudhury, K., 2004. *The Megalithic and Their Associated Remains in Dimoria Area of Kamrup District, Assam*. Ph.D. thesis, Gauhati University, Guwahati, Assam.

Curet, L. A. and J. R. Oliver. 1998. "Mortuary Practices, Social Development, and Ideology in Precolumbian Puerto Rico". *Latin American Antiquity*, 9(3): 217–39.

Devi, P. B., 2011. *The Megalithic Culture of Manipur*. Delhi: Agam Kala Prakashan.

Fürer-Haimendorf, C. von., 1945. "The Problem of Megalithic Cultures in Middle India". *Man in India*, 26(2): 73–90.

Frazer, J.G., 1886. "On Certain Burial Customs as Illustrate of the Primitive Theory of the Soul". *Journal of Royal Anthropological Institute of Great Britain and Ireland*, 15: 64-104.

Gardener, K.M., 1988. *Mortuary Practices and Death Beliefs: The Effects of the Culture Group as a System*. M.A. Dissertation, Texas A & M University.

Gurdon, P.R.T. [1907] 2012. *The Khasis*. New Delhi: Akanksha Publishing House.

Iguaz, D., 1993. "Mortuary Practices Among the Aztec in the Light of Ethnohistorical and Archaeological Sources". *Paper from the Institute of Archaeology*, 4:63-76.

Ingham, J.M., 2001. "Psychological Anthropology". In N.J. Smelser and P. B. Baltes (eds.), *International Encyclopedia of the Social and Behavioural Sciences*. Berlin: Palo Alto, pp. 12349–55.

Jamir, T., 2004. "Megaliths of Nagaland: Reflections of Material Milieu and Social Values". In M. Momin and C.A. Mawlong (eds.), *Society and Economy in North East India*, Volume I. New Delhi: Regency Publications, pp. 105–117.

Jamir, W., 1998. "Megaliths in Nagaland". *Puratattva*, 28: 104–10.

Lamare, S.N., 2005. *The Jaintias: Studies in Society and Changes*. New Delhi: Regency Publications.

Marak, Q., 2012. "Megaliths of North East India". In T.B. Subba (ed.), *Anthropology of North East India*. New Delhi: Orient Longman Private Limited, pp. 34-52.

Mawlong, C.A., 1996. *Megalithic Monuments of Khasi-Jaintia Hills: An Ethnoarchaeology Study*. Ph.D. Thesis, North Eastern Hill University, Shillong.

______. 2004. "Megaliths and Social Formation in Khasi-Jaintia Hills". In M. Momin and C.A. Mawlong (eds.), *Society and Economy in North East India*, Volume I. New Delhi: Regency Publications, pp. 35-57.

Meitei, A.M. and Marak, Q., 2013. "A Study on Megalithic Burial Stones from Jaintia Hills, Meghalaya". *South Asian Anthropologist*, 13 (2): 157-66.

_____. 2015. "A Study of Traditional Mortuary Practices of the Jaintias of Meghalaya, India". *Journal of Indo-Pacific Archaeology*, 39: 74-80.

Mitri, M.B., 2016. *The Living Megalithic Culture of Khasi-Jaintia Hills Meghalaya.* Shillong: Don Bosco Publications.

Mizoguchi, K., 1993. "Time in the Reproduction of Mortuary Practices". *World Archaeology*, 25(2): 223-35.

Peterson, F., 1972. "Traditions of Multiple Burial in Late Neolithic and Early Bronze Age England". *Archaeological Journal*, 129: 22-56.

Playfair, A., 1998 [1909]. *The Garos*. Delhi: Spectrum Publications.

Porter, A., 2002. "The Dynamics of Death: Ancestors, Pastoralism, and the Origins of a Third-Millennium city in Syria". *Bulletin of the American School of Oriental Research,* 325: 1-36.

Rao, S.N., 1991. "Megalithic Practices among Khasis and Nagas of North Eastern India". In J.P. Singh and G. Sengupta (eds.), *Archaeology of North Eastern India*. New Delhi: Vikas Publishing House, pp. 106-24.

Roy, D. 1963. "The Megalithic Culture of the Khasis". *Anthropos*, 58(34): 520–56.

Singh, O.K., 1985. "A Live Megalithic Culture in Manipur". In V. N. Misra and P. Bellwood (eds.), *Recent Advances in Indo-Pacific Prehistory: Proceedings of the International Symposium held at Poona,* December 19-21, 1978. New Delhi: Oxford & IBH Publishing Company, pp. 491-96.

Tylor, E.B., 1871. *Primitive Culture*. London: John Murray.

Ucko, P.J., 1969. "Ethnography and Archaeological Interpretation of Funerary Remains". *World Archaeology*, 1(2): 262-80.

10
The Sociology of Stones in Nagaland

Jelle J.P. Wouters

The very moment a person removes a boulder from its natural position and puts it to use — functionally, ceremonially, or otherwise — it transforms from a natural object into a cultural artefact that derives contextual meaning and significance. The stone is extracted from nature — even while still part of it — shed from its empty existence, and woven into the material and social fabric of a community. Saying so is no different from the axiom that a person may enter the world in a natural state with a biological profile, but immediately after birth acquires a cultural identity. In terms of functionality, stones, as anyone with even the scantiest knowledge of archaeology (including myself) knows, were chipped, scrapped, and flaked by our early ancestors into tools used for gathering, scavenging and hunting, thus starting a protracted process, extending over centuries, during which early humans perfected the art of stone tool-making. However, the practical usages of stones, or the technicalities of stone tool-making, are not my prime concern here. What I am interested to explore are the ceremonial, commemorative, and magical connotations of stones, or what is often loosely called 'megalithic culture', and so with an ethnographic focus on Nagaland.

"If commodities, like persons, have social lives" (Appadurai, 1986: 3), and if individual biographies can be found tied up in objects (Hoskins, 1998), this chapter will illustrate how for the Naga monoliths and other stones are invested with social histories, culturally inflected values, as well as personal biographies. Hence, a study of the social lives of such stones can provide a window into the past, casting rays of light unto a history that has gone largely unwritten and undocumented, although not, of course, unremembered as rich repertoires of oral history flourish from one Naga village to the next. Among the Naga, I draw my ethno-historical and ethnographic insights from a Chakhesang village I shall call Phugwumi (but which remains better known as Kikrüma), and whose inhabitants are the repositories and enactors of a rich megalithic culture with monoliths of various sizes, forms, and significances dotted in and around the village. Within Phugwumi, as among the Naga more widely, the local command of monoliths lies in their robustness. They withstand and endure, unlike wood that rots, clay that dissembles, and unlike humans who decompose.

As early as 1926, J.H. Hutton, then Deputy Commissioner in the colonial Naga Hills, recognised the significance of stones in Naga cosmology, social organisation, rituals, besides their economic usages. He subsequently divided the Naga usage of stones in three types: utilitarian, ceremonial/commemorative, and magical (1926: 71). This division largely holds true today, even though the advent of Christianity has challenged the magical qualities, both benevolent and malevolent, associated with certain stones, and even though, as Hutton also knew, a single stone can have multiple purposes and meanings, thus defying any neat categorization. To illustrate, the elongated and neatly arranged barrage of stones, piled up one above the other into a level, bench-like shape in Phugwumi is not only the memorial of a reputed villager whose family, after his demise, was sufficiently well endowed to slaughter pigs and oxen and distribute the meat (a funeral practice of the wealthy locally called *thüpre* and in commemoration of which villagers had carried and piled the stones), but also became a 'utilitarian' place for villagers to sit and talk. As this chapter unfolds we will discuss multiple types of stones as they have been erected or found in places across Phugwumi.

More broadly, this chapter posits that in a society whose history has largely gone undocumented, as is the case for the Naga, except the incidental jottings found in Ahom *Buranjis* (Tai-Ahom records), chronicles of Manipuri royal courts, and nascent writings of British civil and military officers, the uncovering of sociology and social history of stones — Why were they erected? By whom? And what meanings and values do they embody? — may offer insightful views into local histories. The pages that follow contain conjectural history, or "as told by village elders." However, given that each ethno-historical section we will discuss tends to be subject to multifarious interpretations, conjectures, and indeterminacies, my understanding of them remains best understood along the lines of Edmund Leach who once wrote that: "It is not the anthropologist's task to write history, but if history is to be elaborated with the aid of inspired guesses the special knowledge of the anthropologist becomes relevant so as to point up the probabilities" (1960: 49).

Megalithic Culture in Nagaland

In placing and tracing Naga origins, V.K. Nuh (2002: 1-2) takes Nagas' megalithic culture as a point of departure, and went so far as claiming that:

> "The Nagas were probably the original megalith builders and many of the megaliths that were erected over the world from Europe to America to South-East Asia and Middle East, were in all likelihood erected by them. The reason for this conclusion is not that the raising of megaliths is immune to independent origin, but that these megaliths are connected with a definite and united culture, called the Naga culture."

Nuh's conclusion is presumptuous, to say the least, even though in proposing some sort of universal, uniform megalithic culture he is not far off an argument proposed by C.B. Clarke (1874: 482) based on his study of monoliths in the Khasi Hills. "In all modern treatises of Archaeology and Anthropology the study of monumental stones form an important chapter", he wrote, then continued:

> "Monuments of a remarkable similarity in design are found alike in Europe, Asia, and isolated islands in the Pacific Ocean, and these are in general of such extreme antiquity that they are treated as belonging to the prehistoric age… It is reasonably suspected that a careful study of the Khasi method of raising stones, and of the traditions or customs in according with which they raise them, may throw some light upon more ancient monuments of the same kind, even upon Stonehenge."

Such fanciful speculations aside, amongst the first to research, in some depth, Naga megalithic culture was Major Godwin Austen (1872) who was otherwise known for his detailed descriptions of Khasi stone monuments. First entering the Naga Hills, he was astonished to find that certain Naga communities, the Angami Naga among them, similarly erected upright stone monuments.[1] More fascinating still, to the eyes of Godwin Austen, was that while among the Khasi he had noticed that the custom was "fast dying out", among the Nagas it appeared "in full force" (1875: 144). Colonel Woodthorpe, who travelled far and wide among the Nagas during the second half of the 19th century, similarly expressed his astonishment. He jotted: "[these stones] are either monumental or simply commemorative of some big feast given by a rich man" (more in the next section). The pulling and raising of such monoliths, Woodthorpe observed, demanded great amounts of collective effort on part of villagers who often had to bring them from the river bed or patches of jungle far away:

> "These stones are often of great size, and are dragged up into place on wooden sledges shaped like the prow of a boat, the keel curving upwards. On this sledge the stone is levered, and carefully lashed with canes and creepers, and to this the men, sometimes to the number of several hundreds, attached themselves in a long line, and putting rollers beneath the sledge, they pull it along until it has been brought to the spot where the stone is to be erected" (Woodthorpe, 1881: 54).

But if this custom already struck early travellers and administrators as remarkable, what went altogether beyond them was that stones were perceived as either dead or alive, male or female, and were occasionally addressed, indeed talked to. Hutton wrote how among the Naga stones had a spirit, or a soul, and that it was possible for a stone to decease: "some of them split when burnt, others merely change colour, but in both cases the stone is considered dead, and the virtue departed" (1926: 81-2). A stone could also decease through defamation. On a visit to the Chakhesang Naga village of Khezhakenoma, Hutton had stumbled upon a miraculous dolmen on which paddy laid to dry was said to double in quantity. But not so anymore, the villagers confided. About why the stone had ceased to perform its miracles, Hutton received multiple narrations:

> "The miraculous power was ended, according to one account, by lighting a fire round it, although others say that it was defecated upon, or, again, menstruated upon, or according to a third version, a childless and barren couple performed the sexual act on it" (1926: 82).

While the exact reason thus remained obscure, all villagers agreed that the stone had died. Roughly half a century earlier, Lieutenant Barron (1872) had narrated an event in which two pairs of stones were brought before him by a Naga gentleman. "[They] fell from the heavens" (1872: xii), the owner had explained. Upon inquiry from multiple sources, including passing Fakials and Shans from neighbouring Burma, Barron discovered that one pair of the stones had already deceased: "they evidently thought that some virtue had gone out of [it]" (*ibid.*). The other stone was still considered alive. As the dead stone had become useless, the man agreed to let Lieutenant Barron purchase it "at half the price of No. 1 [the stone still alive]" (*ibid.*: xiii).

As already mentioned in passing, stones were also gendered and male and female stones were treated differently. Witnessing a stone-pulling ceremony in Kohima village, Hutton (1922: 246) observed how one of the two stones was designated as male and the other as female. As they were laced with creepers onto a sledge in preparation of being pulled from the jungle to the village, the stones were addressed the following: "Your place is not here. We have made another for you. You must go to that which we have made for you. Go lightly and go quickly!" (*ibid.*). Throughout the proceedings, Hutton observed how "the male stone took precedence", and while the pullers of the female stone were few and ordinarily dressed, the pullers of the male stones were many and dressed in full attire including headgear (*ibid.*).

This cultural and symbolic significance of stones had a wide-spread across the region now known as India's North East, and was extensively written about during the colonial era. The very richness of such accounts made J.P. Mills declare, in 1933, that "An archaeological characteristic of Assam [then including the Naga Hills] of worldwide fame is the wealth of megaliths" (*cf.* Marak, 2012: 36). But if extensively written about in colonial accounts, in recent decades megalithic culture has received little attention among the Naga and India's North East more widely, bar a splendid recent overview by Marak (2012). For the Naga, this contemporary neglect appears in parts related to the notion, propagated in certain circles, that stone rituals and beliefs are part and parcel of a non-Christian past, a period some seek to denounce, perhaps unfortunately so, as 'heathen worship' that is best forgotten. And yet, the sections that follow seek to illustrate for Phugwumi that the stories and meanings behind monoliths can foster crucial historical insights, while new monoliths continue to be erected, albeit for different reasons than they were in the past.

Stones of Merit

A crucial function of megaliths in Phugwumi was to commemorate the generosity of feast-givers. "This is so and so", *Athe* (a classificatory Chokri term for grandfather), and who I accompanied often on walks around the village, would point to a monolith and utter the name of a villager long deceased. "He was a wealthy man in his time. The owner of fertile fields and abundant harvests. For several times he feasted the entire village." During the feast-giver's life-time, the stone *Athe* now pointed to was erected as a testimony to his generosity and the elevated social standing that came with dispensing one's wealth in the form of successive feasts. Even if the feast-giver himself had long deceased, the monolith continued to commemorate and venerate his deeds, and was a continuing source of esteem for his progeny and the wider clan he had belonged to. There were many such monoliths — which we may call "stones of merit" — skirting the outskirts of the village, and *Athe*, akin to most village elders, seemed to know the story of the particular feast-giver behind them all. The practice of "Feast of Merit", or *zhotho muza* as it was called in Phugwumi, was written about widely during the colonial era, and was seen as a key insight into the Naga social set-up, even though not all Naga tribes practiced it, or did so in the same way. The first trained anthropologist to study the Naga, Christoph von Fürer-Haimendorf, doing so in the 1930s, wrote about "hundreds and thousands of megalithic monuments" with each of them erected to commemorate the 'fame' and 'generosity' of a particular feast-giver (1939: 19). On further inquiry he found that, among the Nagas, one's social status and standing did not rely on the accumulation of wealth, but that social ascendance could be achieved through a person dispensing his wealth by throwing lavish feasts, a social institution that came to be recognized as the Naga "Feast of Merit."

For an aspirant villager to climb the social ladder, to expand his sway and have his voice heard more loudly in the village, a single feast would hardly do the trick. However, in the course of his lifetime an ambitious person was expected to provide a series of feasts. These feasts were ritually sanctioned with each of them allowing the feast-giver a further display of his rising social standing. In Phugwumi, it would start with a feast-giver's right to wear a specifically embroidered shawl (*thüpükhü*), followed by the permission, as he continued his feast-giving, to decorate his house with horns and carvings, to ultimately large monoliths being erected in his name. On a tour through the Eastern Angami area, now Chakhesang, Fürer-Haimendorf wrote how he stumbled onto a large open compound with houses on two sides:

> "Cross barge-boards rose from the gables of one of the houses, like the enormous antlers of some proud stag. Proud, too, must have been the owner of these wooden horns, for they showed that he had given several of those expensive feasts of merit whereby the Naga rises in social prestige and in the esteem of his neighbours" (1939: 9).

In Phugwumi, a complete series would involve nine feasts, after which a row of nine monoliths would have been erected in the feast-giver's name (the first stone would be erected after the fourth feast), a life-long exercise that involved such grandiose expenditures that only three villagers are remembered to have ever accomplished this (Züüzü Yhobu, Lemu Tunyi and Thinou Puro). In fact, most villagers would never find themselves in the position to throw a single feast, and instead relied on the village wealthy to, now and then, enable them to lavish on meat and rice beer. As Fürer-Haimendorf explained:

> "The wealth of the ambitious was employed to provide food and enjoyment for the less prosperous members of the community, for at a feast of merit there was meat, rice and rice beer for every man, woman and child in the village" (1939: 47).

In addition to wealth and social status, Jamir, more recently, asserted the importance of ideas on fertility in connection with the Naga feast of merit. He sees megaliths as "vehicles of fertility":

> "Apart from the fundamental idea of fertility being deeply manifested in agriculture, sex, death and martial prowess, simultaneously, there exists a clear connection with the monolithic erections, where feasting is functionally related to this elusive concept. In fact, on the whole, they often maintain a cyclical motion" (2004: 109).

While few villagers were able, everyone aspired to be a feast-giver, and this ambition, the colonial officer J.P. Mills wrote, had a stimulating impact on local agriculture among the Naga. It is worth quoting him at some length:

> "...the essence of this system [feast of merit] is that every male Naga, if he is to acquire merit and status in this world and the next, must give a series of feasts, every detail of which is strictly prescribed... they begin with the sacrifice of a pig and end with that of at least one domestic bison garnished, so to speak, with quantities of cattle and pigs. An immense amount of rice and rice beer is consumed, and more rice than money goes to the buying of the animals. The feasts, therefore directly simulate agriculture. More important still are the privileges they win for the giver. At stated stages in the series he and his wife gain the right to wear special cloths, which increase in splendour and in the elaborateness of their embroidery the further he advances. He is also entitled to embellish his house with carved posts and beams. It is important to remember that, no matter how rich a man may be, he can win the rights to these cloths and carvings only by giving feasts" (1935: 134).

Seen as a historical social institution, the feast of merit thus seemingly invoked contradictory principles, combining tendencies of economic redistribution and social differentiation, of both socialism and snobbery, but crucially it vested social eminence in a person's ability to act as a provider, not, say, in mere accruing.

It is the abolishment of the feast of merit by mostly American and Welsh missionaries who (mis)interpreted them as an ostentatious wastage of wealth and its free flowing rice beer as inspiring immoralities sorts, that has contributed, so it appears, to a subversion of values, one that stretches from a moral economy of ritualized redistribution to one of clueless accumulation with rich farmers harvesting more paddy than they can possibly eat but without any longer an outlet to distribute it in reward for social ascendance. The alternative of selling one's self-cultivated paddy on the market, while occasionally done, is an option less preferred, and if the ability to redistribute was both a sign and a duty of being rich in the past, today it is the presence of multiple *khi* (a large bamboo barn to store paddy) brimmed with paddy that denotes a person's agricultural skill and wealth, even if some of the *khi* now contain paddy grown too old and musky to eat. The abolishment of the feasts of merit had other consequences too. The same J.P. Mills commented: "a great number of very fine embroidery patterns and carvings designs owe their existence entirely to this system of feast of merit and will continue to exist only as long as the system does" (1935: 134), then lamenting: "one has only to stroll through a Christian village. There may be many rich men with granaries bursting with rice, but not a fine cloth or carving you will see" (*ibid.*).

In Phugwumi today some village elders vividly recall, and feel nostalgic to the feasts of merit they witnessed in their youth. A number of Phugwumi houses still flaunt the meticulously carved wooden walls and cross barge-boards distinctive of the house of a feast-giver. But in Phugwumi, too, the advent of Christianity had demanded sacrifices, and after the majority of the villagers had taken to the new religion (the first villager converted in 1947 but in sizeable numbers from the late 1950s onward), the practice of feast of merit saw a steep decline, and then died out completely. Except perhaps, somewhat paradoxically, on Christmas Day when a Christianized version — that is a feast without its traditionally characteristic ingredient of rice-beer — is invariably organised for the Church congregation by a wealthy villager, usually a politician, successful contractor, or a high-ranking government officer, and while the feast-giver is no longer honoured with a monolith erected in his name, he is still offered a shawl and subsequently collectively prayed for during the Christmas service.

Stones of War

"At the time of the first British acquaintance with them [the Nagas]", Hutton (1965: 19) wrote, then continued: "many villages were still isolated from their neighbours by thickly forested hills and by rivers unfordable for several months in the year, and they tended to be on terms of head-hunting warfare with their nearest neighbours, or at best of an armed and ever suspect truce, almost every village being an independent political entity." Phugwumi's pre-colonial history, indeed, is a history of warriors, raids, and inter-village wars over local status, standing and dominance. Phugwumi's geographical location, perched high on a hilltop from where it stands guard over its neatly excavated paddy fields below, while of inconvenience in several ways (especially in terms of water scarcity), helped the village grow into a strong powerhouse as enemies could be spotted from afar while the steep, rocky slope made for a natural defence wall. By the time British forces surveyed the Naga Hills, Phugwumi had established itself as a monopolistic protection racket that was known and feared widely. It levied tribute from surrounding villages, while it raided many others. Its local hegemony, however, took a blow when it was attacked, and subdued, by a British-led force on the 11th of February, 1851 (Butler, 1855: 208-10), a battle which has gone down as amongst the most ferocious and bloodiest fought in the Naga Hills (Wouters, 2015), and which, in measures, may have contributed to the non-interference policy the British Government adopted towards the Naga just a month later (Puro, 2008). Some stones in the village, this section will illustrate, remember of this chapter of village history, which is often referred to, somewhat crudely, as its "head-hunting period", a feat that was, back then, commonly reported across Naga villages.

In the vicinity of one of Phugwumi's old village gates, of which there were traditionally six, made of large boards of wood decorated skilfully with skulls carved upside down, a stone protrudes the rocky slope. Unlike the stones nearby, this one displays an exhaustive pattern of lines, carved there with sharp spear-points. Some of the lines are thin, probably carved with single scratch. Others are etched deeper, the result of multiple scrapes. What these lines represent are human heads, or, to be precise, enemy heads decapitated by Phugwumi warriors. Each successful warrior — with success here measured in his ability to cut a head — was, on his return to the village, to cross the village gate and scratch his spear on this particular stone, one scratch for each head. The deeper lines, hence, belonged to Phugwumi's most renowned, and most feared, past warriors. Back then, the capturing of a head was not only an act of war, it was also interpreted as a sign of prowess, masculinity, as well as a harbinger of fertility — heads contained 'soul-matter' as Hutton (1928: 403) termed it, which fertilized the village — and an act ritually sanctioned through subsequent war-dances and ceremonies within the village (*see* Fürer-Haimendorf, 1939).

The British 'pacification' (a colonial euphemism for the slaying and subduing of recalcitrant populations) of Phugwumi, and of the Naga Hills more widely, added by the gradual infusion of Christian practices and principles, brought a halt to such erstwhile head-hunts, and not a few in Phugwumi now refer to the old village gate and the stone as an eerie place best avoided. That said, narratives of past battles, heroic deeds, and brave warriors remain an essential part of Phugwumi's repertoire of oral history. The names of the brothers Nyiho and Müshuirü, and of Yosü and Masa, among many others past warriors, for instance, continue to be recalled in the village, and remain part of the general knowledge children in the village receive as they grow up, even though multiple generations have now gone by.

Yet another example of stones that link to Phugwumi's "head-hunting past" can be found in two stones found at the village outskirts. Oral history tells that these stones, today overgrown with scrubs, were once reputed warriors belonging to the neighbouring Sumi tribe then bent on invading Phugwumi. Arriving at night, and in large numbers, the Sumi warriors intended to attack the village by surprise. Before launching their assault, they, however, dispatched two of their bravest warriors to explore the village defence barriers to find the most suitable place to launch their attack. The two Sumi warriors were never to return. This was not because they were spotted and slain by Phugwumi villagers but because, the story goes, they met a spirit benevolent to Phugwumi which instantly recognised the looming danger and froze them into stones. As both warriors did not return, the other Sumi warriors took this as a bad omen and abstained from attacking the village.

Stones of Peace

If inter-village hostilities, raids, and wars were part of pre-state village life, so were pacts of peace. Over time, Phugwumi engaged in peace deals with multiple villages, both with direct neighbours and those at further distance. One such treaty remains symbolized in an elongated monolith erected in the middle of the village, and which asserts and reasserts the peace between Phugwumi and the Angami Naga village of Mezoma. This peace treaty, agreed in 1880, had been preceded by numerous bouts of raids and violence, often lethal in their effects. As the peace was concluded it was further resolved that once every generation (counted as thirty years) the villagers would meet, taking turns in hosting and visiting, to commemorate the peace with lavish feasts, traditional dances, and games, a practice which continues till date with the last such fraternity conducted in Phugwumi in 2011.

Erecting a stone to commemorate a peace treaty was common practice among the Naga. During the colonial era, Captain Butler witnessed such a ceremony and wrote how a "stone of peace" was erected along with the words: "As long as this stone stands on the earth, no differences shall occur between us" (*cf.* Hutton, 1922: 146). In Phugwumi, elders recall that a peace-ceremony also involved an exchange of spears. In this ceremony, the eldest person of both villages would meet to gift and receive a spear, meticulously sharpened. Also part of concluding a peace was an oath-taking ceremony. The formula, also observed by Captain Butler, ran as follows:

> "If any man in my village break this peace first then, so long as water flows in my spring and so long as the sun and the moon remain in heaven, shall my men be defeated, and all the forest and red earth shall not be enough to cover my corpses and much blood shall flow on my side" (Butler cited in Hutton, 1922: 146).

Elders in Phugwumi narrate how their forefathers had undertaken a similar oath-taking ceremony with the Mezoma villagers, as well as with other villages they had concluded peace with, although the words spoken, while conveying the same spirit, could be somewhat different. The fact that such oaths were backed up by a 'self-curse' for its defaulters, and that they were spoken in public, made such treaties, in the vast majority of cases, durable.

Speaking more generally; oath taking was crucial to the political order not just between villages, but also within Phugwumi. The village's customary law, for instance, dictates that in case of suspected poisoning, of which cases occurred in the past, the defaulter, if identified, would face excommunication for a set number of years. If the accused was to deny the allegation, he would have to involve a close relative (for instance, his father, wife, son, or brother) and pledge his innocence by invoking a curse on both himself and his relative(s) was his plea to innocence not genuine. While variously remembered, the pledge could assume a formula like the following: "If I have really given the poison, then for all our years on this earth let us be cursed and let us not live happily like anyone else."

If inter-village wars and raids are now of a time bygone, memories and resentments between former enemies may linger, and which led two Chakhesang villages to embark on a road to reconciliation as recent as 2012 when the villages of Lazami and Phek announced their reconciliation in Nagaland's local dailies. Their jointly published statement read:

> "The Phek village and Lazami village along with Yorübami as a witness, consisting of Village Council, Church member, G.Bs, Elders and different organisations held a historicai meeting of 'Apology and Reconciliation'... for the past misdeeds committed by Lazami village of burning down Phek village houses many (9) times during Head Hunting Period."

Finally, it may be added that in the context of the Indo-Naga conflict, too, there exist "stones of peace" such as the monolith positioned in the middle of Mokokchung Town, and which symbolises and commemorates the most recent ceasefire (1997) between the Nationalist Socialist Council of Nagalim (IM) and the Central Government. Its inscription reads: "Peace Monument: Erected on August 1, 2004 on commemoration of cease-fire declaration in Nagalim on August 1, 1997."

Stones of Naga Nationalism

While grave-stones, and their inscriptions (a relatively recent practice), may not qualify as megalithic culture, in Phugwumi some of their inscriptions assume wider historical significance. Among them those who invoke the spirit of Naga nationalism that started to infuse the village from the 1950s onward, and during which a large number of villagers joined the ranks and files of the Naga National Council (NNC), which sought Independence from India.

While Naga political consciousness draws back well into the colonial era, it was on the 14th of August, 1947 that Naga spokespersons declared Naga Independence. India's newly Independent Government, however, immediately rejected the Naga proclamation, and when subsequent talks, negotiations, and attempted treaties failed, it dispatched its military and paramilitary forces to enclose the area. Then Director of the Indian Intelligence Bureau, B.N. Mullik recounted: "troops moved into Tuensang by October, 1955, and the war with the Nagas started from then" (cited in Vashum, 2000: 137). By that time, A.Z. Phizo, then President and ideologue of the Naga National Council, had already assembled a Naga Army which took to guerrilla tactics.

A large number of troops also moved into the Chakhesang area, which was known as an NNC stronghold. As noted, many in Phugwumi joined the Naga Movement, and some of its early cadres are still alive today. They now recall the times they took on the Army, even though they were outnumbered many times over. They also remember the long marches, often at nights, the days they had gone without adequate food, and the general hardship and misery that came with life in the jungle. Those villagers who did not join the Naga Army often helped the NNC in other ways, usually by donating and supplying foodstuffs, clothes, or monetary contributions to the cadres. Some inscriptions on grave stones in Phugwumi now remember of this period. Two of them read:

> "In loving memory of Mrs Chikhuhulu w/o Verhiyo. Born in 1908 she was chairperson in the region for Naga movement [women wing]. Her sacrificial deeds and courageous life given for the nation will be remembered by all. She left for her heavenly abode on 23 March, 1997."
>
> "In loving memory of Mr. Verhiyo Puro s/o Posuyo. Born in 1896 he represented Chakhesang tribe in Naga wrestling during British rule. He had donated a barn of paddy to NNC. He had seven sons and left for his heavenly abode on 21st April, 1992."

If conventional logic dictates that the little space available on grave stones is reserved for a person's most outstanding deeds, clearly supporting the Naga National Council (NNC) was, back then, construed as a higher and admirable good.

While the Naga Movement lingers, over the past decades its texture has changed. Today it stands fragmented into rivalling factions with feuds and assassinations between them causing regular headlines. Signs of this current chapter of the Naga Movement, too, are found on grave-stones within Phugwumi. The following two inscriptions are carved on the burial stones of two Phugwumi National Workers (members of the Naga underground) assassinated by a rivalling underground group:

> "In loving memory of Mr. Kuvetso Kezo s/o Sachi Kezo. First member in Chakhesang region to join in NSCN-IM, 1990. Served in the capacity of APO and Leacy till his voluntary retirement in 1997. A true and dedicated national worker. Died on 3rd October, 2007. A True and Dedicated National Worker."
>
> "Lt. Nuvotso Kezo s/o Lt. Huza Kezo of Kikruma village. 2nd Lieut — NSCN-IM. Join [*sic*] in 1995 at the very early stage who laid his life for our people on 3rd October, 2007. Served as youth Chairman Kikruma Town (2003)."

Seen from a wider angle, such open commemoration of the Naga Movement could be a risky undertaking in the past. To illustrate, in his memoirs the officer Dev, posted to Nagaland at a time of recurring clashes between the Indian and Naga armies, put himself on record stating: "[a source] of embarrassment during my stay at Mokokchung was the incident of the 'epitaphs.' " While touring Ao Naga villages, he noticed how numerous tombstones bore inscriptions such as "killed by the Indian Army" or "we gave our today for your tomorrow" (1988: 85). Representing the Government, Dev found such declarations an "awkward source of discomfiture" and subsequently ordered his subsidiary officers "to ensure that all such epitaphs were either erased or destroyed in a manner they thought fit" (*ibid.*). When one year later, Dev discovered that the same epitaphs where still there, he issued an ultimatum and decreed that all, what he considered to be, "offensive memorials" (*ibid.:* 86) be removed. Dev narrated:

> "There was initial resistance and much grumbling but this was soon overcome in a determined manner and all but two epitaphs disappeared... [however] the one at Aonokpu and the other at a village (the name of which I just cannot recall at this moment) remained. The day after I visited these two villages with a police force, had the memorials taken out, and imposed a fine of Rs. 10,000 on each village" (1988: 86).

The Missing Stone

Stones also figure centrally in many Naga folktales, often as part of origin and migration stories. The Ao Naga, for instance, tell their ancestors sprang up from six stones at a place called Longtrok, which is located in the vicinity of today's Chungliyimti village (Mills, 1926). Others point to a place called Makhel located in the presentday Mao Naga area of Manipur as either their point of origin or the place from where they dispersed. According to Shimray: "A majority of the Naga groups refer to their dispersal point to be Makhel. They erected megaliths at Makhel in memory of their having dispersed from there in various directions" (2007: 24). Again others refer to a mythical stone called *Tso Tawo* in the Chakhesang Naga village of Khezhakenoma and look upon this stone as signifying the place of their dispersal (Joshi, 2012: 32). Although, the origin and dispersal stories associated with Longtrok, Makhel and Khezhakenoma are all very different, megaliths are present in each of them, further pointing to their centrality in the Naga historical and cultural repertoire.

While bordering Khezakenoma, and neither situated very far from Makhel, the historical sequence of Phugwumi, as told by village elders, makes no explicit reference to Khezhakenoma and Makhel, although some elders invoke Makhel as a place their forefathers might have passed through. Before proceeding, it must be asserted that local origin and migration stories generally tend to be mired in controversies, are occasionally obscure, and always sites of contestations. Who founded the village? Where did the ancestors reside before they arrived in their present location? Which clan(s) came first? Which ones settled later, and when? Disagreements about such questions continue to fuel disputes across Naga areas, and writing about these is, therefore, hardly a straightforward exercise. In Phugwumi, too, while most agree on the general outlines of the village's origin story, elders may emphasize different nuances, tweak certain parts, or disagree about names and dates. What follows here is a rough and general depiction of Phugwumi's story, and while I think this version is agreeable to the majority of the villagers, it must be kept in mind that some in the village, if given the chance, might choose to tell it somewhat differently. What stands beyond doubt, however, is that the establishment of the village, its location chosen, in all versions told, was not a human act, but one divinely inspired.

Phugwumi's history draws back many centuries, and while most elders tell of ancestors in places across China and present day Myanmar, let us take up the story for our purposes in Phugwumi's previous dwelling, which is a place known as Chikriphüba, located close to where today's Angami Naga village of Viswema came to be established. For generations, narrations go, Chikriphüba offered its inhabitants a life of relative prosperity. The land was gentle and fertile, and a nearby pond provided sufficient water the year round. As a result, the village was growing in numbers, expanding its sway. This tranquillity and progress, however, came to be disturbed by a mammoth and ever-hungry snake which started to call home the nearby pond. At nights, the snake would conceal itself, but it would slide out of the pond during day time when all able-bodied men and women had gone to work in the fields outside the village. Sliding its way towards the bamboo and thatched houses the snake attacked and devoured the village's toddlers, swallowing them from head to toe. During this spell, not a few children went unaccounted for. At loss about the cause of the disappearances, one villager, known for his physical strength, was assigned to stay behind in the village during day-time to find the cause of the recent misfortune that had struck the village. Hiding on a roof, he witnessed the snake and its hunt after the village's toddlers. As life was turning increasingly miserable, a dream descended on a villager by the name Yinü Vero in which he was told:

> "If you do not leave this place all of you will not prosper and not multiply. There is a better place for you. To reach there you have to lead your people east-wards. As you go, carry with you one unblemished rooster and one dog. Walk until you have crossed two rivers. From the second river you must lift one stone and tie it tightly on your back with reeds. Then keep walking. At the chosen place, the place where you will

> prosper and multiply, the rooster will start crowing, the dog will bark, and the stone will fall of your back. This, and no other place, is where you should rebuild your village."

Yinü Vero obliged and persuaded the other villagers to follow him. With him, Yinü took the rooster and the dog as he had been instructed. When they reached the second river he lashed a stone on his back with reeds. Then they marched, waiting for the rooster to crow, the dog to bark, and the stone to let loose. To the north of present day Phugwumi, they stumbled upon a place Yinü and the others thought was perfect. The land was sprawling and gentle, not steep as the places they had hitherto crossed. Water appeared abundant too. But while the rooster crowed and the dog barked, the stone refused to fall from Yinü's back. Enthralled with the place, and of the prospect of building the village there, Yinü tried to challenge destiny by jumping and shaking his body, hoping that the stone would fall of his back. His efforts, however, were to no avail. As they continued their march they eventually reached a hillock, and it was there that the three divine signs — the rooster's crow, the dog's bark, and the stone falling — ensued simultaneously. Yinü and the others had found the place where they would live to thrive.

For many generations to follow the stone Yinü had lashed on his back remained on the exact spot where it had fallen off. That is, until recently. Until one morning the stone was no longer there. The year and date in which the stone went missing is hard to ascertain, but it might not have been that long ago given that some elders remember to have seen the stone, and can point to the place where it had once been. Within Phugwumi, the disappearance of the stone remains a case unresolved. Taken away by an individual for reasons best known to him? Divinely disappeared? Or simply misplaced (after all, it was not that large a stone)? Possibilities abound but no conclusions. The stone that had led Phugwumi's forefathers to their present location, and from where Phugwumi grew into a large and powerful village, has been declared missing.

Stones of Magic

Hutton (1926), as noted, differentiated the use of stones among the Naga between ceremonial (commemorative), utilitarian, and magical. This section concerns a brief discussion of the latter. Brief, in parts, because the advent of Christianity has worked to diminish the magical associations bestowed upon certain stones, or at least so in public discourse. And yet, most elders can tell of many stones, both large boulders and of the size of a hand's palm, to whom magical and spiritual qualities are thought to be invested, too many to list in full.

Such magical stones in the village were thought to have a life of their own. They came in different kinds, some benevolent, others malevolent. Some could give birth. A few claim to have witnessed it. Others accept that stones could give birth but never inside human purview. Young generations are more sceptical, and ascribe birth-giving stones to the realm of myths. In Phugwumi, one such type of 'magical stone' was called *thüvü,* blackish in colour and shiny in appearance. This stone, traditional knowledge conveys, was inhabited by a spirit, or a soul, and which transferred its qualities unto the person who possessed it. The substance of these qualities could vary including a disposition towards accumulating wealth, an innate propensity to stealing, to emanating a charm near irresistible to women. The owner of the particular stone near mechanically became submerged by the stone's 'nature', and over time developed great affection for it, regardless of the stone's nature being benign or malign. A person who possessed a *thüvü* associated with stealing, for instance, soon turned into a kleptomaniac. No matter how wealthy the owner of the stone might be, or how severely the villagers might punish him for his deeds, he or she would not cease roving about. As such, the owner did not own the stone, but the stone owned the owner. The only remedy was to search the house, locate the stone, and destroy it; episodes which are remembered in the village.

Another stone, larger in size, that was allotted spiritual powers was called *Kütsütapfü*, or "open-mouth stone", which referred to its shape which resembled an open mouth. Inside this stone, so it was said, spirits lived and strange sounds could be heard when putting one's ear close to it. The spirits inside were thought of as malevolent, and soon those villagers brave enough challenged this stone, and the spirits inside, by uttering insults and making demeaning postures in front of it. Over time, daring this stone turned into a sign of prowess, and the story went that only those with the required braveness and internal strength could challenge the stone and remain unhurt. To the contrary, a person failing to have such strength, but still challenging the stone, would instantly feel his muscles tightening, and worse.

Other stones could occasionally give off good signs such as one called *Thicho-o Zerütsü*. It lies in the jungle and is the stone on which a particular spirit was said to sharpen his dagger. When villagers would set out for hunting and notice on the stone that the spirit had recently used it, it was taken as a sign of good fortune in terms of the hunt. A final 'magical stone' I wish to highlight is the *Chimhümi Thivü Rasüh Tsü*, which is a stone on top of which, in days now bygone, the eastern phratry of the village (the western phratry had their own place) would perform the sacrosanct "rooster-ritual" (*ThivüRasüh*). In this ritual, held during the festival of *Sükrinyi*, an unblemished rooster was dedicated to the spirits with the prayer for a year of good harvests, the absence of epidemics, and the avoidance of unnatural deaths. Here, the stone assumed ritual significance. The unblemished rooster, once released on the stone, was said to possess powers of forecasting. For instance, if the rooster, once released, would face east it implied that the climatic conditions would be favourable, if the rooster would bite the soil it indicated a bumper harvest, while if the rooster would fail to crow it indicated a year of trouble.

Stones of Jubilee

If the advent of Christianity, and the new set of beliefs, morals and principles it purported, came at the expense of a till then flourishing megalithic culture, as a cultural expression the pulling of stones has also re-casted its significance in contemporary times. One such adaption in Phugwumi is the erection of monoliths to celebrate and commemorate jubilees of sorts. Such jubilees can be manifold. Among them, the Golden Jubilee of Phugwumi's Baptist Church in 1997 in honour of which a mammoth monolith was erected in the church premises. And when the village's Revival Church, a nascent denomination in Phugwumi, hosted a joint meeting and celebration of the Chakhesang Christian Revival Church Council in the year 2000, the event was venerated by the pulling of a monolith. It was during my stay in the village that Phugwumi's Youth Organisation saw its Golden Jubilee, and its organisers too decided to pull a stone in commemoration of this milestone. Spread across the village we further find stones celebrating jubilees of the village's multiple wrestling associations, one that remembers the inauguration of the badminton stadium built at the fringe of the village, and one that does the same for the market-shed along the road.

If the purposes of erecting stones have changed to primarily the celebration and commemoration of jubilees, so has the technology to pull the monoliths adapted itself to contemporary times. While wooden sledges, creepers, and brute physical strength were the tools available to pull a stone towards the village in the past, today monoliths are heaved in a truck, transported along the road, and erected with the help of a crane. What has hardly changed, however, is the social meanings and commemorative powers monoliths continue to carry, both the ones pulled in days long bygone as the latest additions to the village's rich megalithic assortment.

Conclusion

While megalithic expressions no longer make the headlines they did during the colonial era when British administrators regularly reported about the social significance of stones among the Naga, this chapter has sought to show the continuing vitality of a "social study" of monoliths and stones. Even as local megalithic expressions have waned, they have also re-casted themselves, while the presence of these stones — the tales, meanings, and values invested in them — provide a crucial source for the unpacking of local social histories, as the case of Phugwumi illustrates. The types of stones discussed in the various sections, and the narratives and values invested in them, obviously do not nearly constitute a comprehensive picture of Phugwumi's village history. What they do offer are ethno-historical snapshots of past social institutions and historical episodes. Stones in Phugwumi, and among the Nagas more widely, in a word, have *social lives*; and it is in reconstructing and reporting these lives that we find openings into unwritten pasts.

Note: This is a revised version of an earlier piece I wrote titled: "The Social Lives of Stones: studying the Past in the Chakhesang Naga village of Phugwumi", published in *Anthropology Today — North East Institute for Research in Anthropology (NEIRA)*, 1(1): 21-41, and reproduced here with permission.

Acknowledgements

There are many people I need to thank for enabling me to research and write this chapter. Too many to list here. But here I would like to make special mention of Neisalie Kezo, Athe Beduhü, Kuhupoyo Puro, and Zhoto Tunyi, who have all been of tremendous help. I am also deeply grateful to the villagers of Phugwumi

(Kikrüma) as a whole, whose never failing hospitality and kindness I hope to be ever able to reciprocate through this and future writings on the village.

NOTE

1. During the colonial era, Phugwumi and villages further east were classed as Eastern Angamis. This continued until 1946 when Chokri (including Phugwumi) and Khezha language groups, added by a section of the Sangtam Naga decided to form a tribe of their own, and which they baptized as Chakhesang. Hence, any colonial reference to the Angami Naga may be considered as also including Phugwumi and other formerly Eastern Angami villages.

REFERENCES

Appadurai, A. (ed.). 1986. *The Social Life of Things: Commodities in Cultural Perspective.* Cambridge: Cambridge University Press.

Barron, L., 1872. "Notes on Stone Implements from Naga Hills". *The Journal of the Anthropological Institute of Great Britain and Ireland,* 1: LXII-LXIII.

Butler, J., 1855. Travels and Adventures in the Province of Assam during a Residence of Fourteen years. London: Smith, Elder.

Clarke, C.B., 1874. "The Stone Monuments of the Khasi Hills". *The Journal of the Anthropological Institute of Great Britain and Ireland*, 3: 481-93.

Dev, S.C., 1988. *Nagaland: the Untold Story.* Calcutta: Gauri Dev.

Fürer-Haimendorf, C. Von., 1939. *The Naked Nagas.* London: Methuen & Co.

Godwin-Austen, H.H., 1872. "On the Stone Monuments of Khasi Hill Tribes". *Journal of the Royal Anthropological Institute*, 1: 122-36.

_____. 1875. "The Rude Stone Monuments of certain Naga tribes, with some Remarks on their Customs, etc.". *The Journal of the Anthropological Institute of Great Britain and Ireland,* 4: 144-147.

Hoskins, J., 1998. *Biographical Objects: How Things tell the Stories of Peoples' lives*. London: Routledge Kegan and Paul Ltd.

Hutton, J.H., 1965. "The mixed culture of the Naga tribes". *The Journal of the Royal Anthropological Institute of Great Britain and Ireland*, 95(1): 16-43.

_____. 1928. "The significance of head-hunting in Assam". *Journal of the Royal Anthropological Institute*, 58: 300-408.

_____. 1926. "The use of stone in the Naga Hills". *The Journal of the Royal Anthropological Institute of Great Britain and Ireland*, 56: 71-82.

_____. 1922. *The Angami Nagas: With Some Notes on Neighbouring Tribes*. London: MacMillan & Co.

Jamir, T., 2004. "Megaliths of Nagaland: Reflections of Material Milieu and Social Values". In Momin, M. and C.A. Mawlong (eds.), *Society and Economy in North East India*. New Delhi: Regency Publications, pp. 105-17.

Joshi, V., 2012. *A Matter of Belief: Christian Conversion and Healing in North East India*. Oxford: Berghahn Books.

Leach, E.R., 1960. "The Frontiers of "Burma". *Comparative Studies in Society and History*, 3(1): 49-68.

Marak, Q., 2012. "Megaliths of North East India". In T.B. Subba (ed.), *North East India: A Handbook of Anthropology*. Delhi: Orient Blacksmith, pp. 34-53.

Mills, J.P., 1926. *The Ao Nagas*. London: MacMillian & Co.

Mills, J.P., 1935. "The Effect of Ritual upon Industries and Arts in the Naga Hills". *Man*, 35: 132-35.

Nuh, V.K., 2002. *The Origin of Naga*. Kohima: Vision Press.

Puro, K., 2008. "The Battle of Kikrüma: Fought between Kikrüma People and Britishers in 1851". In *The Kikrüma Students' Union Golden Jubilee Souvenir*.

Shimray, U.A., 2007. *Nagaland Population and Integration Movement*. New Delhi: Mittal Publications.

Vashum, R., 2000. *Nagas' Right to Self-determination: An Anthropological-Historical Perspective*. New Delhi: Mittal Publications.

Woodthorpe, R.G., 1881. "Notes on the Wild Tribes inhabiting the so-called Naga Hills, and our North East Frontier of India". Reprinted in V. Elwin (ed.), 1969. *Nagas in the Nineteenth Century*. London: Oxford University Press, pp. 46-83.

Wouters, J.J.P., 2015. "The Battle of Kikrüma: How a Single Naga village took on the British Empire". *Himal Southasian*. Url:http://himalmag.com/the-battle-of-kikruma/

11
From an Eastern 'Stonehenge' to a Strategic Market Place

Raphael Rousseleau

Introduction

Within the general interest of scholars for Khasi and Synteng megaliths or "huge stone monuments", the funerary and commemorative monuments received more attention than other kinds. Morphologically, similar to the commemorative alignments (*mawbah/maw bynna, see* Rousseleau, 2008 among others), stone monuments erected in market places include standing slabs and large stone tables (*maw-shongthait*), which comprise sometimes very impressive ensembles of hundreds of stones. The most famous example is the Nartiang one. In this chapter, I will first sum up the earliest Western depictions of the Nartiang site (from around 1855), in order to show the comparisons they implied with European archaeological knowledge of this time. Thereafter, I will concentrate on the legendary accounts collected about this place by some Khasi/ Synteng scholars, and on what can be reconstructed from it with complementary ethnographical enquiries on the socio-economic and political context of such an impressive megalithic complex.

Colonial Discourses on Nartiang Stone Monuments

First British Descriptions: The 'Nurtiung Stonehenge'

When the first British travellers crossed the Khasi Hills, they were astonished to find in the very heart of Asia, some peculiar atmospheres reminding them of their homeland. The neighbouring area of Shillong appeared to them as the "Scotland of the East", not only for its 'highlands', but also for the number of megaliths standing in the fog like an 'oriental' reflection of their own supposed 'Celtic' imagery.

At the beginning of the 19th century, European scholars were associating European stone monuments, like the famous Stonehenge in Southern England, with the Celtic people, which later proved wrong. From this supposition, they attributed the same origin to all stone architectures throughout the world (For details *see* Rousseleau 2008).

The first mention of Khasis and other North East peoples goes back to the 18th century, but it was after Assam fell under British rule (after the Yandaboo Treaty, 1826) that Europeans began to know more about the peculiarity of the Khasi customs, mentioned for example by Walters (1932) in the *Asiatic Researches*. Still, the "Note on Kasia Hills and Peoples" by Colonel Yule (1844) really attracted the attention of scholars on Khasi megaliths. Yule was the first to describe clearly the Khasi monuments and to compare them to the Central Asian, Syrian and even European ones. He suggested, for instance, a supposed similarity between the Brittonic word *men* for 'stone' and the Khasi word *maw* for the same.

Quoting Yule, the naturalist J.D. Hooker too, in his *Himalayan Journals* (1855), describes the large ensemble of tables and standing stones in Nartiang in the Jaintia Hills of Meghalaya as another 'Stonehenge', particularly 'picturesque':

> Nurtiung contains a most remarkable collection of those sepulchral and other monuments, which form so curious a feature in the scenery of these mountains, and in the habits of their native populations. They are all placed in a fine grove of trees, occupying a hollow; where several acres are covered with gigantic, generally circular, slabs of stone, from ten to twenty-five feet broad, supported five feet above the ground upon other blocks. For the most part they are buried in brushwood of nettles and shrubs, but in one place there is an open area of fifty yards encircled by them, each with a gigantic headstone behind it. (...) Splendid trees of Bombax, fig and banyan, overshadowed them: the largest banyan had a trunk five feet in diameter, clear of the buttresses, and numerous

> small trees of Celtis grew out of it, and an immense flowering tuft of *Vanda coerulea* (the rarest and most beautiful of Indian orchids) flourished on one of its limbs. A small plantain with austere woolly scarlet fruit, bearing ripe seeds, was planted in this sacred grove, where trees of the most tropical genera grew mixed with the pine, burch, Myrica, and Viburnum. The Nurtiung Stonehenge is no doubt in part religious, as the grove suggests, and also esigned for cremation, the bodies being burnt on the altars.[1] In the Khasia [Hills] these upright stones are generally raised simply as memorials of great events, or of men whose ashes are not necessarily, though frequently, buried or deposited in hollow stone sarcophagi near them, and sometimes in a clay urn placed inside a sarcophagus, or under horizontal slabs.
>
> (...) Returning from this grove, we crossed a stream by a single squared block, twenty-eight feet long, five broad, and two thick, of gray granite with large crystals of felspar (feldspar).

'Rude Stones, Rude Races': From Diffusionist and Evolutionist Comparisons to the First Classifications

Beyond the reports by natural historians and army officers, the Khasi megaliths began to be more systematically investigated from 1872 onwards. In his *Descriptive Ethnology of Bengal* (as Assam was part of the Bengal Presidency up to 1874), Dalton devoted special attention to such monuments, comparing their occurrence in the Khasi hills to the older ones in Europe and to the "Stonehenge found in the Nilgiris" or in the Chhota Nagpur Province (Dalton, 1872: 62, *see* full quotation in Rousseleau, 2012). In the same year, Major Godwin-Austen was the first to give a detailed description of the monuments. In two articles published in the *Journal of the Anthropological Institute of Great Britain and Ireland* (1872, 1876), he stresses the importance of those stones, and compares them, once again, to the 'druidical remains' of Europe. But, far to stop at this general statement, he reported the reasons given by the Khasi themselves to set up the majority of such stones: commemorative and funerary ceremonies. Through some lectures delivered in scholarly societies, his reports were diffused among the anthropologists of that time.

Drawing from Godwin-Austen's works, the first art historian of India James Fergusson devoted some pages to the Khasi monuments in his book *Rude Stones and Monuments in All Countries* (1872). This work is a sort of *Encyclopaedia of the Megalithic Monuments* known at that time, which ought to be the first volume of a planned general history of architecture, which was never completed. Fergusson considered the "rude stone monuments" as an example of elementary architecture, which would have been associated with an archaic religion, a sort of 'stone worship' once diffused by a nomadic 'rude race' of people. He borrowed some parts of this theory from the French archaeologist Alexandre Bertrand, specialist of Celtic Antiquities. But, in Fergusson's perspective this thesis takes a stronger racial aspect, as he sees 'art history' as a "history of the racial influences on arts". This approach legitimised the colonial conquest by claiming the superiority of British achievements in all matters (religion, architecture etc.). In any case, the success of the book contributed a great deal to the temporary celebrity of the Khasis outside India, as a contemporary people erecting stone monuments in a similar way than the European ancestors.

In the meantime, the descriptive term of megalithic monuments was officially preferred to the one of Celtic monuments, during the "International Congress of Anthropology and Prehistoric Archaeology" held in Paris in 1867 (an usage adopted by the Irish archaeologists some years before). The West European megaliths were no more attributed to Celtic people, but rather to anterior Neolithic and Copper Age cultures, a hypothesis fully confirmed today. Furthermore, similar stone monuments outside Europe were considered then as an evidence, not merely of the diffusion of a single people, but of the universality of a "barbaric phase of civilisation" (Westropp, 1869), within the frame of the evolutionist theory of history. This 'barbaric' stage was imagined, nonetheless, through comparisons involving European 'national' past (like the Highlands clans). In consequence, the 'Hill tribes' were presented as proud and independent quite like their supposed European counterparts (Arnold, 2005).

In 1874, in an article in the *Journal of the Anthropological Institute*, C.B. Clarke gave a typology of monuments and an account of the funerary ceremonies linked with the commemorative standing stones and the ossuaries. He mentions the quarries and the techniques of stone extraction, well known to the Khasis who, in his own words, were "good geologists". He rightly remarked that the rude aspect of the monoliths was taken too quickly as a proof of their supposed antiquity, while the majority of them were erected recently, if not just few years before his observation (Clarke, 1874: 493).

Ancestor Commemoration and 'Stones for Sacrifice'

In 1914, Major Gurdon devoted a long chapter of his monograph, *The Khasis,* to their stone monuments and the funerary ceremonies associated with the same. Inspired by the evolutionary theories of J.J. Bachofen and L.H. Morgan, he considered the Khasi traditions as a survival of a matriarchal stage of civilization (based on a primordial 'maternal law'), supposed to be common to both ancient European and modern Indian people. Gurdon (1914: 147) saw the megaliths as a manifestation of an "ancestors worship" characterising a stage of civilization.

But, according to Gurdon, the first Khasi and Syntengs also revered serpent-spirits, and the famous *thlen* legend would be a survival of it, as well as the sacrifices said to be offered for the river goddess Kopili. This river marked the boundary line between the Synteng/Jaintia and the North Kachar territories (Gurdon, 1914), and he mentions sacrifices to this goddess in a nearby tank in Nartiang. Building upon this isolated 'fact' and the evidence of human sacrifice to the goddess Jainteswari in Jaintiapur, Gurdon discusses the possibility that the table stones might be originally sacrificing altars (1914: 151):

> At Jaintiapur and Nartiang, both of which places were the headquarters of the kings of Jaintia, there are very large table-stones. We know for a fact that human sacrifices used to take place at Jaintiapur. Is it possible that human beings were immolated on these table-stones? It would be unsafe to base any conclusion on the solitary folk-tale about the *Iew Ksih* table-stone; but the tale certainly furnishes food for reflection.

Then, while the author recognises the evidence of the commemorative nature of most of the stone monuments of the area, the hypothesis of human sacrifice is stoked by Gurdon again when he describes the Nartiang stones as a case of the last type of his classification of regional megaliths (Gurdon, 1914):

> *Maw-shongthait*, or flat table-stones, often accompanied by vertical stones, which are placed in the market-places and by the side of roads to serve as seats for weary travellers. (...)
>
> It may serve as an example of these stones to describe the very interesting collection of stones at Nartiang *hàt*, or market. (...) These stones are popularly supposed to have been erected long ago by two men U Lah Laskor and U Mar Phalyngki, to commemorate the establishment of Nartiang market, which is called Iew Mawlong. "Laskor" is the Synteng equivalent of the Khasi *lyngskor*, or Prime Minister. "Mar" is a Synteng word meaning a giant, the idea amongst the people being that in the olden days there were giants in the land who performed marvellous feats of strength, e.g. the erection of the megalithic remains at Nartiang and elsewhere. A *puja* is performed upon a great flat stone by the *doloi* and his officers in honour of the founder of the market, but no animals are sacrificed, rice and *rynsi* (balls of rice) only being offered. In the days of the Jaintia kings only the *Raja* could seat upon the great flat stone; hence the name *maw jong Siem* (or Siem's stone). The great upright stone is said to have been brought by U Lah Laskor and a great number of people from Suriang, a place near Nartiang. With reference to the Nartiang stones I would refer to my theory, formulated above, that they were originally connected with human sacrifices. It may be mentioned that at Nartiang there is a bridge constructed out of a single stone, which is also said to have been set in position by U Lah Laskor.

This paragraph contains various insights: Gurdon seems to be the first to mention the local legend about the giant's contribution. He also speculates about the original use of the stone-tables for human sacrifices. Gurdon was influenced by contemporary researches about European megaliths (he quotes several cases in his book). The specialists were collecting folklore in the stones vicinity as well (among which tales about giants), and discussing the already outmoded theory about the dolmens as "altars for human sacrifices". This thesis draws on Roman authors (Julius Caesar, Tacitus) despising Celtic customs as sanguinary 'savage tribes', when the dolmens were interpreted as 'Celtic antiquities'. Most of the archaeologists already abandoned this thesis in 1914, but it still spread in non-professional circles. On the other hand, Gurdon left us some interesting points: the existence of a *puja* performed by the local authorities and the link with the former Synteng Syemship.

After the First World War, the colonial administrator of Assam, J. H. Hutton (1926) wrote "Some Megalithic work in the Jaintia Hills", after a survey he made in October 1925. Hutton identified directly the stone works with the Synteng dynasty of Nartiang and Jaintiapur (in the plains of Sylhet, in present Bangladesh). Passing through Nartiang on October 18th, he was "struck" by the ancient appearance of the village and its market place or *bazar*, "a wonderful collection of menhirs and dolmens" (1926: 335). He did not give clues about this particular spot, but he added that an oral tradition exists similarly about the Dimapur alignments of carved monoliths (now at the entry of Nagaland) as occupying "the site of the ancient market-place of the Kachari capital".

Going down the hills, he notes the paved causeway linking Jowai to the capital of the junior branch of the Synteng dynasty: Jaintiapur. There, Hutton (1926: 342) saw various ruined monuments fallen down with the great earthquake of 1897, but:

> Except some single slab bridges and some very fine menhirs and dolmens of the Khasi type, some of them, as at Nartiang, under the compound walls of the old palace or temple enclosure, I saw no megalithic work at Jaintiapur itself except the remains of a large round stone pillar at the top of the steps of the plinth of what was once the durbar hall.

Inside the palace, he further identified the former altar for the dynastic goddess and, in front of it, a built circular platform said to receive human sacrifices. The dry well was also said to receive the bodies of the victims. Hutton received this explanation most probably from the local informants, maybe the heir of the royal family (*Nripa*) with whom he visited some places. Later, influenced by Sir James Frazer's theories and his further studies of Naga groups, Hutton (1933) concluded that the megaliths illustrated an archaic fertility cult: according to him, the standing stones were imagined as transmitting the fertility forces coming from the ancestor's world to the fields and to the living beings.[2] I close here the chapter on history of the theories to enter into more recent knowledge.

Relocating Nartiang in Jaintia Ethnology

History of the Jaintia Kingdom

Jaintias, referred to as Syntengs by the western Khasi, prefer to call themselves *Pnar*, a word which defines their peculiar (Austro-Asiatic) language as well. They claim to come from the plains, but we do not know the history of their possible migrations, only a legendary account of the first Jaintia kings. The dynasty traced its origins from the previous *syiem* (king) of Sutnga, who claimed descent from a magical fish-woman (Ka Lih Dohkha) captured in the Umwi river, and married by their founder, U Loh Ryndi (Gurdon, 1914). According to Hutton (1926), the fish-girl had two daughters, ancestresses of the two royal branches, the elder in the hills, the younger in the plains. This is a common way of hierarchising the clans among hill tribes. While the *syiem*s were men, succession followed the female line, the heir of the crown being normally the *syiem*'s sister's son.

From an historical perspective, the Jaintia kingdom is known through coins and inscriptions on copper-plates, as well as mentions in chronicles such as *Ahom Buranji*, *Jayantia Buranji*, *Kachari Buranji*, *History of the Koch kings*, *Râjmâla* or *Chronicles of the Kings of Tippera* etc. (*see* Gait, 1906; Devi, 1968), since the beginning of the sixteenth century. Beyond the diversity of accounts, it is clear that the kingdom played a role in the political game between the kingdoms of the time (Cooch-Behar, Ahom, Kachari etc.), and that one king called Parvat Roy in the plains, that is the 'Mountain King' conquered the Jaintia Parganas in the plains (north of the Barak river, Gait, 1906), around this period. According to Chowdhury (1996), his descendant Bar Gossain (towards 1548-64) is said to have shifted his capital from Nartiang (summer capital) to Jaintiapur (becoming then the winter capital), and is also credited to have improved the shrine of the goddess Bam-Janga, in Faljur. Whatever may be the chronicles show that one recurrent key issue was clearly the commercial roads the Jaintia kings controlled between the Assam plains and the Sylhet ones, the tax they imposed upon the traders, as well as the markets settled in the 'doors' (*duar*) of the hills (Dimarua, Gobha, Neli, Khala, *see* Devi, 1968). Jaintiapur itself was then a crucial trade centre and "great *entrepot*" for the exchange of cotton, iron ore (an important product from the Khasi and Jaintia Hills), wax, ivory, betel leaf and cloths against salt, rice, tobacco, fish and goats (Robinson, 1841; quoted in Chowdhury, 1998: 69). The Hill quarries were also the main supplier of limestone to the delta region of Bengal (Gurdon, 1914).

The British came into contact with the Jaintia kingdom upon receiving the *Diwani* of Bengal in 1765 (Gurdon, 1914). In 1824, due to the Burmese War, the king Ram Singh was compelled to sign a treaty of allegiance to the East India Company. In 1832, the colonial Sylhet authorities brought charges against the Jaintia king to have let the chief of Gobha abduct four British subjects, who were subsequently immolated to Kali (according to the colonial reports), except one who managed to escape (Chowdhury, 1996). Upon this charge, they asked him to hand over the supposed culprits, and later for the payment of a heavy fine. In the meantime, the old king died, and the new one, Rajendra Singh was unable to answer to all such conditions. So, his territory was simply confiscated, and he was deposed on March 15, 1835. From then on, the plain area was administrated directly by the colonial rule and the hilly area indirectly.

Beyond the latter implications, the human sacrifice story should be taken cautiously. On the one hand, the accusation of human sacrifice was variously used as a rhetorical device, by the colonial power, in order to justify annexation of territories (for example in Odisha or Chhattisgarh, *see* Bates, 2006). On the other hand, we also find various local narratives about its actual occurrence. In a special article, Gait reported the existence of annual human sacrifices at the *Shakti pitha* of Faljur (site of the fall of the left thigh of *Sati*, the wife and energy of Shiva), and occasional ones at the shrine of Jainteswari at Nijpat-Jaintiapur. According to the narratives he collected, willing devotees were declaring their wish in advance to be immolated to the goddess, on the *Navami* day of the *Durga puja*. The whole scenario points to a possible *Shakta* tradition, supported furthermore by the mention of Kandra yogis said to eat the lungs of the victims, while the royal family had to partake a small quantity or rice cooked in their blood (*cf.* Gurdon, 1914: 103). One may add that a long sword is shown to the visitors in the goddess' shrine (and Shiva) in Nartiang, said to be used for human sacrifices by the present priests, who claim their descent from royal *pujaris* (personal enquiries at the Nartiang former fort, 2001). Still according to them, the heads of the victims were rolling down to the local river below. Be it real or only rumours, the recurrence of such stories testifies its role in the indigenous symbolic economy of power. In Sanskrit texts invoked for such event, a sword over which *mantra* have been uttered (*khadga*), is called "Chandika's tongue", and supposed to confer extra-powers to the king who patronised the ritual (Kooij, 1972). This indication gives us another clue about the hinduisation of the rulers: the fact that the Jaintia kings borrowed Sanskrit names, patronized Bengali *pujaris* and performed *Shakta* rituals can be interpreted as a matter of power and prestige, more than a conversion of beliefs. Most probably, this was part of their *kshatriyaisation* (Kulke, 1993), which did not implicate the abandoning of previous gods and ancestor worship for the *syiems*, let alone for the Synteng people (Bareh, 1997).

Thanks to the Archaeological Survey of then India and now Bangladesh, Jaintiapur, the winter capital of the Jaintia kings, keeps some parts of what Hutton reported ninety years ago. The Jainteswari temple is lying now dilapidated. In the former palace (Rajbari) built with bricks by the King Lakshmi Narayan at the close of the XVIIth century according to an inscription on the gateway [Gait (1906)1963: 316], only the gate, the compound walls and some structures remain. Among the latter, we can recognise the famous keyhole shaped platform and the well, both believed to be used during sacrifices. Outside but close to the walls are platforms of large flat stones (showing traces of quarrying works). Several others can be seen on the northern side of the Nayagang river (in the midst of tyre repair shops). A more complete list is probably available in the local Archaeological service.[3] It is now time to go back to Nartiang site, from a folklore and then ethnological point of view.

From Folklore to Ethnology

In *Khasi and Jaintia Tales and Beliefs* (1966), Ivan M. Simon reported the lore of the giant (*mar*) Phalingki, said to have been entrusted by the then king of Jaintiapur to built the stone constructions (road, bridges, market place) in Nartiang area. Following his steps, a native of the place, U Nobait Swer narrated an extended local version of the story, more focused on the foundation of the market. Widely known, the story begins with the older market settled in Raliang. In short, the Nartiang giant went there, to buy some products, but was surprised by the rain on his way back. Asking an old lady something to protect himself from the rain, she refused to give him anything. Enraged by such unhelpful behaviour, he picked up a stone slab, which was in the market and covered his head with it, up to the outskirts of Nartiang where the rain suddenly stopped. So, he just threw it on the road side and proceeded home.

After some time, the sound of a large crowd of people speaking and quarrelling, was heard on the side of the Umtisong lake, abode of a river goddess (to which was offered a *Basari puja* in the water, every year), while nobody was actually there. This strange noise occurred every Mawlong day. The local main authority, the *doloi* had to go to Jaintiapur in order "to receive puja materials from the king" before *Durga puja* (Swer, 1992: 15, 18). So, he relied on the two *pators* (one in charge of the Eastern part of Nartiang territory, the second of the Western part) and *basans* (councillors) to enquire about the matter. At last, they all came to a *darbar* (council meeting) and the diviner/ "the one who communicate with the god" (*U Luh Blei*), after a ritual, concluded that Phalingki has unwillingly stolen the stone of the market goddess of Raliang, and deposited it near Umtisong. As this market was held every Mawlong day, the invisible crowd was actually the 'fairies' who attended the bazar and followed the goddess (Swer, 1992).

Interestingly, the shift of the goddess was attributed to her own choice: if she managed the event in such a way, it would mean that Raliang people had done some wrong deeds. A new enquiry was made, and a culprit was found: the stingy lady (*ka Ron*) who had denied help to the giant. She was entrusted with the collection of taxes, being a wealthy relative of the Raliang *Doloi*. The latter recognized that he heard about her greed but underestimated it. After a trial, she was banished, and the market shifting matter settled between the *dolois* and the king. Swer (1992) adds that the Raliang people say also that they returned the goddess slab to their village, but it came back to Nartiang again. So, they agreed with the Nartiang people to make a Raliang sacrifice in the new market every year. On the other hand, the Raliang people fixed a new stone in their own village, in order to perform rituals there. The first day of the Nartiang market, the king sacrificed a goat to the goddess, in front of the stone slab. This was the first "market goddess ritual" (*Ka Pam Blang Iew*). After that, the market was declared open for buying and selling. The ritual was nearly abandoned in recent times, and done only towards 1905 (according to U Nobait Swer and his grandmother).

The Doloi and the local lineages had still no special seats. So, they proposed to the King that in order to beautify the market, monoliths and table stones should be placed. This would enable the dignitaries and Durbaries to sit there to view the market and stalls (Swer, 1992: 60).

The king then summoned a territorial council in Nartiang, and explained the matter: to bring stones 'to dignify' the site and collect toll and speak with the people coming from faraway places. The proposal was agreed, so the giants as well as experts in stone found suitable stones. People assembled to pull it with iron chains, but without success. The diviner, once again, claimed that the stones should be tied with 'gourd stalks' from Mikir Hills (Mynsgngat, Kdiap, Mawbakhon), and it was supposedly adhered to. This enabled the stones to be successfully pulled.

U Mar Phalingki saw two very long and regular stones in Sanirang area, and he told the king that his "name would remain for ever" with such stones erected in a public place. It would definitely confer prestige to Nartiang and the ruler. Then, on another market day, the dignitaries called the people again to come to participate. In the meantime, the roads were levelled, temporary bridges were built, and a wooden carriage was prepared. On the said day, the king and dignitaries walked at the head of the procession, followed by drummers, singers and dancers, and then the pullers of the stone. On it, sat a man waving a flag and singing a "rhyme-word song" (Swer, 1992: 69). Swer adds that "the inferior in rank walk(ed) behind the stone and waited for their turn to pull the stones." When they reached the place, the crowd dispersed, but came back the day after, in order to erect the monolith. When they attempted to erect it, they dug deeper and deeper, but the slab never remained straight inside its hole. The diviner was summoned again and declared that the stone required human blood. As a boy was passing by, he was asked to get something in the hole and was crushed to death under the stone. Since then, this tallest stone remains standing, while the smaller Sanirang one fell down during the 1887 earthquake. According to U Nobait Swer (1992), the flat stones were brought thereafter, to complete and to fit with the grandeur of the standing ones. Some say that the tallest slab was brought by U Laskor.

This narrative is obviously recent and legendary, but still reflects meaningful ideas, as well as plausible facts on the procession and technical aspect. From an ethnological perspective now, we may develop on the main socio-political status mentioned (*syiem, doloi*), and their economic and symbolic links with markets, as well as with a market goddess.

First of all, the *syiem* was the main head of indigenous states (*Hima*), that Gurdon (1914) qualified as a voluntary association of villages or groups of villages (but some federations of villages had different names for the same function). The *syiem* presided over the council (*darbar*), which was the real repository of the decisions. He was elected in one lineage by area, by representatives of the dominant and founder local lineages, who were also participants of the council. He was then an arbiter between the local clans, in charge of maintaining peace as well as punishing offences against the local order and customs (*niam*). For this reason, he also had frequently ritual prerogatives ("exorcism, clearance of evil", Bareh, 1997: 235). The fact that various *syiem*s came from outside can be interpreted as a guarantee of such neutrality, as well as the legends of alliances between a dynasty founder and local divine women may be seen as a legitimation of their rule. By comparison, the myth of the 'stranger-king' ruling over landowner/indigenous clans is actually a common feature in myths of Polynesia or Africa (*see* Sahlins, 1985).

As Chowdhury (1998: 157-58) noted after David Roy (1963), the exact name for the state was *Ka It ka Hima* ("the state with its border or extent"), as the borders were fluid and the relation between the villager-citizens and the state/*syiem* was of allegiance, more than territorial. In the case of the Jaintia kingdom moreover, the *syiem*'s personal rule and possessions prevailed on the conquered territories of the plains, while the hills were administrated by *dolois* (see above). The allegiance of the latter was manifested through annual tribute of he-goats to be sacrificed in Jaintiapur (Gassah, 1998). The *syiem* had no power to collect land tax (he owned some lands but was not the "master of the soil" as most often in India), and the state economy was based mostly on toll and taxation upon the *khrong*, local market transactions (Chowdhury, 1996, 1998).

This particularity explains the importance of weekly markets (*iew*) in economic terms, but also as public events and socio-political and juridical institutions (Ramirez, 2014). The cycle of the successive markets were also used for the time reckoning, as the day of the week (8 days week in the Upland) takes the name of the main market place of the said day (Gurdon, 1914; Ramirez, 2014), the fourth being the Mawlong/Nartiang one. The market places were the main sites for public ceremonies indeed. For example, the investiture rituals of the Syiem of Cherra involved various he-goat sacrifices in front of the market altar, while the Mylliem state has an annual goat festival performed at the Shillong market (*Iewduh*), by the five founder-clans' representatives, on a cluster of sacred table stones (Bareh, 1997). Following this description, Barey (1997: 243) quotes a similar model for some *dolois*: "In Narpuh, a new *daloi* is mounted over a sacred stone slab at the market when, the head of a *Pator* clan approaches him and winds a turban round his head, citing solemn addresses. An exchange of benediction follows. Liquor and betels are distributed accompanied by the sprinkling of the holy water."

The *doloi* title was widely found in India (and former Ahom kingdom) for the chief of an army troop. In the Jaintia context, he was the head of an administrative area (*Elaka*), helped and controlled by a council of elders. According to Bareh (1997) and Gassah (1998), the *dolois* were elected among leaders of the local founding clans, but confirmed in their office by the *syiem*. From my own enquiries in 2002-03, I may add that the case of Nartiang points towards possible foreign origins of the *doloi* as well. There, according to local informants, the then office-bearer was Don Dkhar, and he could be chosen among three lineages/titles only — Dkhar (said to be of mixed origin), Dhar (Bengali) and Lamari (Khasi/Mikir?). Whatever may be, the Jaintia Hills were known as the "land of the twelve dolois" (*Ka Ri Khad-ar Doloi*), the first ones being Sutnga and Nartiang. They had, in a way, more powers than the *syiem* himself, being able to decide matters conjointly without having to wait for his agreement, or even to rebel against a tyrannical *syiem*. They had juridical and ritual privileges as well (Gassah, 1998).

Regarding "the stones of the *syiem*" (*ki maw jong Syiem*), or the present labyrinth of about hundred gigantic tables and standing stones, I was told that the stone alignments grew up from originally clanic divisions, bordering two main ways. The *syiem* and *darbar* would have ordered to settle groups of stones by clans, each one corresponding to market stalls. A priest (?) called *sangot* conducted the *puja* in the name of the *doloi* (sacrifice of one pig and one hen, cooked with rice distributed to the peoples, except the head given to the goddess). Then, the elders (*basans* including *doloi*, *sangot*, *pator* and *dan* or tax collector) shared the money collected from the market tax, and ate on the large flat stone. One part of the tax was used for ritual functions.

Such examples show clearly that some stone monuments were

not only "associated with the foundation of markets and were erected in commemoration of political associations and allegiances of clans forming a civil authority" (Bareh, 1997: 6). Moreover, they were highly visible manifestations or tangible proofs of the foundation and maintenance of the political contract between the clans and the head of the political unit. In the legendary account, we learn not only that the two biggest slabs of Nartiang came from Sanirang, but that all the peoples of the political unit were involved in the pulling of the stones. It was a ceremonious act, in which all male citizens participated according to their ranks (a process close to the Jagannath festival in Puri, where all devotees try to touch the cords of the divine cart). The erected stones commemorated, and immortalized in the local memories, this whole conjunction of forces. As for the table-stones, the longer ones were devoted to be the 'seats' of the council (*darbar*) of dignitaries, while the rest of the peoples could participate (at least sometimes), but seated on the ground (Bareh, 1997). From my own researches in other parts of India, I may safely add that this juridical and political aspect of the megaliths was actually widespread.

The very frequent references to 'market *puja*' can now be seen from a more socio-political perspective (Gassah, 1998; Ramirez, 2014). The market gods and goddesses seem to be mostly the divinities of the foundation of the event. In the Nartiang case, the founding stone of the place was considered as the seat of the presiding market goddess, and received some offerings before the opening of the regular exchanges. Gurdon (1914) reported only a rice offering to the founders by the *doloi*. But when we have some details on her identity, the market goddess is described as a local interpretation of Lakshmi, associated with rice, but also with welfare more generally (my own enquiries, as well as Ramirez, 2014). I would insist upon this second aspect, which would explain the double reference: to the market founders and to a goddess. The ritual was a celebration as well as an invitation of prosperity. Now, on the location, according to Swer (1992: 60), the goddess stone abode could be seen under a shed which was built in December 1955 (following the visit of the Governor of Assam, Shri Jayram Daulatram, a visit the author attended personally). But now-a-days, a different interpretation prevails, which gives a male identity and a more spectacular location to the divinity:

In Nartiang on market days, a rite is performed at the foot of the great monolith in order to worship "the Market god of Nartiang" (Pn. *ka Knia Blai Iaw Nartiang*). Worship is carried out by the *doloi* and the *pator,* i.e. the head of Nartiang *elaka* territory and his assistant. Furthermore, an annual sacrifice used to be made to the Market god. It was reintroduced in 1997 after a lapse of 41 years (Ramirez, 2014: 104-6).

Other Important Megalithic Market Places in the Area

Except Nartiang, two other main groups can be seen in Nongkseh and Laitlyngkot, both former seats of local political powers. Located at about five kilometres from Shillong, Nongkseh (or Bisi) was the capital of Khyrim, one of the two kingdoms (with Mylliem) which formerly occupied the present Shillong area. Nongkseh preserves the remains of its erstwhile market place. Gurdon (1914) considers that the tallest stela of the site was called *u mawkni Syiem*, the "stone of the Syiem's maternal uncle", and formed the centre of an alignment belonging to the local *basans* (officials) clan, who provided the principal sacrificer of the Khyriem Syiem. In the present Shillong town, during winter, the representative of the Mylliem district (*Raid*) still offers a *puja* on the stones located in the centre of the Bara Bazar market (*Iewduh*). Within the present market place of Laitlyngkot village, an imposing group of short alignments with large stone tables can be observed. People continue to use it, showing that the flat slabs are the former stall tables, used to display the proposed goods for barter or trade.

Conclusion

I would like to draw now some general conclusions. First of all, the earlier examples show that the evolutionist and racial perspectives on tribes and megalithic cultures were cast by a 'romantic' history and ethnography. Within this frame, the Nartiang 'Stonehenge' was considered as a "picturesque scenery", reflecting the ancient battlegrounds of "heroic tribes" (Arnold, 2005), often compared with European "Druidical/Celtic Antiquities" (so-called then). Such lyrical evocations progressively left ground to more scientific descriptions of megalithic remains around 1870, with the specialization of both archaeology and (here colonial) ethnology. Then Nartiang stones came to be considered as commemorative and possibly linked with fertility cult and human sacrifices, interpretations which can be now fully ruled out.

Eventually, the folklore collections allied with historical and ethnological enquiries showed that such monuments should be seen from economic and socio-political angles, to deliver their whole meaning. Stone-tables are used as stalls and seating platforms in a very practical way, but also as visible signs of power and prestige. For such reasons, and as local heritage, the stone monuments deserve to be protected. Some sites (Nartiang, Laitlyngkot, Nongkrem) have been fenced some years ago, and some others have been cleared from the vegetation, thanks to Meghalaya State (Department of Art and Culture) and other institutions. Even families maintain the old monuments commemorating their own clan members.

This chapter is a contribution to show the complexity and the richness of the megalithic monuments, among which Nartiang is a great example. At present it is important to trace the history of the principal sites and collect the surviving local memories among the people related to them. By this process, the megaliths can be rightly re-appropriated by the Khasi and Pnar/Synteng citizen as an essential part of their cultural and artistic heritage.

Acknowledgements

I take the opportunity to thank Mr. Freeman Kharlyngdoh, former Director of the Department of Art and Culture of the Government of Meghalaya, and above all Mr. Gabriel Sumer, archaeologist, as well as Prof. Ivan M. Simon, and the authorities of Assam and Meghalaya for their help and kindness at the time of my short researches in Meghalaya (2001 and 2003). In 2001, the first survey was financed by the joint Project "Genetic and Languages" LACITO – *Musée de l'Homme*, Paris, co-directed by François Jacquesson. In 2003, a one month mission on the megalithic monuments of Assam-Meghalaya was financed by the Lerici Archaeological Foundation (Polytechnic, Milano, Italy).

NOTES

1. In the case of Nartiang, this interpretation is now doubtful.
2. For more development about the theories on megalithic cultures of India, and more recent conclusions, *see* Rousseleau, 2008 and 2012.

3. If we believe the present reports on the website, the oral traditions in Jaintiapur still transmit the idea of human sacrifice: http://bangladeshunlocked.blogspot.fr/2011/03/jaintiapur-palace-blood-on-stone.html. Recent excavations in Jaintiapur: http://ethnoarcheology.org/%E0%A6%96%E0%A6%A8%E0%A6%A8-%E0%A6%95%E0%A6%BE%E0%A6%B0%E0%A7%8D%E0%A6%AF/

REFERENCES

Arnold, D., 2005. *The Tropics and the Travelling Gaze: India, Landscape, and Science 1800-1856*. Delhi: Permanent Black.

Bareh, H. [1967]1997. *The History and Culture of the Khasi People*. New Delhi: Spectrum Publications.

Bates, C., 2006. "Human Sacrifice in Colonial Central India. Myth, Agency and Representation". In C. Bates (ed.), *Beyond Representations: Colonial and Postcolonial Constructions of Indian Identity*. New Delhi: Oxford University Press, pp. 13-42.

Chowdhury, J. N., 1996. *Ki Khun Khasi-Khara (The Khasi People)*. Shillong.

_____. 1998. *The Khasi Canvas*. Shillong: Jaya Chowdhury.

Clarke, C.B., 1874. "Stone Monuments of the Khasi Hills". *Journal of the Anthropological Institute*, 3(3): 481-93.

Dalton, E.T., 1872. *Descriptive Ethnology of Bengal*. Calcutta: Government Press.

Devi, L. [1968]1992. *Ahom-Tribal Relations (A Political Study)*. Guwahati: LBS Publication.

Fergusson, J., 1872. *Rude Stones and Monuments in all Countries, their Ages and Uses*. London: J. Murray.

Gait, E. [1906]1963. *A History of Assam*. Calcutta: Thacker Spink & Co.

Gassah, L.S., 1998. *Traditional Institutions of Meghalaya. A Case Study of Doloi and his Administration*. New Delhi: Regency Publications.

Godwin-Austen, H. H., 1872. "The Stone Monuments of the Khasi Hill Tribes". *Journal of the Anthropological Institute*, 1(2): 122-43.

_____. 1876. "Further Notes on the Rude Stone Monuments of the Khasi Hill Tribes". *JAI*, 5(1): 37-41.

Gurdon, P.R.T., 1914. *The Khasis*. Calcutta: Government of Eastern Bengal and Assam.

Hooker, J.D., 1855. *Himalayan Journals: Notes of a Naturalist*. Vol. II. London: J. Murray.

Hutton, J.H., 1926. "Some Megalithic work in the Jaintia Hills". *Journal of the Asiatic Society of Bengal*, 22: 333-46.

_____. 1933. "Megalithic work in Assam". *Current Science*, 2 (5): 167-169.

Kooij, K.R. van. 1972. *Worship of the Goddess according to the Kâlikâpurâna*. Part I. Leiden: Brill.

Kulke, H., 1993. *Kings and Cults. State Formation and Legitimation in India and Southeast Asia*. Delhi: Manohar.

Ramirez, P., 2014. *People of the Margins. Across Ethnic Boundaries in North East India*, Guwahati/Delhi: Spectrum Publications.

Rousseleau, R., 2008. "Stonehenge d'Orient. Les tribus 'mégalithiques' dans les discours britanniques sur l'Inde (1740-1945)". *Gradhiva*, 8 (nouvelle série): 96-111.

_____. 2012. "Megalithic landscapes: cultures and Identity in North East India". In Nicolas Laîné and Tanka B. Subba (eds.), *Nature, Environnement and Society: Conservation, Governance and Transformation in India*. New Delhi: Orient BlackSwan, pp. 17-35.

Roy, D., 1963. "The Megalithic Culture of the Khasis". *Anthropos*, 58(34): 520-56.

Sahlins, M., 1985. *Islands of History*. Chicago: University of Chicago Press.

Simon, I. M., 1966. *Khasi and Jaintia Tales and Beliefs*. Gawahati: Department of Tribal Culture and Folklore Research, Gauhati University, Gawahati, Assam.

Swer, U. N., 1992. *The Story of the Sanirang Stones in the Form of Dialogue*. Shillong: Ri Khasi Press.

Yule, Colonel. 1844. "Note on the Kasia Hills and People". *Journal of the Asiatic Society of Bengal*, Vol. XIV (2): 612-631.

Walters, H., 1832. "Journey across the Pandua Hills, near Sylhet in Bengal". *Asiatic Researches*, XVII: 499-572.

Westropp, H.M., 1869. "Cromlechs and Megalithic Monuments". *The Journal of the Ethnological Society of London*, I (1): 53-59.

Section-III

LAND, CHANGE AND CONTINUITY

12
Social Markers of the Garos: Looking at a Tradition Undergoing Change

Gangotri Bhuyan and *Tengnang Dawa Sangma*

Introduction

Megalithic structures and the tradition of erecting megaliths, are found among many communities all over the world. Erecting a megalith to commemorate a merit or in memory of the deceased has been present since prehistoric times, and still continues in some communities. In North East India, the tradition of erecting a megalith is a 'living' tradition. Marak and Jangkhomang (2012) referred to the existence of the living tradition of megalithic monuments and their linked beliefs among the living tribal communities, as *living megalithism*. Megalithism represents a form of ancestral worship and it seems to have been accompanied with elaborate rituals and a complex system of beliefs including the existence of soul and life after death (Rao, 1973; Devi, 2011). Megaliths are found scattered in North East India, spreading through parts of Arunachal Pradesh, Assam, Manipur, Meghalaya and Nagaland.

The megalithic tradition seen among the Garos are different from the usual megalithic traditions and structures which are observed in other parts of India. Playfair (1909) mentioned that the type of megalithic practise observed among the Garos are modified in nature, as they use carved wooden posts (*kima*) (*See* Fig. 12.5) instead of stones to build megalithic structure in memory of the deceased. Along with the carved wooden posts (*kima*) several other structures form part of the memorial megalith. Apart from the structures, the rituals and the associated functions of the structures in their culture, the taboos (*marang*) attached to the building and maintenance of the structures makes the study of megaliths much more interesting. Elaborate reference to the *kima* and the rituals associated with the erection of the *kima* and related structures are found in Erik de Maaker's *Negotiating Life: Garo death rituals and the transformation of society* (2006).

There are various types of megaliths found in North East India based on structure, function and raw materials used. Hence, classifications or grouping these megaliths into specific categories, are not easy. Witness stones, boundary stones, clan stones, village foundation stones, sacrificial stones, sacrificial posts etc., are noticed in Garo Hills, though rarely in practice. Some of the early attempts to classify or group the megaliths of Garo Hills were made in the writings of Mawlong (2003) and Marak (2012).

Megalithic Structures in Garo Hills

The megalithic structures are found in most of the villages in Garo Hills. But the ritualistic practices take place only in the *Songsarek* (non-Christian) villages, whereas the Christian Garos do not practise these rituals anymore. Exploring the different locations revealed that almost every village has one or the other megalithic structure indicating that there were traditional believers especially in the form of village foundation (*kosi*) (Fig. 12.1) and boundary stones (*a·mal*) (Fig. 12.4). Some of the villages in Garo Hills where megalithic structures are found are given as under:

1. **Nokat Apal**, located in the headquarter of North Garo Hills District, Resubelpara, lies at 25°55' 43.91' N latitude, 92°35' 13.42' E longitude, and 175 m AMSL. Nokat Apal is a well-known place of interest due to the supposed *sivalingas* found and the tales related to its existence.
2. **Mandalgre**, located in Samanda of East Garo Hills District, lies at 25°30' 30.18′ N latitude, 90°22′ 04.45′ E longitude, and 998 m AMSL. It lies across the Simsang river and has a total population of 379 individuals residing in the village. Located in a difficult terrain, Mandalgre had the largest collection of *kosi* as found during the exploration.

3. **Rombhagre** under East Garo Hills District lies at 25°33′ 27.40′ N latitude, 90°21′ 22.31′ E longitude, and 497 m AMSL. Situated along the Tura-Williamnagar Road, Rombhagre consists of 79 families with a total population of 470 individuals (Census, 2011).
4. **Chidaogre**, under West Garo Hills District, at 25°37' 26.93'N latitude, 90°09' 53.35′ E longitude, and 376 m AMSL, is located 17 kms from Goeragre towards Chibragre, ahead of Babadam. Chidaogre is situated about 25 kms from the sub-district headquarters Rongram and 37 kms from the district headquarters Tura, where traditional beliefs and practices are still being followed. The village consists of 37 families with a total population of 186 individuals (Census, 2011).
5. **Boldakgre** and **Mikalpara** under West Garo Hills District lies at 25°36′ 58.59′ N latitude, 90°06′ 11.20′ E longitude and 305 m AMSL, and located in Selsella Tehsil. It is situated about 9 kms from sub-district headquarters Selsella and 46 kms from district headquarters Tura. The present location is the new settlement area. The old village lies about 1-2 kms away from the present location.
6. **Selbalgre** forest reserve lies at 25°34′ 33.20′ N latitude, 90°17′21.77′E longitude, and 171 m above sea-level, in the village of Selbalgre under Rongram Tehsil in West Garo Hills district of Meghalaya. Sub-district headquarters Rongram lies about 15 kms away where district headquarters Tura lies 30 kms away. Selbalgre is one of the oldest villages in Garo Hills. The present village has about 124 families with a total population of 682 individuals (Census, 2011).
7. **Sadolpara** located in the Dadenggre Tehsil of West Garo Hills District lies at 25°39′26.79′N latitude, 90°07′47.63′E longitude and 246 m AMSL. Situated 18 kms away from the sub-district headquarters Dadenggre and 43 kms from district headquarters Tura, it is one of the villages where the Garos still follow their traditional beliefs and practices.

Structural and Functional Descriptions

In the study of megalithic structures in Garo Hills, we classify them into two broad categories on the basis of raw material — (a) Stone Structures, and (b) Wooden structures.

The stone structures that are witnessed are morphologically of the menhir category of different dimensions. The height varies between 1-1.5m, breadth between 3-55 cms, thickness 22-40 cms and circumference between 9.5-1.37 m as found from Mandalgre, Rombhagre, and Boldakgre. They are mostly found in clusters of 4/5 to 40.

On the other hand, wooden structures (which we club under megaliths) are only those that have a sacred function to it. Therefore, it stands to reason that these wooden structures, unlike the stone ones, continue to have a living tradition to them among the traditional believers (*Songsarek* Garos). The *kima* (Fig. 12.5) measures about 4-5 feet in height, the breadth and thickness depends on the wood used for carving, as seen in Sadolpara and Chidaogre. The *jaktap* (Fig. 12.2) found with the *kosi* cluster in Boldakgre had the dimensions of 100 cm × 19 cm × 22 cm (length × breadth × thickness).

In the following Table (Table 12.1) a classification of the type of megaliths is given :

Table 12.1: Types of Megaliths in Garo Hills

Sl. no.	*Structure*	*Raw material*	*Function*	*Place found*
1.	*Kima*	Wood	Memorial post	Sadolpara, Chidaogre
2.	*Kosi*	Stone	Village foundation stone; also used as sacrificial stone	Boldakgre, Mandalgre, Selbalgre
3.	*A.mal*	Stone	Boundary stone	Watregre (New Bibragre)
4.	*Dilang*	Wood	Carved box-shaped structure used for funerary purpose	Sadolpara
5.	*Kimindam*	Wood	Religious altar	Chidaogre, Sadolpara
6.	*Chura amudam*	Bamboo	4-legged structure to ward off diseases	Chidaogre, Sadolpara
7.	*Te.eng*	Wood	Y-shaped post	Chidaogre
8.	*A.sirokgipa jaktap*	Bamboo	Sacrificial altar	Boldakgre

Stone Structures

The following are the type of stone structures seen in Garo Hills :

Kosi

Kosi is a generalised term used for megalithic structure (morphologically a menhir) erected either as sacrificial stones or as foundation stones among the *A·chik* or Garos of north-east India. *Kosi*, thus, has a dual purpose — for sacrificial rituals, judicial proceedings and village foundation. *Kosi* in wooden and stone forms can be seen in most of the *Songsarek* villages which project their traditional philosophy and principles that has been propagated since time immemorial.

Fig. 12.1: *Kosi* in Rombhagre

These are implanted either to depict the political power for administration, for judgement or to invoke the spirit or *mite* (a common term used for spirits) — *a·king guri nokgipa* and other lesser spirits. *Kosi* are also treated with reverence by the *kamal* (priests), *nokmas* (village chief), and the villagers although it has certain taboos (*marang*) attached to it. Sacrificial offerings of animals like golden *langur*, hoolock gibbon, goat, dog and roosters are made for ritualistic ceremonies like *A·song tatta*, *A·song songa*, *A·song denna* etc.

There is an erected bamboo with a conical basket placed within the circumference of *kosi* known as *A·sirokgipa jaktap* (Fig. 12.2). This structure is ritualistic in function, erected to keep the offerings and relics while practicing the ritual.

Among all the sites visited, Mandalgre provided the largest cluster of *kosi*. While exploring the surroundings in Mandalgre, we were led to a dense reserve forest area where numerous *kosis* were found, mostly fallen and overgrown with vegetation, but not weathered. The thick forest cover has kept them hidden and safe from human vandalism.

Fig. 12.2: *A·sirokgipa jaktap* in Boldakgre

Kosi Rongdu or A·song Songa

Kosi rongdu or *A·song songa* (Fig. 12.3) is a village foundation stone erected by *a·king nokma* (village chief and land owner) for establishing a new settlement area and agriculture plot for a particular clan under his chieftainship and jurisdiction. *A·king nokma* along with other *nokma* erects a foundation constituting a union of two or more villages' heads residing within the land of *a·king nokma*. Prior to *a·king nokma*, other *nokmas* implant the *kosi* accompanied by other men while women prepare for the feast. The significance of this megalith is to protect villages from all diseases and bring prosperity by the spirit *Kalkame*. It is also entrenched to notify every villagers and outsiders to visually be aware of the centre of settlement and administration.

Before the pre-colonial period, head-hunting and conflicts between other invaders was prevalent; hence, the strongest and the bravest were selected to defend the village at the expense of their life. Therefore, the foundation was also erected to commemorate their contributions and it was a sign of respect and dignity given for a chief and warriors. The beginning and end of administration and *nokma*-ship is also signified through the entrenchment of new *kosi*. Several *kosi* portray different generations of *nokma*'s administration. Depending on the stability and settlement of the villagers the numbers of *kosi* sum up. Today the settlement area where *kosi* are present is known as *songgitcham* which literally means "old village or abandoned village". Eventually, the old village becomes the sacred groves and reserved forest where people are not allowed to violate certain rules of *songgitcham* approved by the *nokma* for the safety of its people.

The same *kosi* has multiple functions as it was also utilized as a sacrificial altar during the foundation and an annual ritual called *A·song Songa* was practiced by *a·king nokma* along with the villagers in the *Songsarek* society. *A·song Songa* is basically an act of implanting a *kosi*. Worshipping and honouring of these stones symbolized the presence of deities and spirits bestowing strength, protection, abundance of fertility and good health among the worshippers.

Fig. 12.3: *A·song songa* in Selbalgre

During *A·song songa* ceremony, rituals are performed chronologically as it has been followed traditionally by their forefathers/mothers. Earlier, when Garos were head-hunters, heads of the enemy were buried below before entrenching the *kosi*. Sequentially, it was replaced by the heads of hoolock gibbons, golden *langur* and other animals. The sacrificing and burial of human heads indicated the practice of head-hunting in the society of the Garos during the pre-colonial period. The implantation of *kosi* is also associated with the succession of *nokma* or *a·king nokma* where he entrenched his own *kosi* during the ceremony. The blood of the goats and other animals are smeared on the *kosi* for lesser spirits. Through this practice the chief along with the villagers believed that the social institution and other characteristics related to the Garo society could be maintained and the covenant between the spirits and *a·king nokma*. It is an annual ritual celebrated during the month of March before agricultural cycle ceremony known as *A·galmaka*, a ritual of slashing and burning of *jhum* field. Thus, this sums up the integration of a Garo community through the reverence of *kosi* to attain security and gain fertility in relation with the land holding system during the ceremony of the *Songsarek A·song songa*.

A·song Kosi and A·song Nokpante

The culture of driving away of spirits and invoking spirits through sacrifice can commonly be seen in most of the tribal cultures all over the world. Similarly, an altar for sacrifice, and selection of a specific site for performing rituals are also seen in most part of the *Songsarek* villages and abandoned villages of Garo Hills, Meghalaya. *A·song kosi* and *A·song nokpante* are two such kinds of sacrificial altars and worship sites where numerous menhirs or *kosis* are entrenched.

A·song kosi is erected at the heart of the village; either near the *nokma's* house or at the entrance of the village whereas *a·song nokpante* is erected farther from *a·song kosi*. *A·song kosi* means '*kosi* of the province' while '*a·song nokpante*' means '*kosi* or province of the bachelors'. *A·song kosi* and *a·song nokpante* are inter-connected. These *kosis* are revered and sacred rituals are conducted annually in March. *A·song tatta*, a ceremony is celebrated to drive away the diseases and bad spirits from the villages and through this ritual their social institutional belief is safeguarded. During *A·song tatta* ritual, a golden *langur* is captured; it is beheaded; and its head kept in *a·song nokpante* by *nokma* and other men at *nokma's* courtyard. Elders create an effigy of a human figure out of wild grass and leaves and undertake a procession towards *a·song kosi*. The procession passes through every house along with the crucified golden *langur* on a bamboo while some men hit the wall of each house to drive away the diseases and bad spirits dwelling in the village.

A·mal

A·mal (Fig. 12.4) is a boundary stone commonly erected in the valley and other areas marking the territory of the village by the chief of the village. Also, similar menhirs are raised by the villages' head representatives in alliance with various clans living within the authority of *a·king nokma*. This act of integration is called *a·mal jikse*. Besides *a·mal*, there are also natural boundaries through which the territories are decided by the *nokma*. River, streams, and particular trees like *bol gisim*, *bol sil*, and *mandal* trees are planted by the *nokma* to mark one's boundary.

Fig. 12.4: *A·mal* in New Bibragre

Wooden and Bamboo Structures

Kima

Kima (Fig. 12.5) is the wooden post carved out in the shape of the deceased, decorated with the items of the deceased and erected in front of the house of the deceased person. The relatives of the deceased person to commemorate the deceased one, erects a *kima* on the second day after the death of the person. Commonly used wood is that of the branch of jackfruit tree, belonging to the deceased person's house or garden. The *kima* is always carved out by any person with particular skill for carving on wood, and often measures around 2.5 to 4 feet in height and 5-10 inches thick. The decoration of the *kima* with the belongings of the deceased indicates the belief of the people on life after death. *Kima* consists of a pair of posts stuck to the ground, one resembling the deceased person and the other with notches to support the horns of the bull sacrificed at the cremation (Playfair, 1998).

Fig. 12.5: *Kima* in Chidaogre

Kimindam

Kimindam (Fig. 12.6) is vertically erected bamboo altar commonly used among the *Songsarek* during the agricultural cycle rituals. This is not technically a megalith, but is mentioned here due to its functional attributes. The altar is wide, standing straight inter-wined into small square bamboo frames. Sacrifices, chanting and recitations are associated with this ritual while *nokma* (village chief) or *kamal* (priest) perform necessary acts. The altar is made for the deity *Minima Rokime*, the giver and keeper of crops.

Fig. 12.6: *Kima* in Chidaogre

Te·eng

Te·eng is the Y-shaped wooden post with one arm shorter than the other, found in the front yard of the deceased's house. The purpose of this post is to hang the head of the slaughtered cow sacrificed for the dead. It is mostly associated with the *kima*.

Dilang

Dilang is a miniature house carved out of wood as a memorial for the dead and kept for one month in front of the house along with *kima* (memorial wooden post). The house is kept along with grains, food, ash and broken burnt bones and skull of the dead. After a one month ritual of keeping the house in the courtyard, the *dilang* is burnt to ashes on the full moon.

Ga·leng

Ga·leng is a platform to lay down the human effigy made out of bamboo and other wild leaves. The function of this platform is to lay down the hunted head (of human) which is re-enacted and replaced by a human effigy during the *A·song tatta* ceremony.

Chura amudam

Chura amudam (Fig. 12.7) is a four bamboo post altar tied along with paddy entrenched for offering and driving away diseases and ill health from the village. This ritual is conducted by a *kamal* (priest) to cure hearing disabilities, visual problems and speaking difficulty seen among patients from the village. This ritual is known as *Chura amua*.

Fig. 12.7: *Chura amudam* in Chidaogre

Conclusion

Playfair (1909) in *The Garos* compared the Naga stone monoliths to the Garo *kima*, where the functionality is similar with the minor difference in the raw material used. Hence, studying megaliths is complex, especially since a variety of functional and socio-cultural norms are attached to it and the existence of structural variations. The megaliths found in Garo Hills do not fall into the conventional categories or types. Some are combinations and some variations in different raw material. The functional aspect of the Garo Hills megaliths pointed out the respect the living has for the deceased and that they are still revered. Not only there is respect for the deceased but commemoration of the victorious one as well. With the acceptance of Christianity and education and advent of development, the ritualistic practices no longer take place in most of the villages of Garo Hills.

The *Songsarek* Garos are the only ones still practising the traditional rites and rituals in a handful of locations which is fast changing. The condition of the village foundation stones and boundary stones indicates the time elapsed since establishment of the village. Some of the people were nostalgic of the times when the ritualistic practices were performed annually. That was the time when the whole village would come together irrespective of their age and sex. The taboos (*marang*) attached to the rituals and the maintenance of the structures was strictly followed.

Research on megalithic culture in Garo Hills appears promising. Nokat Apal (Resubelpara) is significant due to the presence of huge *menhirs*, which are touted to be '*Sivalinga*'. However, in this chapter we included Nokat Apal due to the age-old tales passed on through the word of mouth among the inhabitants of the area as well as others, making it a popular tourist spot for Garos and non-Garos alike. Similarly, interviews with local residents in different areas reveal more possible areas for the existence of *kosi, a·mal* etc. The collection in Mandalgre is quite impressive, as are the tales related to the existence and erection of these *kosis*. The dearth of both secondary and primary data for many of visited sites acted as a limitation towards the exploration. Proper documentation of the sites is to be done, including exploration of new sites. Considering this as a beginning in megalithic research in Garo Hills, further explorations are anticipated in the coming years to get a complete picture of the ritualistic and cultural significance of the megalithic tradition among the Garos.

REFERENCES

Binodini Devi, P., 2011. *The Megalithic Culture of Manipur*. Delhi: Agam Kala Prakashan.

de Maaker, E., 2006. Negotiating Life: Garo death rituals and the transformation of society. Ph.D. Thesis, Leiden University.

Marak, Q., 2012. "Megaliths of North East India". In T.B. Subba (ed.), *North East India: A Handbook of Anthropology*. New Delhi: Orient Blackswan, pp. 34-53.

Marak, Q. and Jangkhomang. 2012. "Matriliny and the Megalithic Practices of the Jaintias of Meghalaya". *Indian Anthropologist*, 42 (2): 67-82.

Mawlong, C. A., 2003. "Megalithic Elements among the Garos". In M. Momin (ed.), *Readings in History and Culture of the Garos: Essays in Honour of Milton S. Sangma*. New Delhi: Regency Publications, pp. 98-112.

Playfair, A. [(1909) 1998]. *The Garos*. Delhi: Spectrum Publications.

Rao, S.N., 1973. "The Neolithic Culture of Sarutaru, Assam". *Bulletin of the Department of Anthropology*, Dibrugarh University, 11: 1-9.

13

Wood Engravings as Cultural Memories of the Chakhesang Nagas

Ditamulu Vasa

The state of Nagaland surrounded by hills and mountains comprises various tribes with variant cultures and living traditions. Naga culture encapsulates an array of vibrant and diverse material culture with fleeting glimpses of the living megalithic tradition that continues to be practiced till the present day. Megalithic tradition in Nagaland is considered to be a place of worldwide fame which is of prehistoric origin (Jamir, 2014) and the megaliths are considered to be "the most common object for transmitting social memory" (Blackburn, 2008:265). Social and cultural memories exist in the form of representations of the past which can be incorporated with the Naga oral histories relating to megalithic culture and the associated feast of merit. Megalithism is a prehistoric phenomenon, but in Naga society part of it is still a "living tradition associated with their social, religious and economic activities, though with much lower pomp, magnitude and many changes" (Khongreiwo, 2014: 292). The feast of merit which is associated with megalithic culture has been recognised as an informative agency about the domestic and social activities with the community in a series of rituals. Feast of merit is the most important social ceremony in Naga society that is performed by a married man and who have gathered sufficient wealth in terms of livestock and food grains. The feast incorporates feasting with the whole population of his village and "consists of a series of feasts, each more costly than the preceding one, and each higher in status" (Lotha, 2008: 52). The details of the feasts vary but the basic pattern is consistent: animal sacrifices comprising of mithun, pigs and chickens, and the distribution of meat which earns the sponsor not only increased rank or a higher status but also the privilege to wear certain clothes particularly a shawl and decorate his house in a special way (*see* Blackburn, 2008). However, differences are also noticed on the decoration of the houses of the feast giver who extends his feast to a different village. Such instances occur particularly, if the spouse hails from a different village, wherein all the people of the spouse's village are invited to partake in the feast.

The oral narratives for performing such feasts differ from tribe to tribe. To the Lothas, the oral tradition says that God sat on a beam in Mentsuru's house while the tribe was in Mansoria and instructed him to perform a series of feasts for his well-being (*See* Lotha, 2008: 52). For the Aos the feast is to establish not only one's status and honor in this, but also gain favour of the spirits and prosperity of great men of the past (*see* Mills, 1962). Thereby he wins the "coveted right of wearing certain cloths and ornaments and of decorating his house in a particular way, and the animals hanging in the outer room bring prosperity not only to him, but to his heirs who inherit them after him" (Mills, 1962: 257). Likewise among the Angami and Chakhesang tribes although they fall under the Tenyimia group the number of feasts and the method of celebrating differs from village to village. But the entitlement to decorate and adorn his house with carved beams, and the honor for the wife and husband to wear certain types of clothes, remains almost the same.

In the last decades studies on the living megalithic cultural tradition was focused on the stone dragging/pulling ceremony and the erection of megalith, and also dealt with the numerous megalithic monuments scattered in Angami and Chakhesang villages, most of them erected on the approach to the village signifying a living and vital part of Naga culture. But little or no detail documents on the cultural memory, that is visible on the decoration of the house of a feast giver have been addressed. The traditional domestic houses of the varied communities is an exception in the field of creativity particularly because this region is considered a domain of traditional crafts that signifies their individuality and cultural personality both in community life and as an individual. This cultural inheritance in terms of their tradition, indigenous technology, culture, customs, beliefs and practices is manifested in their art and culture of living. This chapter is a report on the reflective anecdote of a feast giver and the symbolism that can be interpreted through the indigenous house designs and the recognition that lives as a cultural memory among the Chozuba and Runguzu villages of Chakhesang tribe.

The common indigenous dwelling houses are square/ rectangular in form that is constructed using resources that are locally available employing simple construction methods. The traditional knowledge on the use of bamboos, thatch and timber is one common feature that is adapted with the economic resources of land, forests and water which are controlled at the village, clan, lineages and individual levels. The houses are varied, built with simple structures of light-weight and pliant wood and bamboo, sometimes raised on stilts for houses that are built on the slopes (Fig. 13.1). It has been noticed that houses raised on stilts has certain advantages such that not only does it provide a panoramic view of the distance, but also provides security during the night from wild animals. In width, the houses vary but most of the houses are divided into two or three compartments according to the need of the owner. The entrance is provided with a space where all agricultural implements are stored, and firewood is stacked in addition to many other household items. All the houses have wooden walls in the front (Fig. 13.2); the side walls are generally made of interlocked bamboo and plastered with mud, whereas for the people having enough wealth, it is made of wood. The roofs are provided with thatch, mud flooring and inside the houses one can see wooden benches and low stools to sit on. All the houses have a fire place which is used for cooking and to keep warm during the winter months. The houses are located close to each other dotted all along the slopes of hill. Having a kitchen garden is not a very common sight though people have started maintaining small manageable kitchen gardens in the backyard.

Fig. 13.1: A view of Runguzu village, Phek District, Nagaland

Fig. 13.2: Houses in Runguzu village, Phek District, Nagaland

Greater differences are noticed on houses of rich families or a person with higher social status who have performed the feast of merit. The selection of method and style of construction varies in terms of the number of feasts that a person has hosted as they define their individuality and identity. In Naga society the social designation of a rich man or a noble family is not accumulating wealth in terms of his surplus crop harvests and his huge resources of livestock, but in the way he utilizes them.

The wealth distribution is done in the form of organising feasts for the whole village which is called "Feast of Merit". A person or a family can perform such feasts for several times. By doing so he gains a social status which is indicated by the structure of his house. The front gable is often decorated with various wooden carvings and the roofs slope off towards the sides (Fig. 13.3). This type of roofing is designed as a precaution against the high winds. Traditionally, the roofs are made of thick thatch intermingled and bound on with a neat ridge at the top to a get protection against both torrential rain and the scorching heat of the sun. The bamboos provide an excellent building material, which is locally available, splinted and plaited, and are used for the wall while the narrow strips form ligatures and used for binding. The traditional Naga houses are without windows and are dark inside even during the daytime.

Fig. 13.3: A rich man's house with a *ceka* structure

Fig. 13.4: A closer view of *ceka*

Distinct from the other common house, in addition, his house, is indicated by a grand horn-like projection signifying his achievement and his special status. Only the person who has hosted this feasts several times get the entitlement to decorate his house with such projection locally called *ceka* (Figs. 13.3 and 13.4).

In order to attain the full decorations of the house there are different levels or stages. A person who has performed a feast once is entitled to decorate the ridge of his roof with criss-cross bamboo splits without the house horns. The next feast he performs, he is entitled the grand horn-like projections at the front roof. And if the person's wife is from a different village and during his feast invites the entire village of his wife, then he is entitled to erect the horn-like projections in the front of his house as well as the back. The only difference is that the projection at the back is made slightly smaller. Nevertheless any feast giver has the entitlement to carve animal heads on the front wall of his house (Mills, 1962) (*See* Figs. 13.3, 13.5, 13.6, 13.7, and 13.8). The house posts at the front too can be carved only after he performs the second feast. The motif of the carvings resembles the banana fruit stalk, which is purely aesthetic in nature (Fig. 13.6).

Fig. 13.5: Carvings on the walls of the house of a rich man

Fig. 13.6: Carved decorations on the walls

Fig. 13.7: Carvings of animal heads

Fig. 13.8: A replica of a house of a rich man

The carvings of animal head and the female breast-like designs are symbolic in nature and appear to be associated with fertility and prosperity. The number of animal head motif denotes the number of animal one sacrificed for the feast and also during the rituals and ceremonies for the constructions of the house. The carvings of mithun heads are a symbolic depiction since this animal is ritually held in the highest esteem among the rest of other animals. The reason for carving this animal heads is because it signifies prosperity denoting a symbol of wealth.[1] Arrangement of female breast-like motif signifies the enormity of food grains possessed by the owner. These carvings are made with a belief that the house will protect the villagers from any untoward incidences such as famine and natural disasters.

According to village elders, these symbols are carved to show that the people of the village are prosperous and their land is fertile. It is also a belief that the house is blessed with benevolence and that the villagers will not suffer to live in hunger. As a newly born baby gets his/her first food from their mother's milk, likewise this house will protect his people from famine and disasters. Some houses have carvings of human head which signifies or is related to head-hunting.[2]

The arrangement of the feasts differed from village to village but essentially the series of feasts is performed with rituals where both the host and wife had to regale the whole village. Not more than one feast can be given in a year. The informant from Runguzu village also shared his memories on how every feast of merit was more elaborate and costly than the previous one. With this, the feast giver's status rose up further with the entitlement to wear certain ornaments and shawls and also adorn his house with carvings of animal heads and birds. Another interesting feature is the number of stones erected for the host and his wife. Each series of feasts is incomplete without dragging stones and erecting them in a suitable area, the number of stones gets doubled in the subsequent feast or feasts in a series of 2, 4, 8, 16, and 32. With this a person is considered to have completed one full cycle of feast of merit. He is then given a symbolic rebirth by carrying him in a basket dressed up like a small boy. Eventually status differentiation in terms of wealth is differentiated from the number of stones that represents the feast donors.

Skulls of wild beasts and animals hunted by the person during the time of construction or collective activities of hunting game are also decorated above the main door (Fig. 13.9). The craftsmanship in wood carvings is depicted on the houses to distinguish persons of higher social status from the common people. Such type of wood carvings is also noticed among the other Naga tribes who practiced the Morung system, also translated as social institutions. The house opens to a big hall where the huge grain storage baskets, pounding plantation are hung overhead, this is seen in almost all the houses (Fig. 13.10).

Fig. 13.9: Skulls of animal heads hung by the roof

Fig. 13.10: Grain storage baskets with bunches of corn hung overhead

The house designs with carvings are symbolic, whether of power

The house designs with carvings are symbolic, whether of power or wealth but it depicts cultural ideas gathered through social and cultural memories. It also reflects the inflow of traditional skills passed down through generations glorifying indigenous cultural life and harmonious community living. The interpretation of the symbols, alone or in combination remained difficult because the elements of rituals and ceremonies became non-functional with the advent of Christianity, such that it has not happened in generations that finally led to the customs and its practice being forgotten altogether. As such oral texts are the only source from where we can glean information of past lives and also give us information about the past by interpreting oral traditions and folklores in the form of historical narratives and traditions interspersed with mystical and ritual symbolism held sacred by the community (Aier, 2014). As such it is also evident that to document such practices that existed in the past "folklore is another aspect which may lead us to many unknown facts of these communities" (Sarma & Hazarika, 2014: 53). The present data merely discusses on the information gathered from Chozuba and Runguzu villages respectively which is to say that particular types of designs may have been favoured by particular cultures and that the same may not be seen in other Naga cultures.

NOTES

1. From personal communication with Mrs. Khwupoprülü, Chozuba village.
2. From personal communication with Mr. Shwüpu, Rünguzu village.

REFERENCES

Aier, A., 2014. "Archaeology and Oral Tradition of North East India: The Need of a Dialogue in Interpreting the Past". In T. Jamir and M. Hazarika (eds.), *51 Years after Daojali Hading: Emerging Perspectives in the Archaeology of North East India, essays in honour of T.C. Sharma.* New Delhi: Research India Press, pp. 227-35.

Blackburn, S., 2008. "The Stories Stones Tell: Naga Oral Stories and Culture". In M. Oppitz (ed.), *Naga Identities: Changing Local Cultures in the North East of India.* Ethnographic Museum of Zürich University: Snoeck, pp. 259-69.

Jamir, W., 2014. "Affinities of Naga Megaliths: An Ethnoarchaeological Study". In T. Jamir and M. Hazarika (eds.), *51 Years after Daojali Hading: Emerging Perspectives in the Archaeology of Northeast India, essays in honour of T.C. Sharma*. New Delhi: Research India Press, pp. 333-39.

Khongreiwo, R., 2014. "Landscapes, Monuments, Collective Memories: Understanding Pre-Christian Belief Systems and Socio-religious Practices of the Nagas". In T. Jamir and M. Hazarika (eds.), *51 Years after Daojali Hading: Emerging Perspectives in the Archaeology of Northeast India, essays in honour of T.C. Sharma*. New Delhi: Research India Press, pp. 292-317.

Lotha, A., 2008. "Naga Identity: Enduring Heritage". In M. Oppitz (ed.), *Naga Identities: Changing Local Cultures in the North East of India*. Ethnographic Museum of Zürich University: Snoeck, pp. 47-56.

Mills, J.P. [1926]1962. *The Ao Nagas*. London: MacMillan & Co. Ltd.

Sarma, P. J. and M. Hazarika. 2014. "Situating North-east Indian Archaeology in Chronological Perspective: Fresh Observations". In T. Jamir and M. Hazarika (eds.), *51 Years after Daojali Hading: Emerging Perspectives in the Archaeology of Northeast India, essays in honour of T.C. Sharma*. New Delhi: Research India Press, pp. 37-59.

14
The Megaliths of Cherrapunjee in Changing Times

Sukanya Sharma

Introduction

The megaliths of Cherrapunjee picture the enduring traditions and of timelessness that prevails in the land. As exemplars of moral order and aesthetic harmony, the landscape of Cherrapunjee with the megaliths has achieved the status of a national icon (Daniels, 1993). The identity of the Khasis of Cherrapunjee in particular and Meghalaya in general is defined by the landscape dotted with megaliths. The tallest and biggest of the megaliths about 8m × 2m × 0.46 m (height × breadth × thickness) is located at Nartiang in the Jaintia Hills District of Meghalaya. These are memorials depicted in works of art, on film, in novels or even in music of the area. Through them people make sense of who they are and the social relations that structure their lives. The landscape of Cherrapunjee (with the megaliths) has been communicating aspects of identity and power of the Khasis and the Jaintias. They have also been well documented and have been studied as important research problems in the nineteenth and twentieth century by British and Indian scholars. To mention a few they are Godwin-Austen (1872), Hutton (1929), Rao (1973), Roy (1963), Mawlong (1996, 2004) and others.

Cherrapunjee is a small town located on the southern edge of Khasi Hills, a dissected plateau at an altitude of about 4823 feet

(1484 m) AMSL. It is the headquarters of Sohra Civil Sub-Division and falls in East Khasi Hills District of the Indian state of Meghalaya. The study area is located at 91.70°E longitude and 25.30°N latitude. The area is approximately 469.04 km^2. The flat top of the plateau is barren with a thin layer of top soil. The steep slopes in the gorges are covered by tropical rain forests. Coal mining is a common occupation of the population of the area. Large areas are being brought under mining and with the construction of roads and development of transportation networks this activity is further increasing. As a result of this, megaliths, like menhirs and dolmens, strewn over the landscape are uprooted.

People have gained easy accessibility to remote areas, where the megalithic fields are, because of the construction of good roads. Various other activities like erection of transmission towers for mobile telephone network, electricity transmission lines and poles, house building etc. are also affecting the megalithic fields. These are developmental activities which cannot be stopped. Good roads, electricity, telephone networks are almost birth right of people now. But, it is also true that if the megaliths disappear from the landscape, a very strong part of their identity will also go with it. They are part of a prehistoric cultural tradition which is intricately woven with their socio-cultural life. They can help in tracing back a link from an uncertain present to a past whose achievements are seen as significant and remarkable. These relics have contributed a great deal in building up pride in Khasi art, technology and traditions. It affirmed the historical continuity of the land and cultural continuity of their traditions.

According to the 2011 Census of India, the literacy rate of Cherrapunjee city is 92.59 per cent. The census projects only 32 per cent as employed in Cherrapunjee but during the fieldwork it was noticed that majority of the young men of the area work as petty contractors — either in the government funded infrastructural development projects or in the private sector. Besides this, people are also employed as government servants, school teachers, in the private sector, mainly tourism, as farmers and daily wage labourers. The people are literate and they aspire to 'develop'. Tourism is beginning to unfurl the hopes of the people for a better life. That is why they want roads to be built; they want telephone connectivity, financial institutions like banks, resorts, hotels, eateries, shopping plazas etc. In this changing situation even if the megaliths are not threatened they are ignored. Real material changes in the nature of society and the economy in the latter half of the twentieth century have resulted in new identity formations in Cherrapunjee and this has undermined some of the presumed certainties of cultural identity (Carter *et al.*, 1993). In the process we are losing the megaliths, a primary archeological record.

In the light of the problem stated above I undertook a project in Cherrapunjee funded by Indian Council of Historical Research (ICHR). A survey of India toposheet (no.78 O/12) has recorded these megaliths in 1966-67 and in the surveyed area approximately 297 clusters were recorded. As part of this study a GPS survey undertaken in 2008 recorded approximately 85 clusters in the same area. Within this I have excluded the disturbed sites and the 85 include the non-disturbed sites only. This project aimed to document local community attitudes regarding the megaliths, understand how the community accessed, interacted and used the sites at present, and develop a framework for managing archaeological heritage as a cultural resource by integrating global and local conservation approaches.

Megaliths of Cherrapunjee

Most visible in the landscape today are the *menhirs* or standing stones. They are called *mawbynna* or the stones to mark and remember (Roy, 2010a, 2010b).) It is erected at the end of all the mortuary rites. Rows of 3 menhirs and a dolmen, 5 menhirs and a dolmen are also commonly sighted in the landscape of Cherrapunjee today. Sometimes this might also extend to 7, 9 or even more in number (Mawlong, 2004). The central menhir is always higher than the ones on its side and the average size recorded in the study is 283 cm × 100 cm × 25 cm (height × width × thickness). The central stone is known as the *mawkni* or maternal uncle stone while the ones on the side are *mawbud, mawpyrsa* and they represent the younger male members of a clan, such as brothers and nephews (Mawlong, 2004). The average size of the brother or nephew stones is 160 cm × 82 cm × 20 cm. The associated dolmen or *mawiawbei* is the ancestress stone, also called *mawkynthei*. Average diameter of the circular dolmens is 47 cms. During my fieldwork I recorded a set of 3 menhirs without the associated sitting stones or dolmens, erected beside the ancient pathway of Mawmluh village. The central one was taller, 130 cm than the two on the sides. The height of the menhir on the right was

97 cm and the menhir on the left was 90 cm. This cluster known as *mawkyliem* was supposed to have been erected in that strategic place because they were meant to mark adultery. In Khasi *maw* means stone and *kliem* is adultery.

The Khasis and Jaintias cremated the dead before they converted to Christianity. The bones or *shyieng* were gathered and placed under a stone *mawshyieng.* The first cist is called *mawkynroh* or *mawphew* and it is near the house of the deceased and for his or her bones alone. Average size of *mawkynroh* is a diameter of 8 feet 8 inches, and a height of 1 foot to 8 feet. This consists of a flat circular stone supported by vertical stone pieces. They keep odd number of stones for men and even number of stones for women. They also kept the articles that were frequently used by the deceased while alive, like utensils, wooden stools etc. After a year, it is transferred to a second and larger *mawkynroh* where the bones of other members of the family are also kept. The average size of the recorded *mawkynroh* are – back slab 123 cm × 81 cm × 15 cm (width × height × thickness); side slab 110 cm × 89 cm × 15 cm; three small door slabs 32/33 cm × 78/75 cm × 15/14 cm. They organize a feast and celebrate the day as auspicious. It is believed that the deceased then moves to heaven to meet his relatives (Roy, 2010a, 2010b).

Later the bones are transferred to the third cist called *mawbah* (big stone). If the clan has to built a second *mawbah* they mark the event by erecting a set of triliths called *mawniam* (stone of the religion or more accurately, of religious ceremonial) and it is the final resting place of the bones of all the members of the clan. The other kinds of stones are also connected with the mortuary ritual though they are not repositories of bones. The *mawbah* is usually twice larger than the family *mawkynroh.*

There is also *mawkjat-mawlynti,* stones of the leg and stones of the path which are erected on the path leading to the *mawbah* to guide the spirits and also to provide a resting place to the spirits of the deceased and their ancestors. *Mawksing, mawkait* or *mawja* are all triliths and also in sets of 5 standing menhirs with dolmens erected a year or two after the *mawbah* ceremony. These stones are not distinguishable in appearance from *mawbynna* and the term *mawbynna* is often loosely used for them (Roy, 2010a). These are all part of the mortuary rites erected at different stages. Then there is the *mawbri-mawsam* or boundary stone. During field-work I recorded a *mawbynna* in Mawmluh village and villagers call it the "victory stone". The size of this single menhir 180 cm × 92 cm × 20 cm (height × width × thickness). These types of single menhirs were erected by individuals for miscellaneous purposes. They are also called ancestral stones.

Fig. 14.1: Individual *mawkynroh* or *mawphew*

Fig. 14.2: Family *mawkynroh* or *mawphew*

Fig. 14.3: Clan repository or *mawbah*

Fig. 14.4: *Mawkjat-mawlynti,* stone of leg or stone of path with dolmen

Fig. 14.5: *Mawbri-Mawsam* or boundary stone

Fig. 14.6: *Mawbyna* or victory stone

Fig. 14.7: Ancestral stone

In the 469.04 km^2 area surveyed, there are few undisturbed sites. Some have been disturbed in the past by coal mining activity while some are disturbed now by various activities like road construction, electricity and telephone installations etc.

Majority of the people have converted to Christianity. A miniscule number have not converted but even among them the tradition remains only to the extent of cremation and the internment of the bones inside the family and clan cists. No erections of menhirs and dolmens have been recorded in the recent times.

The antiquity of these megaliths has not been established yet. This is because habitation deposits have not been excavated and dated in the area, as this have not been located yet. Prolonged mining activity and deforestation in the past have completely washed away the top soil as noted earlier. The cist chambers lie open as they have been heavily disturbed by humans in search of grave goods. A common occurrence with these megalithic clusters in Cherrapunjee is iron slag. A correlation between the two has not been established but half done menhirs and dolmens lying around the sites are intriguing. Maybe iron tools were manufactured and used for building these monuments. Megalithic sites in rest of India are frequently associated with the Copper–Bronze or Iron Age. A recent study by Prokop and Suliga (2013) established with the help of radiocarbon dating of charcoal and the results of chemical, microstructure and phase composition of iron-ore and slags, that the smelting of iron in the Khasi Hills was initiated at least 2000 years ago. From the Nonkrem site the charcoal extracted from the slag layer at a depth of 270 cm was dated at 2040±80BP (353 BC–AD 128). In the Raitkteng site, the radiocarbon age of charcoal from the bottom of the profile is dated at 1110±30 BP. According to the authors relatively large charcoal particles up to 0.5 cm in size probably indicate the main phase of deforestation. Land must have been cleared for wood and for erecting megaliths. Similar developments during the same time period had taken place in other parts of India and the world. Modern pollen assemblage data from 65 sites of Cherrapunjee and adjoining areas indicates large scale deforestation and massive soil erosion, resulting in the formation of present day grassland under a drier climate (semi-desert type) (Bhaumik, 2008). The occurrence of abundant xerophytic grasses, along with trace value of fern and fungal remains, supports the inference (Basumatary *et al.*, 2012).

Findings

The first concern of the study was to find out if economic changes have resulted in the formation of new identities for which the importance of the megaliths is undermined. Reconnaissance Survey was undertaken for collecting data. This included foot survey, GPS documentation, GIS mapping, non-participant observation and interview method. GIS mapping of the area was done with three objectives: (a) to geo-reference the megaliths documented; (b) to understand the topography; and (c) to find out if the distribution of the megaliths on the landscape followed a pattern.

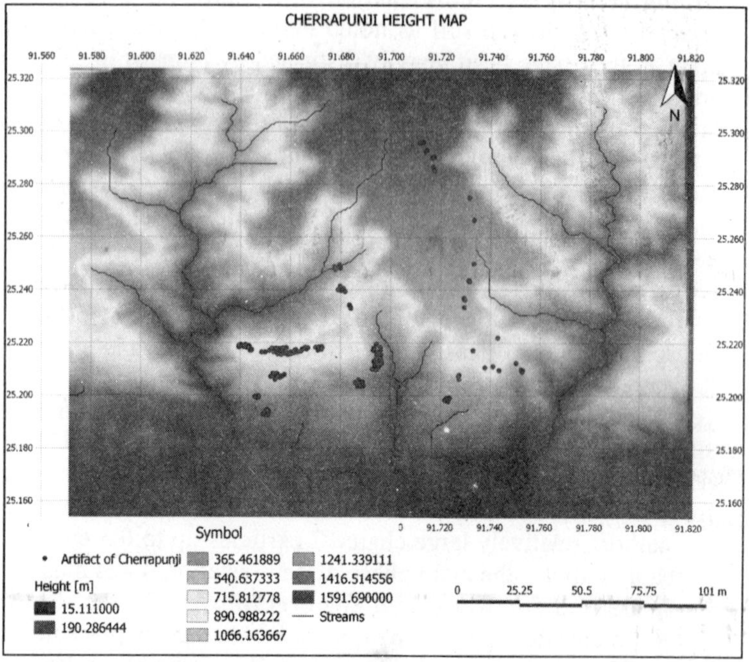

Fig. 14.7: Megaliths, with Cherrapunjee height map as base map (scale 1:95382)

Note: Different colours show different height of the study area. Most of the megaliths are located on light green to green colour, which show minimum height of the hill as well as flat part. Most of the megaliths are located between 800-1591.69 m height which is relatively flat.

The maximum height of the study area is 1511-1680 m AMSL, and the minimum height is 0-167.9 m. Most of the megaliths are located between 800-1591.69 m height which is the rocky and undulating table top. To ensure stability and longevity of the monuments the builders chose the relatively flat areas of the landscape. They exist in clusters but some also stand in isolation winding across the landscape indicating probably an ancient pathway. The thick clusters are located beside a modern village. This was a strong indication that the people of the area cared for the megaliths.

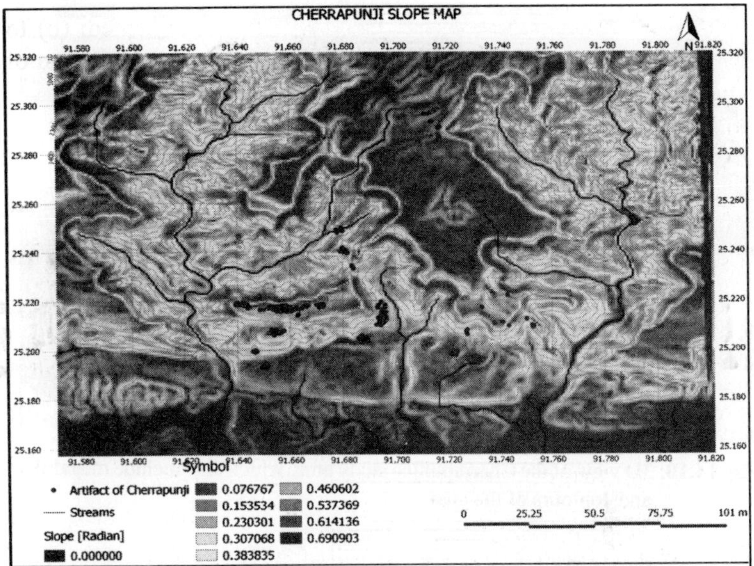

Fig. 14.8: Cherrapunjee Slope map (Scale 1:90000)

Note: It includes megaliths and streams as a layer, for different slopes different colour have been used, red shows minimum and green shows maximum slope of study area. Most of the megaliths are on red colour, which has 0-13.17 degree and these are flat area of the hills.

Fig. 14.9: 3D view of the Cherrapunjee study area

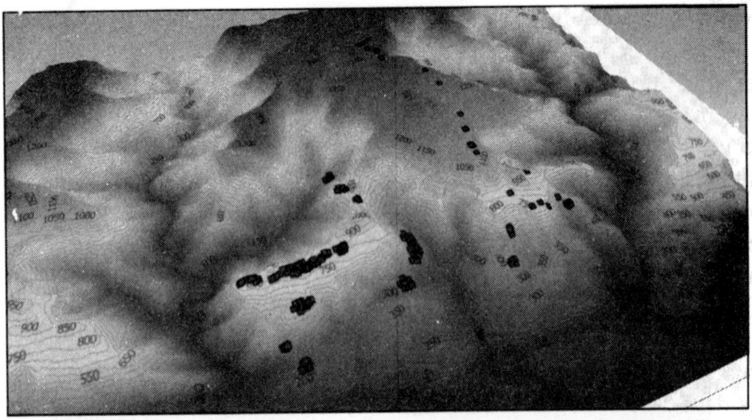

Fig. 14.10: 3D view of the Cherrapunjee study area, which also include megaliths and contours of the area

Socio-Cultural Parameters

With the help of an interview schedule the people were approached to ascertain their attitude towards the megaliths. 500 individuals within the age group of 15 to 40 years were interviewed from the study area. Interviews were taken in high schools, community centres, market places, residents,Governmental and Non-governmental Offices located in the area. The results of the interview gave a picture of the attitude of the people of the area towards the megaliths.

The first question asked was whether they considered megaliths as their heritage. The overwhelming positive response established that the megaliths are still respected, but it was the group of people between the age group of 15-20 years who were more concerned. This might be because issues of identity trouble them the most in the global homogenized world and the megalith provided them a cultural symbol. To the question of whether they felt that the megaliths need to be conserved, over 99 per cent of the people replied in the positive. Again interestingly to the question whether megaliths should be removed for the purpose of development, over 90 per cent replied in the negative.

Thus, the following observations were made — (1) People are very much concerned about their heritage and have a strong feeling to preserve it but they do not know how; (2) People see it as their cultural identity and have strong feelings for megaliths; and (3) A negligible number advocate for destroying them if required for development activities.

Though economic changes have resulted in the formation of new identities in Cherrapunjee the importance of the megaliths has not been undermined. The context might have changed. At present for the inhabitants of the study area besides being visible markers of culture the megaliths are also good symbols in their landscape. The spirits of the deceased ancestors attached with the megaliths are believed to be sources of fertility. Megalithic constructions in the past were strategies of domination and in the present too the locals of the area in the light of modern economic developments are interested in continuing this same strategy. This has triggered a process of recontexualisation. The past have been reanimated from the dead into living forms. They are part of the material culture of the present day inhabitants of the region among whom majority are Christians. Today as cultural identity markers they are sold as curios, projected in the works of arts, ornamentally erected in front of public buildings etc. With this recontexualisation the megaliths have been ripped out from its matrix but this production and use of the megaliths has to be regarded as a contextualised social act. Through the process of duplicity there is recollection and recovery. The recontexualised archeological record is considered to be the material culture of everyday which purports to operate in the service of life.

The Solution

This archeological record is struggling against the onslaught of 'development'. The younger generations as the interviews indicated share a strong bond with their culture and tradition. A group was advocating for marking a particular place for preserving megaliths, which is a practical approach to keep them safe. Another group was in complete denial. With the help of *darbar* and headman (local system) some places can be marked and the responsibility can be given to some people. Lack of funding was a main concern for everyone. They strongly believe if they get support from any institute or government they will be able to safeguard it properly. This was the conclusion of a discussion held in Nabon Sawain Memorial Presbyterian School, Mawmluh held on 17th April, 2010. After organising a few of these meets in a span of 2 years it was decided that the development activities damaging the megaliths must be mapped.

An area within the study area was sampled for developing a list of activities causing damage to the sites. This sampled area consisted of ten villages—Laitkynsew, Nongwar, Mustan, Tyrna, Mawmluh, Mawlong, Mawkhlah, Mawsmai, Mahadeklaityra and Cherrapunji town.

A list of activities causing damage to these sites was made. It was as follows:

(a) Ramkrishna Mission School – Construction
(b) Market – Construction of road
(c) Megaliths Near RKM school – Construction of road
(d) In Fields near RKM – Construction of road
(e) School towards Laitrrya – Construction of building
(f) SDO office – Construction of building
(g) Eco park – Construction of building
(h) Awsmai Megalithis – Mining
(i) On road near Mawsmai – Mining
(j) Lad Ryngud Village – Electricity poles
(k) Way to Thangkharang park – Mining
(l) Laitrrya – Mining
(m) Shiv mandir in Laittrya – Construction
(n) Megaliths in fields on the way – Mining
(o) Megaliths on the way to Sohbar – Mining
(p) Sacrificing place – Mining
(q) Cairns biggest (10 feet diameter) – Construction of house

The list contains most of the common causes of damage. Completely stopping these activities will not be possible but the loss can be minimised.

Administrative power of each village in the area is with the village *darbar*. These are village councils comprising twelve selected members. There is one *sardar* or head of the council, one secretary, two *matehbar* and eight executive members. The tenure of the council or *darbar* is five years.

During the programme in 2010 the Mawmluh village council decided that a part of the village where megaliths are dense will be fenced and protected. No construction will be allowed in the area. In consultation with the village *darbar* the study concluded by framing a policy document.

The following is the policy document emerging from the meeting on 23rd August, 2012. The aim of this policy was to manage and sustain the significance, authenticity and integrity of the tangible and intangible cultural heritage resources for which the darbar is responsible for the enjoyment and benefit of all inhabitants of Cherrapunjee and of the world.

1. The *darbar* acknowledged Cherrapunjee's rich cultural heritage and was committed to ensuring the safeguarding of this heritage in the areas under its jurisdiction.
2. The *darbar* accepted responsibility for ensuring that the effective protection, preservation and sustainable utilisation of cultural resources is integrated into the process of village public welfare schemes.
3. The *darbar*'s trusteeship should include the cultural heritage component, that the cultural assets be taken into account in development projects and that the needs and values of especially local/neighbouring communities are honoured in this respect.
4. In the case of any developments or projects relating to Cultural Heritage all villages concerned should liaise and consult with the Manager for Cultural Resource Management and Indigenous Knowledge which in this case is the *darbar*.
5. Complete integration of cultural heritage and indigenous knowledge into the physical and development planning process as well as management of village public welfare schemes.
6. Informed decision-making based on national priorities; respect for culture and traditions and the *darbar*'s conservation and development priorities.
7. Public consultation and involvement in policy development and decision-making.
8. An inclusive approach to determining resource significance and value so that the values of all cultural objects represented in Cherrapunjee are embraced and reflected.
9. *Darbar*s must ensure that negative impacts on all forms of cultural heritage are mitigated and positive impacts are enhanced for the benefit of present and future generations. There should be codoperation and negotiation between stakeholders, executive agencies, consultants and specialists

in the CRM field as a basis from which to develop effective and appropriate management strategies, policy, procedures, codes of practice, guidelines, mitigation techniques and methods, norms and standards, etc.

10. *Darbar*s should use cultural resources in a sustainable way in order to meet present and future human needs, history reconstruction, capacity development and image building.
11. *Darbar*s should resolve potential and real conflict between preservation and development and to enhance the *darbar*s continuous efforts to safeguard the future of Cherrapunjee.
12. *Darbar*s should ensure greater sensitivity and respect to cultural perspectives and beliefs during archaeological research including excavation of sacred and burial grounds as well as other forms of research practices.
13. *Darbar*s should promote a multidisciplinary approach to research on cultural resources as well as perspectives on cultural resource management and indigenous knowledge.
14. *Darbar*s should identify with and seek to promote the following principles: (i) To ensure that heritage resources are effectively managed; (ii) The skills and capacities of persons and communities involved in heritage resources management must be developed; (iii) Provision must be made for the ongoing education and training of existing and new heritage resources management workers; (iv) Heritage resources form an important part of the history and beliefs of communities and must be managed in a way that acknowledges the right of affected communities to be consulted and to participate in their management; (v) Heritage resources contribute significantly to research, education and tourism and they must be developed and interpreted for these purposes in a way that ensures dignity and respect for cultural values; (vi) The identification, assessment and management of the heritage resources of the *darbar*s must — (a) take account of all relevant cultural values and indigenous knowledge systems; (b) take account of material or cultural heritage value and involve the least possible alteration or loss of it; (c) promote the use and enjoyment of and access to heritage resources; in a way consistent with their cultural significance and conservation needs; (d) contribute to social and economic development;

(e) safeguard the options of present and future generations; and (f) be fully researched, documented and recorded.

Conclusion

With the help of the policy document the village councils or *darbars* should be able maintain a database to review projects or activities that could potentially affect the megaliths. Active village councils of the area decided that all projects or development activities would require a review to assess the level of threat to the megaliths of the area and to determine the degree of mitigation, if any, required for removing or limiting the effects of the threat. Through the work a dialogue has been opened up between tradition and perceived science or best professional practice of heritage management. Under the changing economic conditions it is important to integrate the global and local issues for an effective heritage management plan. There is a definite change in the image of archaeology among the local population and its presentation during the field work. In India, heritage conservation laws and policies do not allow participation of the people. It is a subject of the state which is all about protection but not about management. The Government agency decides which heritage property should be preserved. The magnificent looking Nartiang megaliths have been preserved as a heritage monument. But all the rest of the megaliths facing the threat of 'development' are not considered. As a cultural identity marker of the landscape of the area they are not just monuments but imprints, symbols of a past which is relevant to the present.

The project helped to discover how cultural heritage professionals and locals especially descendant communities communicated matters of cultural heritage. This can aid in developing heritage awareness programmes and a legislative basis for conservation.

Acknowledgements

The initial part of this work was done with a research grant of the Indian Council of Historical Research (ICHR). I am grateful to them for the grant. I am grateful to the Department of Humanities and Social Sciences, IIT, Guwahati for all the logistical help while doing the project. Special thanks to my students Pankaj Singh and Yogesh Kumar for helping me in my project work. I deeply acknowledge the help of Abhishek Samrat, M.Sc. student from Indian Institute

Tyrna, Mawmluh, Mawlong, Mawkhlah, Mawsmai, Mahadeklaityra and Cherrapunjee town with whom I constantly interacted during the period of 3 years — A big thank you to them for all the help.

REFERENCES

Basumatary, S.K., S. Dixir, S.K. Bera and R.C. Mehrotra, 2012. "Modern pollen assemblages of surface samples from Cherrapunjee and its adjoining areas, Meghalaya, north-east India". *Quaternary International*, 298 (2013): 68-79.

Bhaumik, S., 2008. "World's Wettest area Dries up". *South Asia News*. Calcutta: BBC.

Carter, E., J. Donald and J. Squires. 1993. *Space and Place: Theories of Identity and Location*. London: Lawrence & Wishart.

Daniels, S., 1993. *Fields of vision: Landscape Imagery and National Identity in England and the United States*. Cambridge: Polity Press.

Godwin-Austen, H.H., 1872. "On the Stone Monuments of the Khasi Hill Tribes, and on Some of the Peculiar Rites and Customs of the People". *Journal of the Anthropological Institute*,1: 127-28.

Hutton, J.H., 1929. "Assam Megaliths". *Antiquity*, III (2): 399-408.

Mawlong, C., 1996. *Megalithic Monuments of Khasi-Jaintia Hills: An Ethno-Archaeological Study*. Ph.D. Thesis, North Eastern Hill University, Shillong.

_____. 2004. "Megaliths and social formation in Khasi-Jaintia Hills". In M. Momin and C.A. Mawlong (eds.), *Society and Economy in North East India,* Vol. I. New Delhi: Regency Publications, pp. 35-57.

Prokop, P and I. Suliga. 2013. "Two thousand years of iron smelting in the Khasi Hills, Meghalaya, North East India". *Current Science*, 104(6), 25 March.

Rao, S.N., 1973. "The Neolithic Culture of Sarutaru". *Bulletin of the Department of Anthropology,* Dibrugarh University, 11: 1-9.

Roy, D., 1963. "The Megalithic Culture of the Khasis". *Anthropos*, LVII: 548-50.

_____. 2010a. "The Megalithic Culture of the Khasis–I". *The NEHU Journal*, VIII (1): 1-13.

_____. 2010b. "The Megalithic Culture of the Khasis–II". *The NEHU Journal*, VIII (2): 1-20.

Index